T0375060

PALACE OF ASHES

PALACE *of* ASHES

CHINA AND THE
DECLINE OF AMERICAN
HIGHER EDUCATION

MARK S. FERRARA

JOHNS HOPKINS UNIVERSITY PRESS · BALTIMORE

© 2015 Johns Hopkins University Press
All rights reserved. Published 2015
Printed in the United States of America on acid-free paper
2 4 6 8 9 7 5 3 1

Johns Hopkins University Press
2715 North Charles Street
Baltimore, Maryland 21218-4363
www.press.jhu.edu

Library of Congress Cataloging-in-Publication data

Ferrara, Mark S.
  Palace of ashes : China and the decline of American higher
education / Mark S. Ferrara.
     pages cm
  Includes bibliographical references and index.
    ISBN 978-1-4214-1799-8 (hardcover : alk. paper) — ISBN
978-1-4214-1800-1 (electronic) — ISBN 1-4214-1799-5
(hardcover : alk. paper) — ISBN 1-4214-1800-2 (electronic)
  1. Education, Higher—Aims and objectives—United States.
2. Education, Higher—Aims and objectives—China. 3. Universities and colleges—Standards—United States. 4. Universities and colleges—Standards—China. 5. Education and
globalization. I. Title.
  LA227.4.F47 2015
  378.73—dc23   2015004322

A catalog record for this book is available from
the British Library.

Special discounts are available for bulk purchases
of this book. For more information, please contact Special
Sales at 410-516-6936 or specialsales@press.jhu.edu.

Johns Hopkins University Press uses environmentally
friendly book materials, including recycled text
paper that is composed of at least 30 percent post-
consumer waste, whenever possible.

For my mother, Nicole Ann Jones,
an angel of light for so many who are ill and suffering

CONTENTS

ACKNOWLEDGMENTS

In the writing of this book, I am indebted to many people along the way. My wife, Liangmei Bao, helped to proofread the manuscript, but above all provided the space in which to write it. Regrettably, this thin volume is all there is to show for many hours that we might otherwise have spent together.

Several former professors deserve acknowledgement for their teaching, which continues to inform my life and work. Walter R. Coppedge introduced a lost business major to the wonders of world literature, changed the course of his studies, and continues to clarify his work. Cliff Edwards, the hidden sage, imparted the philosophy of emptiness, though the author has been slow to put it into practice. Marcel Cornis-Pope introduced new theoretical approaches to literature and cultural studies, and W. Scott Howard directed the dissertation that opened the way to other book-length projects, including the one in the reader's hands.

Robert A. Rhoads of the University of California at Los Angeles most generously shared his excellent work on China's rising research universities; having access to it facilitated the timely completion of this study. Special thanks also to Haun Saussy at the University of Chicago and Robert Hegel at Washington University in St. Louis for their encouragement of my work on Chinese literature and culture.

Professor Huang Yongmin, now retired from Fudan University, deserves my gratitude for his sincere support over many years, and I thank Steven Lee from the English Department at the University of California at Berkeley for extending an invitation to be a visiting research scholar during the spring 2015 semester. The final revisions of *Palace of Ashes* were completed on the Berkeley campus.

William Simons and Robert Compton, our campus union leaders, encouraged me to write as a way of bringing attention to the crisis in American higher education. My colleagues Toke Knudsen and Brian Dolber have been tireless in forwarding articles on the state of the academy, many of which are referenced below. Wesley Graves lent his careful eye to the manuscript, and conversations with Matthew Voorhees, Charles Nelson, Bambi Lobdell, Ho Hon Leung, Matthew Hendley, Charles Ragozzine, Adam Spingler, and many others helped to shape the claims found herein.

While campus administrators are generally not portrayed positively in the following pages, I remain grateful to the former president of Drake University, David Maxwell, and particularly to his provost, Ronald Troyer, for showing me what effective, student-centered, and democratic campus leadership looks like. The English Department at SUNY Oneonta warrants credit for firing the author's zeal to make a thorough examination of the decline of American higher learning.

The early drafts of this book were completed during the summer of 2014. In contrast to the forbidding winters in the northern foothills of the Catskill Mountains, the summers here are lovely and lush — many insects, flowers, deer, chipmunks, rabbits, and other beings pleasantly sped my writing along under a friendly pagoda. Amidst all of that seasonal commotion, my neighbor Robert Shultis died, and though I did not know him well, it seems appropriate that his passing be acknowledged here, at least as part of the great transformation of the ten thousand things.

In addition to expressing my appreciation for the work of the librarians and staff at Milne Library in Oneonta and the UC Berkeley Libraries, I extend a heartfelt thanks to Toby Miller, Henry Giroux, Gaye Tuchman, Bill Readings, Derek Bok, Stanley Aronowitz, and the many other academics who are fighting — by writing. It is my earnest hope that more of us will put away the fear that is so pervasive in the academy today, and follow their example.

. . . .

Palace of Ashes

FIFTEEN YEARS INTO the twenty-first century and the outlook for higher education in the United States is more dire than many would imagine. Although the country still boasts of a handful of universities that lead world measures of excellence (such as research spending, patents, number of international students, and invention), a well-documented decline in the overall quality and stature of its institutions of higher learning took place over the past three decades.

Everywhere one looks in the American academy, "marks of weakness, marks of woe"[1] abound: generational state and federal defunding, administrative bloat, unsustainable tuition growth, an unconscionable reliance on part-time faculty, growing student loan debt, the adoption of corporate governance models, the rise of an audit culture that props up a new managerialism, increasing standardization and vocationalization in the curriculum, the diminution of the humanities, and a forfeiture of the ideal of higher education as a public good.

In the pages that follow, an important story unfolds. It places the development and decline of American higher education in a historical context to illustrate how the forces of globalization are helping rapidly developing Asian nations (such as China and India) to transform their major universities into serious contenders for the world's students, faculty, and resources within just a few generations. What this phenomenon suggests about the future of global higher education may surprise some readers, particularly those convinced of the superiority of American colleges and universities.

Together, we shall examine the social and economic trends that underpin the dual narratives of the rise of Chinese higher learning in the late twentieth century to the present and the corresponding decline of it in the United States during the same period. To best accomplish that task, we take a broad historical approach to the origin and development of the modern university in both countries. In reaching back to the ancient world, the very beginnings, a pattern of movement from divergence to convergence will be revealed — one that has accelerated in the twenty-first century.

For the sake of example, the advances of the industrial revolution and the spread of European colonialism during the eighteenth and nineteenth centuries meant that the economic benefits of globalization went to a few players. It was therefore a time of great economic disparity when the global balance of power favored nations like Britain, France, Germany, and the United States. In our own time, the processes of globalization are entering a new phase of economic convergence in which peripheral and semiperipheral countries are closing in on the production levels of the developed world at a hitherto unimaginable pace.

One consequence of that global convergence is increased international competition for a finite set of human and natural resources. Consider, for instance, that over the course of a few decades (from the 1950s to the 1990s), Japan, South Korea, and Taiwan transformed themselves into developed countries that now contribute significantly to the world economy. The same global economic processes that led these countries to prominence on the world stage in the twentieth century are now at work in China, India, Indonesia, Vietnam, and elsewhere in Asia. China is the second-largest economy in the world today, but most serious estimates suggest that it will overtake the United States in a generation or two (barring unforeseen political, social, or economic events).

Each of the chapters in this volume helps to illustrate the primary reasons that the United States is particularly ill-prepared for the great convergence underway in global higher education. Because human resources are highly mobile, angling to attract human capital is increasingly integral to the creation of international hubs of innovation (driven by top-flight colleges and universities that compete internationally). Recognizing this reality, the Chinese government has invested hundreds of billions of dollars in its higher education de-livery system to train the scientists and engineers its economy needs to grow. Moreover, China plans to enable its flagship universities to contend more directly with elite Western institutions in the coming years, including those in the American Ivy League.

As part of those efforts, China seeks to move away from the tradi-tional emphasis on rote learning and vocational training; its fledgling knowledge economy needs workers who can create and innovate (and not simply reverse engineer). Meanwhile, colleges and universities in the United States are embracing science, technology, engineering, and math (STEM) in place of a long-standing tradition of broad hu-manistic learning—and they are increasingly adopting centralized, hierarchical, and authoritarian policies with no meaningful histori-cal antecedents. Such inversions of tradition are just one of the many paradoxes that we will encounter as we ponder the implications of the global convergence taking place around a single model of the "world-class university."

A world-class institution can be defined as a super-research uni-versity that enjoys international stature and where faculty members consistently produce important scholarly output. Its main focus re-mains on science and on the commodification of the products of the scientific method. Thereby, the world-class university encourages its faculty members to shift from open and free independent inquiry to team-based research on real world problems that can be brought to the marketplace, to seek diverse sources of funding (from corpora-tions to private donors), to recruit students and faculty worldwide, and to undertake collaborative work with NGOs and multigovern-mental organizations.[2]

In this new international paradigm of the world-class university, the humanities are mistakenly viewed as ill-suited to producing the engineers and scientists needed by modern postindustrial economies, and they are increasingly marginalized and underfunded. In the Unit-ed States, the abandonment of liberal learning started in earnest dur-ing the 1980s when tax cuts and the systematic defunding of higher education became a part of the culture wars between liberals and their conservative rivals (who saw universities as bastions of counterculture politics in the 1960s and 1970s). Similarly, China's own long-enduring tradition of humanistic learning grounded in Confucianism has yet to stage a meaningful comeback—although there are stirrings of one.

Having taught at universities in China, South Korea, Turkey, and the United States, I find the historical, cultural, and economic trends outlined in this book to be very real. I see them not only through the lens of the intensive research that informs this study but also through my own personal experiences living and teaching abroad. Perhaps as a result of this background, the cases of China and the United States seem to most poignantly illustrate the processes of global convergence. Not only are China and the United States the world's largest economies, they have also built the most extensive higher education delivery systems in the world, making them ideal candidates to illustrate the consequences of internationalization in global higher education.

My concern is not that the quality and reputation of Chinese higher learning will overtake that of the United States per se; for that achievement, we must wait. Rather, my worry is that the current downward trajectory of American higher education is unsustainable in a new era of rapid globalization. It is not simply that we are gradually falling behind the rest of the world, but that the American academy seems to have lost its way by jettisoning key features of its own historical and cultural heritage. The academic edifice is falling into disrepair as higher education becomes a commodity bought by an individual consumer to provide upward social mobility via professional training, rather than a civic good funded from public coffers. This shift, from altruistic values to self-interested ones, can be attributed to the adoption of neoliberal ideology, which is sweeping through international higher education.

According to the philosophers Pierre Dardot and Christian Laval, the principle characteristic of neoliberal rationality is "the generalization of competition as the behavior norm and of the enterprise as a model of subjectivation." Rationality, they argue, is not simply a euphemism for the word capitalism, but in fact neoliberalism "is the rationality of contemporary capitalism—a capitalism freed of its archaic references and fully acknowledged as a historical construct and general norm of existence." As such, a new mode of government of human beings is now in ascendance, by which the universal principle of competition has become embedded in the discourses, practices, and apparatuses of power.[3]

Neoliberal ideology is pernicious not because it is a mindset or belief, but rather because it is a system of norms "now profoundly inscribed in government practices, institutional policies, and managerial styles," all of which are extensions of a logic of competition between individuals.[4] This universalized logic of competition justifies the transformation of institutions established for the public good, like universities and hospitals, into enterprises that rationalize inequalities among workers and administrators as a side effect of economic Darwinism (where the fittest rightfully survive and the weak are left to fend for themselves).

Because they are embedded in the world-class model, neoliberal practices are being adopted in higher education systems around the globe. In the United States, the thoughtless embrace of neoliberalism has meant moving toward educational practices that include high-stakes testing, skill-based teaching, standardized curricula, and memorization drills. Left unchecked, neoliberalism threatens to transform global higher education into an adjunct of corporate power and values.[5] Already, most models of university governance in the United States "mimic corporate structures by increasing the power of administrators at the expense of faculty," thereby reducing the professoriate to a mostly temporary and low-wage workforce — and their students to customers.[6]

As they are transformed into corporate and entrepreneurial entities, American colleges and universities increasingly bear little resemblance to their predecessors, which eschewed ties to business and profit (as corrupting influences on pure research and the ideal of liberal learning). The current rush to transfer academic research to the practical needs of the marketplace as quickly, and as profitably, as possible — as well as to pass the costs of college onto the "consumer" through higher tuition and fees — is also very much in keeping with neoliberal doctrine.

In my view, there is more at stake for the United States than the loss of a mode of decentralized governance that combined with a distinctive civic idealism to make American colleges and universities the envy of the world between 1949 and 1980. In making such an assertion, which will be supported below, I do not intend to downplay the shortcomings of the academy during those years, or to succumb to a soporific nostalgia for a bygone era. We must not forget that prior to the 1960s, the American university was an elitist space that largely excluded people of color, women, and the poor. We seek instead a new paradigm, one that retains the best attributes of the academy of yesteryear, accommodates them to the realities of the new world of convergence, and features a diversity of representation in terms of students and faculty. As it stands, neoliberalism is driving global standardization, which means institutions of higher learning in the United States will resemble those found in Britain, Australia, and New Zealand—as well as in China, India, Singapore, Kenya, and elsewhere—despite the distinctive historical traditions of higher learning found in each of these countries.

In dealing with such complex topics as the origins of the great convergence of higher education in China and the United States, I draw upon a considerable body of scholarly work concerning the historical development of higher learning in both countries, as well as my own experiences teaching at Kyungnam University in South Korea, and in the Foreign Languages and Literatures Department at Fudan University, in the mid- to late 1990s. It was a wonderful time to be in East Asia as an expatriate. The streets of Shanghai were still gritty and edgy, and they buzzed with incessant activity as people reveled in newfound freedoms to buy, sell, and speak more openly than in the previous forty years. Dilapidated wooden hutongs (胡同) from another era gave way, seemingly overnight, to bizarre postmodern structures of steel, tinted glass, and chrome. Soon those shiny buildings were demolished and rebuilt again in a dizzying display of economic prosperity (and Chinese-style urban planning). For example, I lived near the Wujiaochang area for almost two years and saw it reconstructed once during that time. When I returned some five or six years later, it was so unrecognizable that it might have been in another city altogether.

As director of the Chinese Cultural Exchange Program at Drake University from 2004 to 2007, I visited China regularly to create partnerships with colleges and universities of all sizes (from two-year colleges to major research universities) in Hebei, Jiangsu, and Sichuan provinces. This experience helped to sharpen my understanding of the important transformations taking place in Chinese higher education, including a doubling (along with enrollment) of the number of institutions of higher learning in the country. During these years, I was continually amazed to find sprawling new campuses outside of almost every Chinese city or town that found its way onto the travel itineraries. Often, such institutions would operate an old campus in the middle of an urban area (where it was founded) as well as a new one located on the outskirts of the municipality. A good example of this model would be Nanjing University, but there are now many Chinese institutions of higher learning that boast of multiple campuses.

In contrast to the growth, development, and optimism found on campuses across China, a deep concern about the direction of American higher education led me to start blogging on the crisis in the academy in 2013[7] and to undertake this comparative study of higher education the following year, so that readers might gain a better understanding of why global convergence has meant progress and improvement for China, but decline in the United States. For one thing, the Chinese government has been deliberate about developing research and improving teaching, growing scholarly productivity, and establishing connections with industry as well as better articulating promotion processes and enhancing faculty recruitment.[8]

Even so, institutions of higher learning in China still fall short in terms of those features that once distinguished the American university in the world community, namely institutional autonomy, meaningful tenure protections, shared governance, free inquiry, administrative transparency, and a lack of censorship. For example, I happen to be writing on the twenty-fifth anniversary of the 1989 Tiananmen Square massacre, a tragic event that has effectively been wiped out of the Chinese collective memory through strict controls over the media and education. When one of my relatives, an engineering student at a local Chinese university, visited the United States last year, he was quite surprised to learn of the Tiananmen student protests.

Although Chinese higher education promises to make further progress in the years ahead, it can advance only as far as its authoritarian single-party political system will allow. In a real sense, as long as the country remains under Chinese Communist Party control, it may never realize an environment conducive to the academic freedom that once characterized the higher education systems found in advanced Western democracies. Censorship and surveillance on this scale might be accepted practices under authoritarian regimes, but they have no place in true higher learning.

On the other hand, ongoing revelations from Edward Snowden have made clear the unprecedented (and perhaps unconstitutional) scope of U.S. government surveillance of its own citizens. In the face of such covert operations and widespread use of the technologies that enable large-scale collections of data, the real prospect of loss of the spirit of free inquiry on American campuses is chilling. Signs of that forfeiture appeared following the September 11th attacks, with the adoption of the Patriot Act in 2001 (and its reauthorization in 2006), which granted the Department of Homeland Security the power to "target universities" and the "free pursuit of knowledge" in many ways. This included granting the Federal Bureau of Investigation (FBI) access to "book circulation records, Internet-use records, and registration information stored in any medium" as part of ongoing investigations related to terrorism or intelligence gathering.[9]

In embracing centralized models of administrative control that blend quasi-authoritarianism with the corporate values associated with neoliberalism, American higher education is restrictive, rather than expansive. The depletion of democracy resulting from the rise of the entrepreneurial neoliberal state is mirrored in the loss of faculty governance on campuses across the nation. Without question, observes David Chan, global higher education today is seen "as a knowledge industry and a prime instrument for upgrading national economic competitiveness." East Asian countries are adamantly trying to transform their national higher education institutions into international ones so as to compete with other global players.[10] As Amy Roberts and Gregory Ching show, the elusive "world-class" designation that so many countries around the world are striving for is ultimately positional and subjective because of the lack of an absolute set of performance criteria and measures to define it.[11] Yet, this absence of a clear rubric has not dimmed global enthusiasm for creating world-class universities.

The relentless pursuit of world-class universities, often referred
to inside higher education as "internationalization," actually dis-
guises a process of cultural imperialism, and more specifically of
Americanization, since the dominant model of the university is
drawn from elite institutions in the United States (such as Harvard
University and the Massachusetts Institute of Technology). In the
case of China, internationalization means using English (rather than
Mandarin Chinese) as the language of instruction. Likewise, the
English language has become an important component of the dreaded university entrance examinations in South Korea, Japan, China,
and other East Asian countries. Yet, faculty members in South Korea's flagship universities often have difficulty using English in the
classroom and publishing with prestigious international journals
and elite presses.[12]

Based on my own experiences in South Korea during the mid-
1990s, and more recently during a brief stint at Hankuk University
of Foreign Studies in 2013, Korean students who do not gain admission to top universities in their own country now go abroad, rather
than attend second- or third-tier institutions at home. In fact, nearly
240,000 South Korean students studied abroad in 2013, contributing
significantly to "brain drain" in the country.[13] To combat this flight of
students, a fevered competition is brewing among Korean universities
to attract international students, which has resulted in complaints of
lower admission standards for foreigners and campus segregation
between international students and nationals.[14]

Like other countries around the world aspiring to compete for students, faculty, and resources in the global arena of higher education,
Japan is finding that the implementation of English-based instruction in its elite universities has had unintended consequences. Despite best efforts, Japanese students still struggle with English, have
difficulty with Western models of instruction and evaluation, and
complain of foreign pedagogies being adopted without contextualiza-
tion.[15] The widespread reception of American international models of
higher learning brings with it other unintended consequences as well,
including the erosion of traditional teaching methods, the privileging
of English as a lingua franca, and the imposition of American models
of university governance and organization.

In the case of China, global convergence ironically means the adoption of an entrepreneurial model of the world-class research university by a communist government, which sees its own continued existence as inextricably tied to its ability to keep lifting Chinese citizens out of poverty and into the middle class (by transforming its manufacturing economy into a knowledge economy). In order to manufacture a citizenry that can think creatively, China is also implementing a modified version of the American university. This comparative study of China and the United States provides a different perspective on the paradoxes and contradictions that accompany the processes of internationalization in higher education.

For instance, the current neoliberal trends in American secondary education of privatization, standardization, and core curricula are gradually being foisted on higher education. President Barack Obama, whose administration championed the much-maligned "Race to the Top" program, proposed to tie federal funding for higher education (already in decline for three decades) to performance-based "data indicators" like graduation rates, graduate earnings, degree completion times, and other metrics.[16] Global convergence means that such "metrics" (which ostensibly make institutions more easily comparable to one another) may help the United States attain educational outcomes for its citizens that resemble those currently found in China, namely, the production of highly specialized professionals who lack the critical thinking and creative cognitive skills associated with making groundbreaking innovative and technological advancements.

As the Chinese Communist Party moves to create institutions based on Western models of the modern research university, the United States is allowing neoliberal ideology to turn the majority of the faculty into part-time knowledge workers, known as "adjunct" or "contingent" professors. The systematic dismantling of other American traditions in higher education over the last thirty years, such as intellectual freedom protected by tenure and the liberal arts curriculum, has subordinated the principles of free speech and liberty to those of the marketplace.

Thus far, by way of introduction, we have considered the symptoms of the crisis in American higher education, the global quest to establish regional centers containing clusters of world-class universities, and the influence of neoliberalism on the standard model. Readers alarmed by the state of American higher education may wonder what can be done to reverse course. We should first understand what made American colleges and universities truly distinctive between 1945 and 1980 — as well as grasp the processes of internationalization that are standardizing higher education delivery around the world — in order to articulate a new paradigm based on a progressive vision, one that incorporates humanist thought and a greater diversity of representation.

To begin with, we may best position higher learning in the United States in the twenty-first century by understanding those aspects of its educational heritage that led to unrivaled global preeminence after the Second World War and adapting them to the new realities of convergence in which we live. Jonathan Cole asserts that an unusual amalgamation of values once informed the American academy, including universalism, organized skepticism, the creation of new knowledge, the free and open communication of ideas, disinterestedness in financial gain for those ideas, free inquiry, international peer communities, peer review, and working for the common good.[17] These principles will be the benchmarks by which we measure the recent decline of American higher education in a comparative and historical context.

Noting four major shifts in the development of higher education, Robert Paul Wolff observes that the academy was first a sanctuary of scholarship dedicated to the study of the literature and arts and to the discovery of universal human truths. The American college and university next became a training ground for professionals where individuals gained social status through certification (as doctors, lawyers, accountants, and so forth). In the "multiversity" that emerged during the mid- to late twentieth century, sprawling schools of every sort were run by centralized administrations whose chief duty was providing workers for the industrial military complex. Most recently, the American university has become a capitalist firm with a board of directors, and it manufactures educations that students buy.[18] Such a downward momentum should be of grave concern to those working inside the academy as well as to those individuals viewing it critically from afar.

Over the past two decades or so, "everything in higher education, worldwide, has been moving in precisely the wrong direction. The corporatization of education has proceeded apace, with profitability replacing knowledge as the measure of institutional success, and students ever more strongly dissuaded from following the arc of their curiosity by crippling loan burdens."[19] Yet, at their best, argues former president of Stanford University Donald Kennedy, institutions of higher learning in the United States provide "the opportunity to give others the personal and intellectual platform they need to advance the culture, to preserve life, and to guarantee a sustainable human future."[20]

The ideal of academic freedom that arose in American universities in the early to mid-twentieth century insulated professors and their institutions from political interference, thereby protecting heterodox thinking and sanctioning unconventional behavior. As a consequence, creative people were permitted to live creative lives with a loose structure and minimal interference. This arrangement helped to distinguish Henry James's "ivory tower" from the "real world."[21] Today, that distinction is being eroded as more universities seek corporate ties and court private donations, as a way to offset declines in state and federal funding for higher education.

Once enshrined in the tenure system, the guarantee of academic freedom was a defining feature of the American academy. In the 1960s, more than 70 percent of all faculty positions nationwide were tenurable; today that number has dwindled to just 23 percent. Deplorably, the majority of faculty members in the United States now work on a part-time contingent basis, and they are frequently paid wages that put them (and keep them) in poverty. When temp services like EDUStaff are hired to essentially outsource adjunct professor hiring and payroll duties,[22] then we know neoliberalism is slowly exhausting the American university of its intellectual capital.

Moreover, whereas faculty once helped to run the university, power in today's academy has shifted to administrators who make final determinations about nearly all university issues. Stanley Aronowitz suggests that this appropriation of the tradition of shared governance is symptomatic of a more general incorporation of America.[23] The causes for the decline in the quality of American education can be found in shifts from shared governance to a centralized corporate managerialism, the near-disappearance of the tenure system, the deprofessionalization of the faculty, administrative bloat, skyrocketing tuitions, the loss of the humanities in favor of vocationally oriented STEM programs, and the unjustified reliance on adjunct faculty as a cost-saving measure.

Admittedly, in the short term, there may be little danger of Harvard, MIT, or Yale ceding their positions as the preeminent universities in the world to the likes of Beijing, Qinghua, or Fudan in China. Yet, as we shall see, even elite colleges and universities in the United States — with their billion-dollar endowments — are not immune from neoliberalism. The current supremacy of American colleges and universities on the world stage is a consequence of lingering perceptions of excellence, which no longer accord with reality. Because that reputation, outside the top-tier colleges and universities, relies on creditability established long ago, it cannot sustain the academy in perpetuity. At the same time, countries such as China continue to make massive investments in higher education and brazenly imitate Western models of the college and university to create world-class institutions. Chinese educators are also slowly learning how to teach creativity, which propels the innovations upon which economic success rests.

As regional hubs of higher learning (containing concentrations of world-class colleges and universities) take shape around the world, they will compete with each other for an international pool of students and faculty who will be learning, not in decentralized spheres of critical engagement for the public good, but in spaces where city-states and corporations work together to train their knowledge workers. Consider the fact that even as the United States remains the first choice for students around the world, competition from other English-speaking countries, particularly the United Kingdom and Australia, is siphoning off students and attracting faculty. Meanwhile, quickly industrializing nations are investing in the infrastructure projects needed to create their own international (English-speaking) centers of higher learning.

Therefore, the United States has more to squander than the residency of a few eminent scholars and their students by letting its preeminence slip away to other parts of the world. Since the Second World War, higher education has been a major source of international soft power. The exercise of it has always meant welcoming foreign students to our institutions and finding the means for the best to stay after graduation. For those who did return to their home countries, they did so at least with a quality education — as well as some form of cultural assimilation from their exposure to American campus life. Federally funded exchange programs (such as Fulbright-Hayes) brought tens of thousands of international scholars to American shores, and they sent a similar number of American scholars abroad in order to facilitate mutual understanding. American universities "played a significant role in training Chinese doctorates,"[24] for instance, and some of them returned to China having acculturated to a working democracy.

This book finds focus around China and the United States not only because of the author's experience but also because these two countries now share more political and economic interests than possible before 1978. China is America's second-largest trading partner, and it sends more students to the United States than any other country. Moreover, the case of China illustrates the fact that global convergence in higher education benefits developing peripheral and semiperipheral countries by providing them with a (somewhat flawed) template for betterment. To the extent that they can emulate the positive features of American higher education that have helped to shape the dominant model of the world-class university, the United States will gain more rivals for the best faculty and students the world has to offer.

The compelling truth is that the United States has been measurably slipping behind "in a relative sense" since the turn of the millennium due to a steady loss of federal and state financial support, flat wages at public colleges, and a slowdown in the publication rate of American scholars (especially in the public sector).[25] Simultaneously, the advantages enjoyed by institutions of higher learning in the United States (of government support, decentralized competition, openness, and the "first-mover" advantage) are being eroded as graduate programs around the world increasingly attract students.[26] As these trends take firm shape in the coming decades, they will become more apparent to American educators, policy makers, and politicians — who still have an opportunity to respond appropriately.

Time is of critical concern, however, especially in the hard-hit middle and lower tiers of the American higher education system (at two-year colleges, four-year colleges, master's-granting universities, and lower-tier doctoral-granting institutions). It is a matter of time before international students realize that most of their American professors are part-time faculty members who are not treated like accomplished professionals. American scholars of note will start to vote with their feet when other countries offer higher salaries, more resources, and better infrastructure combined with independence and the freedom to pursue pure research—and students will follow them. That more publication is now being done in the European Union than in the United States is a clear indicator that American higher education is losing its edge.

As for China, between 1995 and 2000 the Chinese government spent eighteen billion yuan in support of its policy of establishing "world-class universities" in every region of the country.[27] Some benefits of those investments were clearly visible when I returned to Fudan in 2012 to deliver a lecture on the poet-painter William Blake. In the light-colored brick and concrete building where English literature classes were held in the 1990s, state-of-the-art copiers had replaced purple-ink mimeograph machines, a new humanities library was open and spacious (where the previous one had been dark and dank),and there was even a telecommunications room so that foreign languages and literature faculty members and students could participate in video conferences around the world.

To fully examine the foregoing claims, we start with the radically different cultural assumptions that informed traditional higher learning in China and the United States. Chapter one, "From Mandarins to Mao Zedong," traces the rise of higher learning in China back to the first millennium BCE and offers a detailed overview of Confucianism, the emergence of the imperial civil service examinations, and the formation of the literati class that it succored. The short-lived influences of British, Russian, and American models of higher education in China (after the fall of the last imperial dynasty) are analyzed next, along with the subsequent transformation of the country's first colleges and universities into machines of ideological indoctrination during the rule of Mao Zedong from 1949 to 1976.

The second chapter, "A Shared Humanistic Heritage," traces the origins of higher education in the United States back to its humanistic roots in ancient Greece and its transmission to the Islamic world, where it was preserved and augmented. The Crusades of the Latin Roman Catholic Church helped return Greco-Roman learning to medieval Europe, and its reintroduction inspired the creation of the first universities in the West. We then follow the transmission of the new learning during the Renaissance through the Age of Reason in order to discover the guiding tenets that shaped the first colonial colleges in the New World. The colleges that emerged after the American Revolution were characterized by religious denominationalism, but they gave way to the propagation of public and private liberal arts colleges during the nineteenth century. The first true universities in the United States imitated the nineteenth-century German model of the research institution before making their own way in the twentieth century as sprawling interdisciplinary enterprises of higher learning.

The story of the dramatic reconstitution and expansion of Chinese colleges and universities after 1978 is told in chapter three, "The Chinese Moment." Through a series of carefully calibrated five-year plans and other development strategies that will be reviewed in detail, China created the world's largest higher education delivery system in just four decades. For the sake of contrast, chapter four traces the slow slide of American higher education into crisis starting in the late 1970s. Chapter five attempts to make sense of those two very different paths by considering them in the context of global convergence.

As chapter six, "Pricing the Paradigm Shift," will demonstrate, most American colleges and universities are ill-prepared to compete in our age of global rivalry in the higher education sector. For some readers, the assertion that America's prized system of colleges and universities are mere façades of what they once were (and not so long ago either) may sound alarmist. Yet, a generational neglect of higher education in the United States, coupled with the neoliberal paradigm shift noted earlier, means that the American university requires restoration for a new era of internationalization.

In the brief afterword that brings this book to a close, a series of proposals are put forth for remaking the American palaces of the mind into shining global communities for democracy, freedom, innovation, and creativity. Most institutions of higher learning require reform in order to become decentralized hubs of free inquiry, governed from the bottom up by the faculty, and they can start by severing the corporate ties that have corrupted their nonprofit missions and by streamlining distended campus bureaucracies. At the moment, the United States continues to value higher education as a private commodity rather than a public good — and that means we falter while the world mimics American folly.

CHAPTER ONE

· · · · · · · · · · · · · · · · · · ·

From Mandarins to Mao Zedong

AS THE OLDEST CONTINUOUS civilization in the world, China has a tradition in higher education that dates back thousands of years. We start at the beginning of that history—at the point of greatest divergence between China and the West—in our quest to understand the implications of the acceleration of global convergence in our own time. The ancient Chinese and Greco-Roman traditions of higher learning developed independently of one another, and therefore their pedagogies, educational philosophies, and courses of study reveal to us important cultural presuppositions and innovations passed down to later generations.

In this chapter, we aim to grasp the spirit of Chinese higher education by following its historical permutations, and through them, to arrive at a better understanding of the significance of China's recent departure from its Confucian educational heritage. In chapter two, we trace American higher education to its origins in the classical world and follow its influence into the twentieth century. By historically juxtaposing the Chinese and American humanistic traditions, we seek to better comprehend what has been gained, and lost, for each country in global convergence.

As far back as the Zhou dynasty (1046–256 BCE), perhaps even earlier, a combination of state-supported and private schools first arose to train civil servants in China.[1] From the sixth century to the third century BCE, different schools of philosophy contended with each other for prominence, creating something of a "golden age" known as the Hundred Schools of Thought (诸子百家). Among the better-known schools vying for distinction were Mohism (墨家),

Daoism (道家), Legalism (法家), and Yin and Yang (陰陽家), but far and away Confucianism (儒家) would have the most profound and enduring impact on higher learning. Therefore, any attempt to understand the history of Chinese education is futile without a somewhat nuanced comprehension of Confucian doctrines. Even as Western models of higher learning replace traditional ones in the twenty-first century, core Confucian principles still inform Chinese society.

The Legacy of Confucianism

Confucius (Kong Fuzi, 孔夫子, c. 551–479 BCE) is widely regarded as the first great teacher in China, and although a good deal of his life was filled with suffering, his moral didacticism and backward glance to an earlier era of Chinese history indelibly shaped the contours of Chinese culture for millennia. Born into a period when aggressive martial feudal states led by clan warlords fought each other for dominance, Confucius's father (Kong He, 孔紇) served as a low-ranking officer in the Lu military. Although Kong He had many daughters, in his seventies he took a concubine so that he might have a son. In that desire, he was successful. Yet, when Kong He died just three years later, his long-awaited son and the child's young mother were marginalized, impoverished, and disinherited by jealous family members.

Perhaps because he endured dispossession in his youth, as a young man Confucius worked eagerly at a variety of jobs before becoming a clerk. Little is known about his educational background, but study was undoubtedly of the utmost importance to him, and he gradually established a reputation for being a teacher as well as an honest minor official. Having come of age at a time of fierce warfare and social chaos, Confucius espoused a message of moral rectitude through self-cultivation, which he claimed would lead to a peaceful and prosperous society.

Confucius made the concept of *ren* (benevolence, human heartedness, 仁) foremost in his teaching. The character *ren* consists of the radical denoting a human being together with the number two (in order to give it a pluralistic connotation). Other central Confucian values include *li* (ritual propriety, decorum, 禮), which regulated social interactions along well-defined lines, *qing* (empathy, 情), *xiao* (filial piety, familial obligation, 孝), xing (correct behavior, 行), zhong (loyalty, 忠), and xin (trustfulness, 信). According to Confucius, the superior person cultivates these virtues in order to perfect the self. In doing so, the person simultaneously transforms society positively through an outward manifestation of his or her psychological harmony and order.

This Confucian belief in human perfectibility meant that self-cultivation and lifelong learning became (in a sense) a moral obligation in Chinese culture, for through the transformation of self that continuing education made possible, relationships between individuals could be clarified so as to eliminate strife. For instance, if the head of a household would just practice benevolence (ren) and moral virtue (de, 德) and establish them deeply within himself, then his family relations would be harmonized. And if, by cultivating the self, one's immediate surroundings could be transformed (as the family unit was harmonized through virtue), then it stood to reason that one's town, province, and country would become realms of peace when the emperor was a Junzi (superior person, 君子).

The rulers of the Zhou dynasty developed the concept of the Mandate of Heaven (Tian Ming, 天命) to legitimate their usurpation of the preceding dynasty. They asserted that any right to govern was based on virtue; it was not hereditary or a divine right. If a ruler lost his virtue, he lost the right to lead, and his overthrow was therefore morally justified. Confucius extended this notion of the relationship between virtue and social harmony in his theory of the Junzi. One will know a superior person, argued Confucius, because he "does not seek fulfillment of his appetite nor comfort in his lodging. He is diligent in his duties and careful in his speech. He associates with men of moral principles and thereby realizes himself." Only such a person "may be said to love learning."[2] In this respect, Confucius was quite egalitarian for the time, though he did not extend his generosity to all segments of society. Nevertheless, his ultimate goal was a good society based on benevolent governance and harmonious human relations.

Confucius insisted not only on the "establishment of a social order in which names and ranks are properly regulated, but also the correspondence of words and action, or in its more philosophical aspect, the correspondence of name and actuality."[3] In this way, Confucius attempted to clarify the relationship between sign and symbol, between word and object. Names should correspond closely to actualities, so that on a most basic level, a town named Great Falls would in fact contain waterfalls of a considerable size. If words and actuality fail to correspond, then language will mislead—ultimately resulting in the inability to distinguish right from wrong.

Confucianism took as its central canon a set of texts known as the *Four Books* (四書)[4] and *Five Classics* (五经).[5] They included works of poetry, prose, and history, as well as didactic moral treatises and arcane philosophies. Together with additional texts introduced later, they formed the basis of the imperial civil service examinations. These oral examinations first took place as early as 134 BCE, and successful candidates were granted government positions. They became an important cultural institution from the Tang dynasty (618–907) until their formal abolition in 1905. Most people who studied for the imperial civil service examinations did so not out of a desire to reform society according to the principles of Confucianism but to assume positions of influence, power, and wealth in return for their doctrinal orthodoxy.

In the *Analects* (論語), where many of the teachings of Confucius are preserved, the importance of education is a recurring theme. In the first entry of the first chapter in that collection of aphorisms, the Sage asks: "Is it not a pleasure to learn and to repeat or practice from time to time what has been learned?"[6] According to those who knew him, Confucius genuinely enjoyed discussing poetry, history, and moral values such as propriety, and during his entire life he earnestly sought out ancient teachings.[7] Confucius claimed not to be born with any special knowledge but to have acquired his understanding through a lifetime of diligent study. He was also the first person in Chinese history to assert that in education "there should be no class distinction."[8]

Confucius put into practice doctrines he espoused; he examined himself every day on three points: "whether in counseling others I have not been loyal; whether in intercourse with my friends I have not been faithful; and whether I have not repeated again and again and practiced the instructions of my teacher."[9] In these and other entries, the intersection of education and self-transformation is worthy of note. In fact, so strong was his injunction to cultivate the self through life-long learning that Confucius asserted, "If a superior man is reverential (or serious) without fail, and is respectful in dealing with others and follows the rules of propriety, then all within the four seas (the world) are brothers."[10] In this vision of the unity of mankind, we find a decidedly utopian impulse at the heart of Confucianism—perhaps not so unlike that which pervaded the earliest universities in Europe (and later those in a fledgling nation called the United States of America).

Wing-Tsit Chan credits Confucius with being the founder of private education in China because he had a preference for training students for character over vocation. For this reason, the imperial civil service examinations, whose core curriculum for centuries was based on the Confucian classics, should be considered a distortion of his philosophy (as they fostered careerism). Confucius surrounded himself with gentlemen-scholars, it is true, and over time they became the model for the Chinese literati, who were a mainstay in imperial China throughout most of its history.[11] The literati class was largely composed of individuals who became civil servants (after passing one or more examinations) and assumed various positions of power at local, provincial, and national levels. Since a significant portion of the content of those civil service examinations was made up of literature grounded in moral humanism, for well over a thousand years of Chinese history, students of higher learning, who trained exclusively in what we would call literary studies, occupied a large number of government posts.

As a teacher and civil servant, Confucius pointed toward an ideal way of life (dao, 道), and he insisted on the importance of cultivating friendships with people of integrity, the tireless pursuit of learning, and the cultivation of an aesthetic appreciation of the fine arts. In his twenties and thirties, Master Kong first gathered a band of dedicated scholars around him. Living in his native state of Lu at the time, Confucius earned appointments to minor posts and rose to the level of magistrate in his middle years. Yet, despite that modest success in government, he grew frustrated with a lack of interest in implementing his philosophy among his state's leaders. As his zeal for social reform strengthened, he left the state of Lu and began a period of wandering that lasted more than ten years. He was searching for a forward-looking leader in another state who would appoint only superior persons to the highest ranks of government.

When he failed to discover a leader who would agree with such a radical notion as insisting on virtue among government officials, Confucius returned to Lu and set up a school that eventually attracted thousands of students. There he spent the remainder of his life teaching and editing his beloved classics, including the *Spring and Autumn Annals* (*Lin Jing*, 麟经) and a commentary on the *Book of Changes* (*Yi-jing*, 易经). Although Confucius never found an opportunity to put his ideas for social reform into action in his own lifetime, today higher education throughout all of East Asia, and parts of South Asia such as Vietnam, have been profoundly influenced by his educational philosophy.[12]

We noted that Confucianism exercised an enduring influence in China as the *Four Books* and *Five Classics* formed the basis of the imperial civil service examinations. Since medieval times, explains Benjamin Elman, "imperial dynasties, gentry-literati elites, and classical studies were tightly intertwined in the operation of the civil service examination."[13] When they were formally ended in the twentieth century, the connection between political power and literary culture was severed forever, as China lurched, sometimes haltingly, toward the West and its conception of the university.

The Imperial Civil Service Examinations

During the Han dynasty (202 BCE–220 CE), the civil service examinations began testing candidates on what would become the traditional canon. At that time, kinship and official recommendations were still the traditional methods of gaining access to political and social power, but textual expertise in one of the *Five Classics* was required for appointment to the politically powerful Han Imperial Academy (*Taixue*, 太學), which was formed to ensure the transmission of orthodox texts under imperial censorship.[14] Some estimates suggest that tens of thousands of Chinese students attended "institutions of higher learning" in the Han capital of Chang'an (present-day Xi'an) during the height of its prosperity.[15]

In later centuries, the Chinese civil service examinations became "a cultural arena within which diverse political and social interests contested each other and were balanced." In it, rulers and bureaucrats alike tried to control literati culture through the examinations.[16] As they became political litmus tests, the quest to become a mandarin (scholar-official) and join the literati class soon meant putting self-interest before the public good that Confucius promoted. Success and influence came to candidates "who transmitted the accepted canonical traditions, while those who held dissenting views were shut out of the bureaucracy and banned from any future service." As a consequence of this unfortunate turn from the second century onward, individuals with unorthodox scholarly outlooks (who could not pass the examinations) sought other vehicles for their ideas by founding regional private academies, which thrived toward the end of the Han period.[17]

During the Tang dynasty (618–907), the civil service examinations grew into a two-tier process carried out in the capital. Schools, including those in the prefectures, and successful mandarin officials recommended the candidates who took those examinations. Initially, policy essay questions became the norm, but a turn took place toward "poetry questions and literary formalism in the curriculum" for the Jinshi (進士) examinations after the year 681.[18] A newly centralized Tang government made use of this strengthened civil service examination system to replace aristocrats in government positions with literati court officials (ostensibly following the Confucian emphasis on merit and ability over the birthright of the ruling class). The triennial palace examinations in the capital (held at court from the Tang period until the fall of the last dynasty) were the final hurdle to acquiring the Jinshi designation held by those who passed the final examination.[19]

On the surface at least, the civil service examinations made a nod to the Confucian principle of a meritocracy in the advent of its two-tier (and later three-tier) structure that seemed open to anyone who cared to participate. In reality, however, the emergence of quota systems stipulating the number of passing graduates facilitated geographical, ethnic, and political favoritism. Moreover, the local recommendation process allowed for preferentialism and thereby encouraged corruption. In this manner, the country's system of higher learning gradually drifted away from its Confucian ideals.

Confucius always held that human nature was originally good, but he observed that morally minded people could be lured away from the path of virtue by the promise of worldly profit and pleasure. Over time, the mandarin scholar-bureaucrat gained a reputation for corruptibility that flew in the face of traditional Confucian values. The Confucian emphasis on learning as a means to cultivate virtue became forever transformed, as higher learning became a vehicle not for self-betterment but for worldly success. Such a perversion of higher learning would have come as a great disappointment to Confucius, who declared righteously, "The superior man thinks of virtue; the inferior man thinks of possessions," for the Junzi "understands righteousness; the inferior man understands profit."[20]

Although use of the examination system as a method of insuring orthodoxy and political loyalty among civil servants persisted until the late nineteenth century, by around 1100 shifts in patterns for the appointment of mandarins meant that literati civil officials outnumbered the aristocracy—who slowly became unable to "perpetuate themselves in dynastic offices." Gaining an education that prepared one to pass the civil service examinations, therefore, developed into an important investment once they became "a means to legitimate dominance in the local economy, institutions, and cultural activities."[21]

During the relatively short and foreign Yuan dynasty (1271–1368), Mongol warrior elites employed Muslim and Tibetan outsiders to rule the Han Chinese. Jinshi quotas dropped quickly as the dynastic aristocracy asserted itself, and so most high-ranking government positions were filled by other means, such as recommendations. Between 1315 and 1400, a period of eighty-five years, only twenty-one hundred Jinshi degrees were awarded, a mere thirty-four per year for the entire country.[22]

The founder of the Ming dynasty (1368–1644), the Hongwu emperor (1328–1398), sought the support of the Han Chinese literati after the fall of the Yuan dynasty. During the dynasty's early years, a resurgence took place in the examinations in discourse and policy questions; poetry was eliminated completely from the civil service curriculum (although banned belles lettres "survived as popular genres in private poetry societies"). The Hongwu emperor reestablished the Hanlin Academy as well, and he ordered the creation of schools in every prefect and county in order to carry out an "educational transformation of the people."[23] Although the details of that transformation are beyond the scope of this study, his educational plan was as ambitious for its time as the one undertaken by the Chinese central government in the 1990s.

The first Ming era provincial and metropolitan examinations in 1370 required essay responses expounding upon the interrelationships between the Four Books and the Five Classics. In the second session, candidates wrote a discourse essay, and in the third, they answered a single policy question. As it became increasingly formalized, the imperial civil service examination system significantly shaped what students studied (and rarely did it correspond to the true spirit of Confucianism). For example, incredible feats of memorization were required to deal on the spot with a significant number of canonical texts that each required sophisticated interpretation.

Elman reports that memorizing the Four Books and the Five Classics alone required learning 10,000 different Chinese characters. The extended curriculum of the Thirteen Classics (十三经) meant that students had to remember more than 500,000 repeating graphs. At a rate of 200 per day, it took at least 6 years to memorize 400,000 characters. As a result, memorization became "a pedagogic tool to produce shared linguistic conventions by education."[24] The highly prized ability to memorize as a habit of learning endures to this day in China. Yet, this emphasis on the development of prodigious memories has had the unfortunate consequence of privileging rote learning over the creative synthesis of knowledge; for this reason, China now looks to the West for higher education reform (as chapter three will show).

During the Ming dynasty, there were four main periods of the imperial civil service examination system: from 1465 to 1506 essay writers "stuck close to the original text and its commentaries"; during the years 1506 to 1567 themes and meanings had to be made explicit; between 1567 and 1620 examination responses highlighted verbal cleverness and word play; and in the final period from 1621 to 1644 essays became "genuinely creative."[25] Overall, however, sample essays from study manuals of the period and answers reproduced from memory after the examinations show that good writing during the Ming dynasty consisted of appropriate political language rather than artful craftsmanship.[26]

Whereas a Westerner might imagine that essay responses on the civil service examinations required linear development and evidential support, in fact the nature of the interpretive task faced by Chinese examinees differed considerably, as can be illustrated by the case of the much dreaded "eight legged essay" that was prevalent during the Ming-Qing period. Writers had to open with a proposition around which the essay would be focused and then elaborate on it using brief phrases that suggested the broader scope of the topic. The body of the essay consisted of three parallel comparisons that expressed the moral reasoning of the argument, before a final turn summarized the claim and made clear its moral implications.[27]

Because success on local, provincial, and national examinations was so closely tied to social status and access to power, a variety of schools proliferated during the Qing dynasty (1644–1911). Like the Mongol Yuan dynasty before it, the Qing was also a foreign dynasty. A bilingual state resulted, one in which the power of the foreign rulers from the north was reinforced by the continued use of the Manchu language concurrently with Chinese. During this period, the introduction of traditional nomadic skills such as horsemanship and archery competed directly with the Han emphasis on becoming a Confucian gentleman. Most scholars agree that the Manchus succumbed to a process of sinification during their rule as they gradually adopted Han language, culture, and traditions.

The system of schools established during the last imperial dynasty in China aimed to educate imperials, nobles, and ethnic bannermen (companies of warriors organized under a flag or banner) to serve the Manchu state. According to the eminent Chinese scholar Zhou Ruchang, "princes began their studies with tutors as early as age five, while other royal clansmen started attending government schools at eight. Members of the Lower Eight Banners could start attending government school at age ten. Only the best children of bondservants were selected for the government schools such as Jingshan or Xian'an beyond the age of thirteen."[28]

Pamela Crossley suggests thinking about the relationship between the Qing schools (serving princes, royal clansmen, bannermen, and commoners) as concentric circles, "which from the center out represent decreasing degrees of prestige, state aid, and political demands." In the center was the National Academy (*Guoxue*) for those ennobled by the court (as well as some banner officers). Next were the Imperial Clan Academies (*Zongxue*) that educated those who satisfied the formal requirements for being members of the Imperial Clan.[29]

Further outward still would be the Imperial Household Department Academies (*Neiwu Fu*) where up to 360 youths selected from various departments in the imperial household could study, and there was also a school for the children of palace officers from the Imperial Household Department and the Eight Banners.[30] Each of the Eight Banners (Qing organizational units) contained officers' schools, and further out in the imaginary concentric circles were special state schools "established for the eight military banners (composed of Manchus, Mongols, and Chinese military families)," followed by smaller schools founded for commoners.[31]

Until the late nineteenth century, formal education in China was the privilege of men only. While the social elite of previous dynasties educated their daughters using didactic texts that were largely moralistic, a group of "female scholars" (*nüshi*) emerged during the Qing dynasty to challenge higher education for women that aimed merely to "silence subversives and convert them into participants in the dominant discourse" through circumscribed educational regimens.[32] Because upper-class women were expected to write poetry, which required a high level of cultural literacy, educated females were torn between two contradictory models: the female scholar who transgressed social boundaries and expectations, and the virtuous woman who obeyed and stayed in her place.

Although there were few formal higher educational opportunities for women during the Qing dynasty, some refused to marry (as was customary) and instead became "palace instructresses." Following this unorthodox path, more than a few Chinese women managed to earn fame for their poetry and paintings.[33] For a stirring literary portrayal of female scholars, and an explication of the multiple social pressures they faced, the reader might find the depiction of learned women in the celebrated novel *Dream of the Red Chamber* (红楼梦) of interest. The two heroines, Lin Dai-yu and Xue Bao-chai, studied the same canonical texts as their male counterparts who were preparing for the civil service examinations—and they often proved themselves superior in both wit and erudition to many rather dull male pedants.

As we move toward the profound and manifold shifts in the landscape of Chinese higher education during the later Qing period and into the early twentieth century, let us contemplate for a moment the profound impact that the civil service examinations had on those who took them, on their families, and even on Chinese culture writ large (for their history correlates with the university entrance examination system faced by modern Chinese students). The formal selection process for civil service examination candidates began in the secondary schools. Appointment to an official government post as a mandarin required passing through a series of increasingly selective examinations, and then securing a formal recommendation.[34] Competition for positions was intense, even though the number of individuals who passed licensing and county examinations (held annually and biennially) gradually increased during the mid- to late Qing period, despite the continued use of quota systems.

For example, there was only one licentiate (or successful local candidate) per 2,000 persons in 1400, but by 1700, that ratio was one licentiate per 300 people. These statistics may be initially misleading, however, because the "ratio of licentiates to population became lower and thus less competitive over time" while the likelihood of passing the "higher examinations that entitled them to civil appointments also decreased."[35] By the middle of the nineteenth century, only 1.5 percent of an estimated two million candidates passed licensing and county examinations. Only 5 percent of those individuals passed the biennial examinations, and of the remainder only 20 percent would pass the triennial metropolitan exams. Elman estimates that the odds of success in all stages of the selection process were just 1 in 6,000 (or 0.02 percent).[36] It is a shockingly low figure that speaks to the long tradition of high-pressure examinations in Chinese higher education.

The Ming-Qing triennial provincial and metropolitan examinations were so competitive that young people in their late teens, making a first try, would sit with their elders, some of whom might be on their last attempt after four decades (or more) of futile striving. Feng Menglong (冯梦龙, 1574–1646), for example, failed each time he attempted to pass the metropolitan civil service examinations. Instead of serving in an official post, he devoted himself to collecting and editing popular writings (such as plays and folk songs) in his later years, some of which were translated into European languages.[37]

Corruption (the purchase of degrees, examiner bribery, cheating in the examination halls), the guarantee of hereditary titles for some clans, geographical discrepancies in pass rates, and linguistic barriers all added to the sense of righteous indignation felt by unsuccessful candidates.[38] Because pass rates for the higher examinations were so low, there emerged a whole class of disgruntled individuals who would occasionally turn their pens against the state. Others chose to retreat from what they saw as the co-opting of Confucian principles and scorned those who endeavored, sometimes into old age, to gain official appointment.

Chinese literature is full of vituperative implicit and explicit attacks on the civil service examination system. Cao Xueqin, for instance, "was disgusted by the eight-legged essay" form and in his celebrated novel he called people who studied this self-serving type of writing "career worms" (禄蠹).[39] The civil service examinations were loathed as "a carefully balanced and constantly contested piece of educational and social engineering" that over centuries was "worked out by cooperation between the imperial dynasty and its gentry-dominated society."[40]

Students who made their way through the series of examinations often felt acute anxiety, which they fought off by employing all types of divinations, talismans, interpretations of dreams, and religious rituals aimed at predicting or improving outcomes. These examinations inflicted great emotional stress on the candidates and their families because there was only a small chance of successfully passing them. Like their civil service examination precursors, which resulted in a uniformity of views among the mandarin class (since they were essentially political tests and ideological tools used to ensure political loyalty), modern Chinese university entrance exams in the mid- to late twentieth century also tended to reinforce dominant ideologies (including the cult of Mao).

Early Stirrings of Reform

The mid- to late Qing dynasty marks an important threshold after which Chinese higher education speedily converges with the West following centuries of independent development. The influx of Western learning that began during the Ming dynasty continued steadily into the Qing period. As Western learning became more influential throughout the country, the educational traditions associated with the imperial civil service examinations became a "residual" culture of the past (albeit one that continues to inform the present), while Western models of higher learning became "emergent" in China and in East Asia more generally.

Although Jesuit scholars, such as Matteo Ricci (1552–1610), first introduced Western mathematics and astronomy into China in the sixteenth century, only in the final decades of the Qing dynasty (from 1850 to 1911) did the convergence of Chinese and Western higher education begin to accelerate. For even though elements of Jesuit scientific education were taken up in imperial Qing institutions, including a study plan in philosophy for the Kangxi emperor (1654–1722), "on the whole this influence remained secondary."[41] In fact, Western learning only gained a foothold in China for economic and military reasons. Referred to as the "sick man of Asia" during the late nineteenth and early twentieth centuries, China could no longer compete against the technological innovations of the European Industrial Revolution.

Humiliatingly, the Chinese were forced to sign the Nanjing Treaty in 1842, which ceded Hong Kong to the British (an arrangement that would last until the territory's return in 1997). China would have to contend with similar colonial land grabs into the twentieth century, even having to sanction the creation of French, American, German, and Japanese concession areas that had their own police forces and separate legal systems. The French Concession, for example, was established in 1849 and was not dissolved until 1943.

An impoverished farm boy with a talent for scholarship led the Taiping Rebellion that erupted in southern China from 1850 to 1864. After attempting to pass the provincial civil service examinations four times and repeatedly failing, Hong Xiuquan (洪秀全) became ill. In delirium, he experienced strange visions of an old man with a flowing gold beard. Some time after he recovered, he rediscovered a book outlining the basic principles of Christianity. Reading through it again, he suddenly realized that his visions seemed to be conversations with God in heaven. Such historical intersections of traditions are another feature of global convergence.

After he recovered from his illness, Hong Xiuquan gradually attracted a group of military-minded converts through his preaching of "a strange blend of Christian reform, anti-Christianity, and Confucianism."[42] By 1853, Hong and his impromptu army had taken the important city of Nanjing, and thereafter they gained control over a wide swath of southern China. In due course, Hong declared himself Jesus's younger brother and the second Son of God. He and his converts managed to keep the Taiping Rebellion alive for nearly fifteen years, and its emphasis on reforming social ills (such as gambling, prostitution, and opium abuse) was a harbinger of change that would manifest in such leaders as Sun Yat-sen and Mao Zedong.

Although traditional higher education in imperial China worked fairly well for training civil servants loyal to the court, it was ill-suited for producing the scientists and engineers that the country needed to modernize and industrialize. From the 1860s onward, therefore, Western-style professional schools were established in China to train technicians, and translators began rendering foreign learning into Chinese. Because the civil service examinations were still in place, these Western professional schools remained marginalized until after the fall of the Qing dynasty in 1911.

When the Guangxu emperor (Aisin-Gioro Dzai-Tiyan, 1871–1908) initiated his "Great Reform" in 1898, he created "a country-wide hierarchy of schools, topped by universities" that taught modern as well as classical subjects. A provision was included for Chinese students to be sent abroad to study and for Western subjects to be incorporated into the civil service examinations during their final years.[43] The first three Chinese pupils were sent to the United States in 1847. That number increased slowly, with only 120 students finding their way to the United States in 1872. Today, there are more than 230,000 Chinese students studying in American institutions of higher education.

One reason for the slow start to Chinese-American international student exchanges in the nineteenth century was that the Chinese government directed the majority of its students to European countries—and even to Japan, "where they experienced the European university model with a Japanese imprint."[44] The renowned short story writer Lu Xun (1881–1936), for instance, studied medicine in Japan on a Qing government scholarship starting in 1902, and he returned to the country for further study two years later. Broadly speaking, the advent of Western imperialism in Asia and other parts of the world during the nineteenth century meant the swift diffusion of the European model of the university throughout much of the world,[45] and China was no exception.

Regrettably but undeniably, the Confucian emphasis on an idealized past, perverted though it was by the competitive nature and vocational orientation of the civil service examinations, produced a backward-looking intelligentsia ill-equipped to lead China into the twentieth century. Like Japan before it, China realized that it would have to adopt the weaponry of the West in order to ward off European imperialist desires—and that would mean co-opting Western models of the university. The dire reality of China's economic and military situation meant that the European (and to a lesser extent the American) university model gradually gained a foothold in the country at the dawn of the twentieth century.

The Imperial University of Peking (京师大学) opened its gates in 1898 (and continues today as Beijing University, China's preeminent institution of higher learning). Fudan University in the southern city of Shanghai was founded in 1905, and Tsinghua University followed in 1911, just as the Qing collapsed and ushered in a new era in Chinese history. While it only lasted thirty-four years, a Western-style university system was firmly established in China during what would become known as the Republican period (1911–1949).

When the Qing dynasty fell, traditional Chinese forms of knowledge concerning the natural world were labeled "superstitions" while modern science was championed by Chinese intellectuals "in its European and American forms" as the path to knowledge, enlightenment, and national power. Despite their living legacy in modern civil service and college entrance exams in China after 1911, the end of the Qing marks a clean break from the cultural history of the Ming-Qing civil service examinations as they existed from 1370 to 1905.[46]

From Republic to People's Republic

A revolutionary and cofounder of the Nationalist Party (Guomindang), Sun Yat-sen (1866–1925) was the first president of the Republic of China. Sun went to school in Hawaii as a teenager, spoke English, adopted Christianity, and studied Western medicine at what is now the

University of Hong Kong. He was repeatedly exiled to Japan and several Western countries for fomenting revolt against Qing rule in the southern part of the country. Had his health not failed him, China's path to prosperity through the twentieth century might not have been so tragic. For after he died, the Nationalist Party fractured and Chiang Kai-shek (1887–1975) emerged as China's new leader (by marrying into Sun Yat-sen's family and claiming his political mantle).

Chinese higher education somehow managed to fitfully move forward during the chaotic Republican period. After the utter collapse of imperial China, the normally inward-looking Chinese people were bombarded with foreign products, ideas, and even religious traditions (propagated by eager Protestant and Catholic missionaries whose numbers in China dramatically increased). The return of Chinese nationals studying abroad facilitated this influx of foreign culture, as did the growing flow of trade throughout the former empire.

Around the turn of the twentieth century, the effort to transform the handful of established Chinese universities into institutions that more closely resembled their Western counterparts (in terms of structure and curricula) assumed a heightened urgency. Due to the small number of Chinese Western-style higher education institutions operating in the country, by 1917 foreign-run missionary universities grew to accommodate nearly 90 percent of all Chinese students. In response, the Chinese government began to build new institutions of higher learning, and in the early 1920s, there were at least thirty-five university-level institutions, sixty-eight provincial colleges (to train technicians and translators), and eight teaching (normal) colleges in China.[47]

More secularly minded intellectuals, writers, and professors were lured to China from the West. John Dewey (1859–1952), the great advocate for American experiential progressive education, taught in China from 1919 to 1921. Hu Shih (1891–1962), the equally legendary Chinese scholar and leader of the New Culture Movement (新文化运动), who had studied with Dewey at Columbia, translated for him at Peking University. Hu Shih helped to promote cultural reform in China that was grounded in pragmatism.

The eventual disappearance of Confucianism (and its corresponding humanist vision) in the university curriculum meant that disciplines such as law, commerce, engineering, and agriculture quickly became ascendant, as they were perceived to be better suited to the realities of twentieth-century globalization and industrialization. Although Chinese higher education generally tried to strike a balance between foreign influences and indigenous development during the Republican era,[48] the push to infuse Chinese universities with science and technology during the years 1927 to 1949 meant moving away from Japanese and European models of the university—and embracing an American model. This reorientation of higher education delivery in China gave rise to competition between government-sponsored institutions of higher learning and private ones (which included thirteen American-founded Christian colleges that reproduced American-style liberal arts education).[49]

The Japanese invasion of northern China in 1937 exploited the schism between the Republicans and the Communists in order to further Japanese colonial aims. The imperial occupation severely disrupted the development of higher education in the north from 1937 until 1945 (and it constitutes one of several major setbacks in Chinese higher education reform during the last one hundred years). Rui Yang reports that 91 of 108 higher education institutions in China were damaged during the Second Sino-Japanese War (the first conflict was fought over Korea from 1894 to 1895). Student populations dropped, some colleges and universities were forced to move to remote locations, and almost all colleges and universities struggled to retain the resources necessary to functioning institutions. Even so, higher education enrollments grew in China overall, and by 1945 there were 141 institutions of higher learning in China.[50]

With the defeat of the Japanese Empire by the Allied Forces the same year and the elimination of the Japanese threat to Chinese sovereignty, the Chinese civil war between the Nationalist Party and the Communist Party intensified. Despite continuing financial and military support from the United States, Chiang Kai-shek's grip on power weakened, in part due to corruption in his own ranks, while the armies of Mao Zedong (1893–1976) practiced land redistribution, punished exploitative landowners, set up primary schools, and promised social reforms based on Communist notions of equality. Spurred on by the economic woes that hobbled the Republic of China leading up to 1949, and fanning the flames of thousands of years of exploitation by an elite class (of aristocrats, mandarins, and civil servants), the Chinese Communist Party swelled its ranks with discontented peasants and workers.

As peace talks between the warring factions broke down in 1946, Chiang Kai-shek launched a massive assault against his enemies in the Chinese Communist Party, but the passive defense strategy of the Communists drew Chiang's army into the vast interior of China and gradually wore them down. Within two years, the balance of power in the conflict began to shift, and the Communist forces started to take city after city—and to capture Guomingdang troops and seize much needed equipment.

Mao Zedong and his ragtag Communist army finally overran Chiang Kai-shek in 1949, forcing the general to move his exiled government to the island of Formosa (now Taiwan). On October 1, 1949, Mao Zedong declared the establishment of the People's Republic of China. During what remained of his life, Mao would preside over many tumultuous social transformations in China, some of which would move the country forward, and others that would severely hamper the development of higher education in the country. After less than fifty years of engagement with the rest of the world during the Republican Period, China would once again seal itself off for decades, this time under Communist rule, and it would seek a solution to the pressures of modernity from within, rather than from without.

Lurching toward Modernity

During the Mao era, both higher and lower education were retooled to increase literacy and to inculcate students with socialist cultural values. Similar to the way that Western educated intellectuals like Hu Shih and Lu Xun tried to shift China away from feudal thinking and the backward glance of Confucianism in the early part of the twentieth century, Mao insisted on a new set of moral values borrowed from the West. While the scholarly consensus is that Mao Zedong did little to advance Marxist thought, he did find ways to make its socialist message more central to the Chinese experience. Mao unapologetically used education at all levels to instill a uniform set of values in the population that would help China to embrace industrialization.

Rather than looking to the capitalist United States of America for educational reform, the Chinese Communist Party (CCP) turned logically to the Union of Soviet Socialist Republics (USSR) during the 1950s. The Chinese higher education system thus became the tool of a new political order that wanted to industrialize China's economy in order to catch up with leading Western nations as quickly as possible. Their goal was to create a planned economy under the control of a central government with a hierarchical and authoritarian political order.[51] Higher education fell victim to this centralization, but education played an important role in supporting policies advanced by the CCP leadership, who were closely imitating Soviet models of higher learning.

Between 1949 and 1978, liberal humanist education essentially disappeared in China. All existing private universities and colleges were brought under the jurisdiction of a central or provincial government by 1952. Since missionary universities and other private institutions were regarded as perpetrators of Western cultural imperialism, they were shut down or incorporated into existing establishments of higher learning. To create a socialist, central planned economy, thousands of Russian experts representing many fields of inquiry were invited to China to help develop its higher education system. The curricula, course syllabi, and textbooks that Soviet scholars brought to China were carefully translated and widely distributed. The founding of the Chinese Academy of Sciences dates from this period, although technically it existed independently of the Chinese higher education system.[52]

C. T. Hu rightly observed that the revolutionary changes in Chinese society during the early years of Communist rule shook loose the foundation upon which Chinese society had rested for thousands of years. Hu pointed to the 1954 Chinese People's Political Consultative Conference, whose stated goals included "the raising of the cultural level of the people, the training of personnel for national construction work, the eradication of feudal, compradore, and fascist ideology, and the developing of an ideology of service to the people."[53] Because these reforms aimed to make higher education accessible to workers and peasants, they represent the beginnings of the massification of higher education in China. Moreover, the policy of making higher education open to all of its citizens was a marked departure from the civil service examinations that supported elite power in imperial China. What has unfortunately remained consistent since then is the use of higher education as a means of political indoctrination.

The stated goal of the Great Leap Forward campaign (大跃进) at the close of the 1950s was to overtake British industrial production levels in fifteen years and American output in another fifteen. Such aspirations provided a powerful narrative around which central and local governments could effectively organize the populace into communes. Peasants were taken from the fields to help make steel in makeshift smelting furnaces, and in the enthusiasm created by state propaganda, everyday metal utensils, such as kitchen wares and farm tools, were melted down in backyards and in communal furnaces across China. Even those living in urban centers were encouraged to build steel furnaces and participate.

Mao next organized rural workers and peasants into collective communes so that he could boost agricultural and urban industrial production concurrently (in the hopes of generating much-needed export revenues). To that end, he completely abolished private property by 1958. In the rural communes, which numbered in the tens of thousands at the height of the Great Leap Forward, kitchens were communalized, food and medical care were provided gratis, and alternate systems of accountability and remuneration took the place of monetary wages. Needless to say, this system of social organization, and the new morality that accompanied it, was extremely foreign to most Chinese people. Yet, all attempts to resist communalization were met with party-orchestrated struggle sessions in which errant individuals were subjected to peer pressure and sometimes violence to make them conform to a newly shared reality of communal life.

The central Chinese government put intense pressure on regional and local leaders to demonstrate increases in agricultural and industrial output during the Great Leap Forward. Rather than admit failure, those in positions of power began to falsify output figures, which gave the central leadership in Beijing the impression that its communal reforms were working—indeed faster than expected—when in fact they were an egregious disaster. By the end of the 1950s, signs of famine emerged in the country, which portended a period of extended suffering for the Chinese people.

One economic study of the Great Leap Forward suggests that in 1959 national grain output plunged by 15 percent and decreased "by another 16 percent in the following two years." A three-year run of bad weather exacerbated the results of the poor agricultural policies instituted by Mao, but reductions in labor and acreage used in grain production, reduced work incentives on the people's communes, and the inability of peasants to leave them were all contributing factors to the disaster.[54] In all, tens of millions of Chinese lost their lives to famine between 1959 and 1961. Wei Li and Dennis Yang report, "demographers who extrapolated mortality trends in China estimated the total number of premature deaths during the GLF famine at between 16.5 and 30 million. Even by the most conservative estimates, this famine ranked worst in the loss of human lives in recorded world history."[55]

Somewhat surprisingly, the number of higher education institutions in China grew from over two hundred to just under thirteen hundred from 1957 to 1960, while total enrollments reached nearly one million. Amid this hectic and often uncoordinated expansion, worsening Sino-Soviet relations, and the great famine, the Ministry of Education consolidated the number of higher education institutions in China to just over four hundred, which resulted in increases in the quality of instruction and institutional efficiency.[56] Following the Sino-Soviet estrangement in the early 1960s, the English language was once again introduced in the schools (replacing Russian), but political indoctrination, physical labor for all citizens, and the advancement of science and technology remained the foremost goals of education policy in China.

By the middle 1960s, new rectification campaigns emerged to address problems that Mao saw in the political, ideological, organizational, and economic spheres — and to counter what he viewed as a re-emerging capitalist sentiment among some in leadership positions. Shih Ming Hu observes that the idea of spending half the school day working and half studying, which characterized the curriculum of secondary schools during this period of communist rule, found its correlate in the labor university. The curricula in these Chinese communist labor universities closely coordinated the study of class relations with experimental work and productive labor, but political education was particularly stressed. For example, although half of all classroom time was spent on theoretical material and the other half on labor lessons, "politics was supposed to occupy the largest proportion of time allocated to the theoretical courses."[57]

The unqualified economic disaster of the Great Leap Forward, as well as lingering anger over earlier anti-rightist campaigns that persecuted intellectuals and dissidents unrelentingly, led many in the Communist Party leadership to question Chairman Mao's ability to move China in a positive direction. In retaliation for harboring such doubts, Mao Zedong removed several prominent leaders from power who he believed wanted to temper his radical communal reforms. Writing provocatively in a Central Committee circular on May 16, 1966, Mao urged the full implementation of the Cultural Revolution:

> Socialist society covers a fairly long historical stage. In this stage, classes, class contradictions and class struggle continue, the struggle between the socialist road and the capitalist road continues and the danger of capitalist restoration remains. We must recognize the protracted and complex nature of this struggle . . . Otherwise a socialist country like ours will turn into its opposite and degenerate, and a capitalist restoration will take place.
>
> Those representatives of the bourgeoisie who have sneaked into the Party, the government, the army and various spheres of culture are a bunch of counter-revolutionary revisionists. Once conditions are ripe, they will seize political power and turn the dictatorship of the proletariat into a dictatorship of the bourgeoisie. Some of them we have already seen through, others we have not. Some are still trusted by us and are being trained as our successors, persons like Khrushchov, for example, who are still nestling beside us. Party committees at all levels must pay full attention to this matter.[58]

This quotation is interesting for many reasons: the reference to the Soviet leader, the initiation of another round of cultural struggle against the ills of capitalism, the open encouragement of the continued persecutions of anti-Maoist elements in the party—and Mao's unintentional prescience in terms of his prediction of a "capitalist restoration" (which would indeed take place after his passing).

In his last successful quest to cling to power, Mao Zedong engineered a cult of personality that depicted him as the rising sun, and he
recruited the nation's young people to help him to overturn the "Four
Olds" (四旧), which he argued still plagued Chinese society: old ideas,
old culture, old customs, and old habits. Anything that smacked of
feudalism (and therefore Confucianism), capitalism, or the bourgeoisie was to be overturned. Millions of young people dropped out of
school and attended mass rallies in which public officials, teachers,
doctors, and anyone suspected of harboring "old ideas" would be denounced, purged, or sent to rural work camps. By the time his 1966
Great Proletarian Cultural Revolution (文化大革命) ended completely
ten years later, Mao Zedong would be dead. Within a couple of years
of his passing, a new era in Chinese history would sweep away the
stale ideologies of this Communist era, and in their place would arise
a doctrine of openness and engagement with the rest of the world that
continues to this day.

During the Cultural Revolution, Mao mandated a project of massive relocation in which young people and urbanites were sent to
the countryside to work as laborers, and peasants and workers were
moved into urban areas to fill vacant positions (resulting from persecutions). Jung Chang, for instance, recounts her experience becoming
a "barefoot doctor" in the rural southwest of the country—despite
having no previous medical training. The early Communist drive for
mass literacy through education quickly degenerated into ideological witch-hunts, and schools in many areas were closed. However,
as Chang notes, many peasants did not even want schools, for the
"virtual absence of any chance of a better future and the near total
immobility for anyone born a peasant took the incentive out of the
pursuit of knowledge."[59]

Throughout this period, teachers were "vilified, defenestrated,
rusticated or murdered, as the Confucian bond of loyalty between
students and mentors was ruptured." University entrance examinations were halted, and classrooms across the nation were emptied as
propaganda made scholarly pursuits bourgeois. Farm work and labor
were lauded in their place.[60] For ten years, the country's universities
languished where they had previously progressed by following Russian and American models.

By some estimates, enrollments in Chinese institutions of higher learning declined by more than six hundred thousand between the years 1965 and 1970 to just forty-eight thousand individuals, many of whom were enrolled as "worker-peasant-solider students" based on "political criteria with no consideration of academic qualifications."[61] By 1976, the year the United States was celebrating two hundred years of independence from England, higher education enrollments in China rebounded to more than five hundred thousand, but again most students studied at "workers universities" (with names like "May 7 Cadres Schools"). Flourishing at the end of the Cultural Revolution, their purpose was clear: to instill political correctness and teach technical skills—and "therefore the core curriculum at these institutions was proletarian politics and communist ideology."[62]

From the low point around 1970, China gradually rebounded to become the largest higher education delivery system in the world today. The story of that miraculous renovation and development will be told in chapter three. Suffice it to say, for the moment, the "central purpose of China's modern higher education is to combine Chinese and Western elements." Rui Yang has good reason to assert that such a synergistic relationship between East and West has "never been achieved" in China,[63] but one fundamental claim of this study is that we are witnessing a convergence in global higher education around the model of the world-class university, which is largely an American construction.

We turn now to the historical development of the college and university in the United States, beginning with its ancient classical heritage. In such a comparative context, we realize that the shared importance of humanistic learning and the tradition of elite education in America and China provide a framework upon which the convergence of their higher educational systems is being built.

. . . .

CHAPTER TWO

A Shared Humanistic Heritage

DESPITE ITS CURRENT superpower status, the United States is still a young country with a dramatically shorter history than China. Strictly speaking, American higher education begins in the seventeenth century with the founding of the first colonial colleges prior to the Revolutionary War (1775–1783). However, in order to comprehend the depth of the current crisis in American higher education in its entirety, we should understand its humanistic heritage from the ancient world.

The earliest American colonial colleges drew from an enduring Greco-Roman classical tradition and benefited from the development of the first universities in the late medieval period; ultimately, though, these colleges were based on the northern European university that took shape in the Renaissance and flowered during the Enlightenment. Over the course of time, they would transform that inheritance into a uniquely American model that would become the basis of the modern world-class university, or universal university, around which global higher education is converging in the twenty-first century.

In the previous chapter, we followed the formation of Chinese higher education from the Zhou dynasty (c. 1046–256 BCE) through the twentieth century, putting particular emphasis on the co-opting of Confucianism by the aristocracy, the formation of the civil service examination system, and the manifold changes (some positive, others devastating) after the collapse of the Qing dynasty in 1911. In the West, historians generally recognize the ancient Greeks as the primogenitors of American higher education, yet we might go back further still to the first appearance of formal schools in the Fertile Crescent region known as Mesopotamia, fortunately situated along the Tigris and Euphrates rivers where ancient cities like Uruk, Nippur, and Nineveh would thrive.

Elite Mesopotamian classes controlled formal education until the first millennium BCE, and they educated students to become "scholar-scribes" capable of passing tests on written literature and versed enough in those texts to teach others. Upon completion of these two stages, students could move out into the world of commerce as educated adults.[1] Aspiring students learned to write on clay tablets called cuneiform using reed-like utensils, a technique that dates back to the fourth millennium BCE. Archeologists discovered a narrative, preserved in cuneiform, chronicling the dreary life of an ancient Sumerian schoolboy learning to become a scholar-scribe—a tale so popular that it was repeatedly copied (and reconstructed from more than twenty fragments found at various Mesopotamian sites).

Samuel Kramer attributes authorship of this oft-duplicated tale to a faculty member in an ancient Mesopotamian tablet-house school, though it remains unclear for what reason it was written.[2] In its humorous narrative, the teacher and staff beat a luckless schoolboy repeatedly for his continual tardiness and insubordination. Frustrated by the situation, and seeking to change it, he convinces his parents to invite the teacher to dinner. Strategically, they ply the pedant with alcohol and gifts in a deliberate attempt to butter him up. At the conclusion of the repast, the formerly punitive savant dispenses with the ire that he directed at his pupil, and instead he "waxes poetic and blesses the aspiring scribe in highly reassuring words."[3]

Although the "Sumerian School Days" cuneiform provides some insight into educational practices in the ancient Near East and the role of the scholar-scribe, it likely belongs to an early form of literary satire ridiculing teachers for their avarice. Of course, it is possible that it might also have been a clever way for educators to augment their incomes. We will never know with certainty, but no matter, for to discover a system of higher education recognizable to those of us living in the twenty-first century, we must wait until the first millennium of the Common Era.

Classical Higher Learning and the Origins of Democracy

In ancient Greece, the birthplace of Western democracy, the rise of the city-state (polis; plural poleis) created an environment in which true higher learning (not simply vocational training as in Mesopotamia) could thrive for the first time. The Peloponnese peninsula and its islands have been inhabited since prehistoric times, and following the so-called Greek Dark Ages (c. 1200–800 BCE), city-states like Athens, Sparta, Thebes, and Corinth challenged aristocratic dictatorships and oligarchic rule, as well as the authoritarian tyranny that often accompanied them. They became poleis ruled by landowning citizens who desired new models of autonomy and self-governance. This modest beginning of democracy ushered in the Greek Classic Age in the fifth and fourth centuries BCE.

Due to their different political, economic, and social priorities, Peloponnesian city-states often found themselves in conflict with each other, despite the fact that they would eventually share a spoken language and a common alphabet. The greatest struggle occurred between the military-minded Spartans and the liberty-loving Athenians and their respective allies. In school, Athenian students learned grammar, basic arithmetic, physical training, and music and poetry (as social ornament), while Spartan education trained boys solely in the art of war and girls in the duty of managing the home and supporting the troops.

Homer's Iliad and Odyssey provided Spartans and Athenians with a shared narrative of honor, valor, and praiseworthy conduct in the form of heroic figures who embodied their belief in Greek exceptionalism. These epics primed students for the ideal of civil responsibility,[4] and so it was that Homer gave Athenians and Spartans alike the notion that the citizen's first duty was a militaristic one. As the Classical Period progressed, however, the two city-states diverged.

Spartan life became more militarily regimented and austere, while the Athenians were increasingly driven by a sense of civic duty. They dedicated themselves to the pursuit of liberty and turned to the study of philosophy, architecture, sculpture, history, and literature. In doing so, they helped to shape the course of Western higher education for thousands of years. Arguably, the rise of the American neoliberal university in the twenty-first century is the first wholesale departure from that unbroken humanistic tradition of liberal learning, the arc of which will be traced here and in chapter four.

In Athens, the political forces of change let loose during the Classical Period gave rise to internal conflicts between democracy and inclusion on the one hand and the desire to protect elite power and privilege on the other. Following the reforms of Cleisthenes (c. 570–508), which firmly established its democracy, Athens created a popular legislative assembly open to all male citizens, an elected judiciary, and an executive arm consisting of an elected council of five hundred members.[5]

In education, the newly enfranchised Athenian lower and middle classes did not desire to emulate old pedagogies. They sought instead a course of study that would better prepare the citizenry for the trade and prosperity that led to a "golden age."[6] Into this moment walked the Sophists—itinerant, for-profit teachers of rhetoric, oratory, and useful knowledge (such as law, tactics, diplomacy, commerce, and astronomy). Their nomadic lifestyle evokes the ten-year period of wandering in the life of Confucius, as the sage traveled from state to state in search of a leader willing to institute his ideas for social reform. Of course, Confucius would have found the profit motives of the Sophists, and their use of rhetoric to dissemble, inexcusable. Plato (c. 427–347 BCE) and others scholars would attack the Sophists on just those grounds, as we shall see.

Before the arrival of the Sophists, primary education for the typical Athenian boy meant moving out of the home to an often-improvised learning space (sometimes even a public building or park) where a pedagogue taught the basics of literacy. After approximately three years of study, students would attend a music school, before moving on to the gymnasium, where physical training and sport were the focus.[7] In the fourth century BCE, the *ephebia* emerged as a Greek training school for democratic citizenship and later an aristocratic finishing school for young men. Since *ephebiae* would eventually be found in more than one hundred Greek cities, they were an important force for Hellenization in the region. Aristotle reports, in *Atheniensium Respublica*, that young men would "receive a shield and spear from the state" after one year of study at an *ephebia*, and they then were stationed "on garrison duty" for the next two years. Upon the completion of that martial obligation, students could "take their position among the other citizens."[8] In this way, a completed course of study at an *ephebia* became a necessary condition for the full rights of citizenship.[9]

Out of this early tradition of higher learning, the Sophists rose to pedagogical distinction by promoting the assumption that eloquence used to win an argument was just another iteration of civic virtue. For advocating such a dubious point of view, they were portrayed as "ignorant, evil, pretentious, greedy men who swarmed to Athens between 450 and 350 BCE to deceive the people about the nature of ethical knowledge and political wisdom."[10] Plato, Aristotle, and Xenophon were among their most vehement critics.

Because they were teaching for profit, the Sophists assembled students into large classes, and this increased availability of education had the effect of turning higher learning into a much sought-after commodity among the upper classes. By using rhetoric over reason to win debates, charging high fees, and claiming to instill more learning in students in one year than in twenty years of study in conventional schools, the Sophists "assaulted orthodox educational belief" that men could be "taught to be good," an idea that violated the cultured Athenian principles of character and morality. The Sophists, however, made no apologies for teaching leadership, success, and fame or for "abandoning common men who needed a basic civic education."[11]

Soon, new models of higher learning would emerge that provided alternatives to the *ephebia* and classes with the Sophists. While it only survived for four or five decades, the rhetorical school established by Isocrates predates Plato's Academy. Isocrates turned to teaching only because he lost his estates in the Peloponnesian War (431–404 BCE), but unlike most entering the profession (then or now), Isocrates became fabulously wealthy by training a handful of students and charging them a very high fee. Although versed in the Sophist tradition, Isocrates spoke out against those who educated students in verbal trickery for the purposes of deception and who failed to instill moral values in their students. Isocrates was also suspicious of the Socratic method of questioning. Plato used that position against Isocrates to accuse him of being in the Sophist camp after all. In this way, Plato helped to shape the shady perception of the Sophists that has come down to us today.

Although the course of study at Isocrates's elite school was broad by the standards of the time, Plato's Academy and Aristotle's Lyceum are rightly considered the earliest antecedents of what would become the Western model of the university. Plato's Academy, founded around 387 BCE, often gets credit for the invention of what we call the liberal arts (although there were never any prescribed curricula, degrees, or majors in his academy). The institutions of higher learning founded by Aristotle in 335 BCE, by Zeno in 308 BCE, and by Epicurus in 306 BCE all contributed to the history of higher education (and educational philosophy) in the Western world.[12] For that reason, we should consider them briefly one by one.

After the arrest and execution of Socrates in 399 BCE, Plato fled Athens. By way of memorializing his martyred teacher and mentor, he wrote dialogues using the figure of Socrates to advance his teachings (Socrates left no writings of his own). During his twelve-year hiatus from Athens, Plato traveled widely, associated with the best scholars, and served as an advisor to princes and monarchs, without much success.[13] When he returned to Athens after the threat of being prosecuted for sedition had passed, Plato opened his academy on the periphery of a town near an ancient gymnasium of the same name. There he educated political leaders using the dialectical method found in some of his writings, which he attributed to Socrates. Like Greek educators before him, Plato lauded civic duty, and due to his reputation as an extremely erudite man, Plato could handpick his students from the best families (following Isocrates's example). He trained them to become social leaders.[14] In the context of this pattern of elitism in Greek higher learning, the Confucian principle of valuing character over class seems rather forward-looking.

On the other hand, Plato was an idealist as well, having penned the earliest utopian work in the Western world, The Republic (c. 380 BCE). Its central concern is charting an ethical course, which makes for justice, happiness, and a dedication to progress toward an ideal of shared wellbeing. Plato makes reason (nous) the highest principle around which a society can be organized. In the perfect person, reason rules over bodily appetites, and such a state of mind leads to harmony in the soul. By seeking what is good, Plato argued, one may find wisdom, the goal of all philosophy. Some readers may be struck by the fact that Plato's "philosopher king" resembles the Confucian Junzi (superior person) insofar as, in both of these individuals, right behavior arises naturally from mental harmony, and through its outward manifestation, the political state is transformed into a just entity. Like the Junzi, Plato's philosopher king cultivates a temperate humble character and always chooses knowledge and truth over mere profit. Although observed only in passing, these connections between Platonic and Confucian moral doctrines as intentional vehicles for social transformation are arresting and worthy of note in a comparative study such as this one.

According to Plato, having a philosopher king is a prerequisite for justice and peaceful social accord. A city-state prospers only when a sage rules, for he alone continually eschews the temptations of power and wealth and adheres instead to a firmly established virtue informed by a firsthand knowledge of the Good (the unity underlying the apparent multiplicity of the material world). In his famed "Parable of the Cave" from the Republic, Plato illustrates the fact that precious few ever achieve a perception of the Good, and when they do, they face a daunting task in awakening others to it.

In that parable, "the degrees in which our nature may be enlightened or unenlightened" are presented allegorically using the trope of the cave. In the belly of a cavern, chained facing a stone wall, are a group of unenlightened people. On the wall, all these individuals can see are shadows cast by the light of a fire, which is unseen behind them. Not aware that there is a whole world of light and life above ground, they unknowingly mistake the shadows on the wall for the whole of reality. In this allegory, if one of them unchains herself and ascends upward through the mouth of the cave, she enters the world of knowledge and wisdom, which "is the last thing to be perceived and only with great difficulty." It is, reports Plato, "the essential Form of Goodness." One can become a philosopher king only after seeing the Good and learning to abide in it. The "entire soul must be turned away from this changing world" until its eye contemplates only "the supreme splendor" of the Good.[15]

In Plato's allegory, the person who experiences the Good (that is to say, has experienced the world above ground) must return to the cave and explain to the prisoners that there is more to reality than the shadows on the wall. Because they have no firsthand knowledge of it, those still chained refuse to believe the truth (preferring instead their mind-forged manacles). In this regard, Plato's mysticism reminds one more of native Chinese Daoist traditions than the pragmatic worldly Confucianism that we explored in chapter one. However, Confucius's influence on higher education in China is monolithic in a way that Plato's would never be, making such East-West comparisons more difficult (and less useful) as we move on to Aristotle's Lyceum.

Whereas Plato fixed his perception on the Good, his student Aristotle (384–322 BCE) emphasized the natural sciences and investigation of the empirical world. As a student in Plato's Academy, Aristotle presumably studied the Pythagorean theory of numbers, advanced geometry, and speculations about science with the other students, in addition to exploring "social issues — education, jurisprudence, politics, sex" and other topics in informal lectures or discussions.[16] As a student, and later assistant, in the Academy for two decades, Aristotle may have been inspired to start his own school after Plato's nephew was named to succeed the founder as the preserver of Socratic wisdom and proponent of the Good.

Whatever the case, Aristotle found Plato's emphasis on conceptualism limiting, and after tutoring the son of the Macedonian leader, known to the world as Alexander the Great, Aristotle returned to Athens to start his own school. While the physical grounds of his institution were similar to those of the Academy, "it had a much wider intellectual scope." Aristotle and his associates "were interested in everything, including subjects ignored by Plato." Aristotle's influence on higher education in the Western world is the result of his expansion of the scope of inquiry, as well as his emphasis on the principle that generalizations must be derived from the careful observation and classification of facts rather than from speculation and logic, as Plato held.[17]

Other important schools in ancient Greece were often built around prominent individuals who contributed uniquely to the body of classical thought that informs Western higher education. Although little writing by Epicurus (341–270 BCE) survives, and what we know of his philosophy comes from second-hand sources, we gather that he preached a "basic ethical concept, namely, that pleasure is the ultimate good." In our day, his name is synonymous with coarse sensualism—because his enemies deliberately misconstrued his emphasis on finding happiness, accusing him crudely of hedonism. In point of fact, he encouraged the cultivation of a contemplative state of imperturbable happiness (*ataraxia*) that "follows from self-control, moderation, and prudence."[18] From the garden of his home, Epicurus taught a small group of students the ethics of reciprocity; a theory of atoms that he inherited from Democritus; and a belief in living obscurely but pleasantly (away from the lures of wealth and power). Epicurus also differed from his predecessors and contemporaries in admitting women and slaves into his school.

Zeno (c. 490–430 BCE) taught the philosophy of Stoicism for more than three decades at the Agora in Athens, where he met his students. Like Epicurus, Zeno believed that one could attain a state of happiness synonymous with living virtuously and naturally. In his lessons, he included rhetoric and grammar, which were central to the Athenian spirit of public debate, as well as ethics, physics, and the study of language. Zeno penned an influential handbook of rhetoric, as well as a treatise on Greek education,[19] and he is known for creating a series of paradoxes that intended "to show that ontological pluralism—a belief in the existence of many things rather than only one—leads to absurd conclusions."[20]

As we leave ancient Greece to follow the course of development of higher learning in the West, it is worth noting that Plato's Academy and Aristotle's Lyceum had a more durable influence on subsequent institutions of higher education than did the schools of Isocrates, Epicurus, Zeno, and others. In later years, the Academy and the Lyceum became more esoteric and selective in terms of membership, perhaps due to their informal organization. Consequently, it would be almost fifteen hundred years before institutions of higher learning would arise that more closely resemble the colleges and universities that we know today; yet, there are many important innovations along the way that deserve our attention.

The Transmission of Classical Learning and Its Augmentation in the Middle East

Two further important developments in higher education are the growth of schools based on Greek models during the time of the Roman Empire (27 BCE – 476 CE) and the dissemination of Greek learning to the Middle East, where it was preserved while Europe plunged into the abyss of dismal orthodoxy during the Middle Ages (500–1500). The recovery of classical learning would ignite the flame of the European Renaissance, inspire revolutions in France and the United States during the eighteenth century, and infuse American founding documents (the Declaration of Independence, Constitution, and Bill of Rights) with a soaring idealism.

Most likely, the Etruscans brought the Greek alphabet to Rome before being conquered and absorbed into the Roman state — although it could have arrived via the Greek colony at Cumae around 750 BCE or from any number of Greek cities south of the Italian peninsula.[21] However it happened, we should understand that every boy or girl who learns to read and write in the United States is indebted to the ancient Greeks for transmitting a skill and an alphabet to Rome that spread through the Islamic Middle East into Western Europe, and from there to the New World.

By the third century of the Roman Republic (509–27 BCE), bilingual educators were translating important Greek texts into Latin, including the Iliad and Odyssey. Despite opposition to the continued use of the Greek language, many of these texts remained the focus in schools. Generally speaking, Roman education was practical, aiming for basic literacy, knowledge of the law, and obedience to custom, as well as "the maintenance of religion and morals." As in the schools of their Greek forebearers, curricula for primary and secondary education in ancient Rome were not formalized. Generally speaking, students learned reading, writing, arithmetic, and poetry in grammar school — and history, literature, government, philosophy, science, and public speaking in rhetoric school. Roman students moved from elementary training to grammar school at about age twelve, and from there they went on to a rhetoric school for more advanced study. Roman girls might study with boys in grammar school, but opportunities to continue their education depended on familial support. Following the Greek example, the Romans promoted a form of education that modern Western nations refer to as the "liberal arts."[22]

In the rhetoric schools, orators were trained to serve the Roman state. The ability to speak well "involved effective articulation, knowledge of mass psychology, moral discipline, and speculative intellectual depth." Rhetoric and oratory were taught alongside statecraft and military training, and both became key components of Roman higher education, along with philology, Roman history, literature, law, mathematics, and philosophy. Literary studies were deemed of importance as well, but over time Greek writers gave way to the "lights" of Cato (234–149 BCE), Cicero (106–43 BCE), Horace (65–8 BCE), and Quintilian (35 to 97 CE)—and playwrights such as Plautus (c. 254–184 BCE) and Terence (c. 195–159 BCE).[23]

The orator and statesman Cicero exercised the greatest influence on educational theory during the Roman Republic, and his writings on education provided a template for subsequent development of institutions of higher learning during the Middle Ages. Cicero believed that orators should seek out the broadest possible education and combine it with practical experience. He suggested a course of study that included classical literature, rhetoric, logic, geometry, astronomy, music, physics, history, civil law, and philosophy.[24] In this way, Cicero helped to put in place the outline for liberal learning that spread through Europe and endured well into the late twentieth century in the United States.

During the early Roman Empire, Quintilian advocated for group learning because he found it preferable to individual tutoring, in part for the valuable social skills that it instilled, but also because it created a sense of competition among students (which he thought was better than using corporal punishment as an incentive to learn). Although his curricular recommendations were similar to those of Cicero, Quintilian emphasized mathematics and neglected physical education (one aspect of the Greek tradition that did not get passed down to Rome). Like many educators before him in the Greco-Roman world, Quintilian also stressed the development of memory, and he used moralizing as a primary motivator.[25]

From the period of the Roman Republic (509–27 BCE) to that of the Western Roman Empire (27 BCE–476), formal schooling remained largely the privilege of the upper classes, although an apprentice system did allow for the training of artisans and tradesmen. During the Republic, higher education chiefly consisted of a father taking his son to the seats of government to observe its inner workings firsthand. A young man might also be apprenticed to a family friend noted for his knowledge of public affairs, law, or oratory. At some point, that student would be judged competent in the public sphere and assume an adult role there. Education in the later Roman Republic tended to follow in the tradition of the Sophists (particularly in regards to its utilitarian approach to rhetoric).[26]

The expansiveness of the Western Roman Empire offered students the opportunity for study abroad at any number of academic centers (in Alexandria, Smyrna, Antioch, Athens, and Rhodes, for instance), and therefore travel became an important part of the Roman system of higher education. At the Athenaeum in Rome, Greek and Roman teachers and writers attracted hundreds of students each. Schools flourished all over the empire, catering mostly to local residents, but specialized institutions for the pursuit of the law began to take shape in the wake of Cicero's emphasis on practical education.[27]

After the Roman Empire's expansion made it difficult to govern so large an area, Constantine (272–337) divided these lands into Eastern and Western domains. The Western territories finally fell to invaders and indigenous rebellions when the Visigoths sacked Rome in 410. The Vandals would despoil the city again in 455. With the fall of the Western Roman Empire (variously attributed to the breakdown of social and military institutions, moral decay, inept leadership, barbarian hordes, broken communication networks, Germanic economic expansion, contagious disease, and even the use of lead plumbing in aristocratic households), a long period of darkness settled over Europe that lasted for almost a thousand years. More than five hundred years would pass after the sack of Rome before Europe recovered sufficiently from those economic, political, and social upheavals to form the first universities in the Western world.

Meanwhile, in Constantinople, the seat of the Eastern Roman Empire (330–1453), support for higher education rose and fell with the priorities of those who reigned over it. Theodosius II (401–450) founded what two modern historians call the "State University of Constantinople" in 425. Although under the direct oversight of the emperor and the city council, this institution housed thirty-one teachers and their classrooms in a single building. There students were taught a range of subjects (save for theology, which was excluded by imperial decree). Instructors received a state salary and could retire with a title after twenty years of service.[28] This "proto-university" focused on preparing civil servants for working in the government, much as the Confucian system of higher learning did in China during the same period.

The Emperor Justinian (c. 482–565) tried to raise the quality of existing legal schools by closing the ones that he deemed inferior, and with the help of scholar-teachers, he created new schools with comprehensive curricula. While the Byzantine East had been willing to find bridges between the Greco-Roman and Christian traditions, Western church leaders greatly circumscribed classical learning (due to polytheism and what it saw as an emphasis on sexual desire and bodily appetites). However, after a period of unification and recovery, crusading Latins, Bulgarians, Serbians, and Ottoman Turks gradually tore away the landholdings of the Byzantine Empire. When Mehmet II sacked Constantinople in the fifteenth century and established in its place the Ottoman capital of Istanbul, the Hellenistic legacy of the Byzantines, recorded in its libraries, was preserved in the Islamic world. Europe would recover that heritage only later.

As the Catholic Church grew in power during the early Middle Ages, it took the place of civil administrations by forming districts, or dioceses, controlled by a bishop (whose office was usually located in a prominent church, the cathedral). Diocesan churches might contain cathedral schools, some of which even became important centers of learning in the later Middle Ages. Through these schools, the church ably preserved and transmitted higher learning as its organizations endured invasions, the decay of civilization, and the gradual breakup of civil government.[29] The rise of the Christian monastic community helped to facilitate the transformation of the Church into a social agent for learning amid the "chaos of conquest, disintegration, and barbarization."[30]

Preserved in a few monasteries and among distinguished families, classical learning managed to persist in Europe during the five-hundred-year period between the fall of Rome and the first millennium, although on the whole continuous war and the economics of poverty contained its dissemination. Charlemagne (c. 742–814), the first emperor in Europe after the fall of the Western Roman Empire, was profusely generous to the Catholic Church. Shrewdly, he used her doctrines and personnel as instruments of education and government in order to gain managerial control over the Church—although he did send money to persecuted Christians in foreign lands, negotiated for their fair treatment with Muslim rulers, denounced iconoclasm, "suppressed insubordination in monasteries, and ordered a strict watch on convents to prevent immoral behavior among the nuns."[31]

Charlemagne allowed the clergy to operate their own courts, gave them tithes from the land, and relinquished control over marriages and wills. By working this closely with the Church, Charlemagne initiated the transformation of his territories into a "Holy" Roman Empire (962–1806), so that they would have "all the prestige, sanctity, and stability of both Imperial and papal Rome." This cunning move would deepen the split between Greek and Latin Christianity, but it gave the papacy and bishops a civil authority grounded in ecclesiastical conferment and strengthened the so-called divine right of kings.[32]

In the later Middle Ages, monastic libraries, which had been plundered or purged of classical texts during earlier periods, began to reconstitute themselves in the wake of Charlemagne's reign. Higher education in this period attempted to work a compromise between "pagan" philosophy and Catholic Christian theology. Primary and secondary education in church schools focused on teaching Latin, the lingua franca of the time, so that its graduates could say prayers and conduct services. As students advanced through their studies, they learned grammar (and a smattering of the liberal arts) under the threat of severe corporal punishment. Catechumenal schools emerged to train future clergy and encouraged the preservation of a new emphasis on the otherworldliness of Christianity.

Organized guilds helped to educate people for specific vocations, as well. Such an education took a male student from apprentice to craftsman or journeyman (who traveled to ply his trade) to master.

A formal ceremony inducted the successful apprentice into a guild as a full-fledged member. Once a master, he could train others in an arrangement by which the student would gain the skills of a trade, moral guidance, basic literacy, and religious training. In return, if the student worked hard and kept the secrets of the craft, he could establish himself in business after a period of training that might last up to ten years, sometimes more.[33]

Even though there were few books available at the time, and the ones that were accessible often suffered from poor scholarship or simply were compendia of the past, gaining a formal education nevertheless became necessary preparation for joining the feudal nobility.[34] Training included horsemanship and military exercises, along with an emphasis on courtesy as a social grace, a willingness to protect the weak, and a desire to cultivate honor. According to this new chivalric code, the ideal knight became a soldier, a courtier, and a Christian gentleman. Noble women of the period learned sewing, weaving, handicrafts, music, and dance, as well as basic reading and writing.[35] Chaucer's "The Knight's Tale" presents the ideal of chivalric behavior. This code, not the subject of formal instruction in schools and colleges, is nevertheless definitive in our understanding of that time.

The establishment of the first universities in the Middle Ages, an innovation that we have been anticipating in our brief survey of higher education in the West, takes place as European scholars increasingly grappled with the difficulty of finding ways to synthesize their classical heritage with the Christianity that had eclipsed it. Any solution seemed to mean leaving behind Aristotelian science, classical literature, materialistic philosophy, and humanism, in favor of providing a pathway to Christian salvation in the afterlife. Gradually, however, the study of history, foreign languages, and even the traditional *trivium* (grammar, rhetoric, and logic) and *quadrivium* (arithmetic, geometry, astronomy, and music) began to get worked into the standard curriculum because they served the interests of the church.[36] Benedictine monasteries, for example, preserved parts of the classical legacy for Christian use,[37] but the uneasy relationship between the classics and the Christian canon in the early Middle Ages remained entrenched for generations.

Twelfth- and thirteenth-century scholars developed a scholastic tradition that eventually reconciled ancient philosophy with Christian doctrine. Pierre Abelard (1079–1142) found ways to accommodate Aristotelian logic in his teaching and writing, which proved prescient. However, it was incursions into southern Spain and the Middle East during the Crusades that unexpectedly facilitated a reconciliation of traditions, as Christian scholars came into contact with the Arabic learning that reconnected them with classical learning, which had been preserved and expanded upon for centuries in the Middle East.

Under the Abbasid Caliphate (750–1258), Persian, Egyptian, Spanish, Jewish, Greek, and Syrian cultural influences from its conquered territories coalesced in Baghdad. While Europe largely wallowed in shallows of self-imposed ignorance, the Islamic world enjoyed the fruits of classical enquiry and scholarship; the House of Wisdom (Bayt al-Hikma) in Baghdad became a place for translation and research. It shared with Cordoba in Spain a reputation as an outstanding center for higher education in the Islamic world.[38] Islam had a common language in Arabic that disparate cultural groups used to communicate with each other, plus an umbrella of faith under which they could collaborate. Therefore, Islamic scholars were able to freely study a variety of subjects, which included literature, medicine, astronomy, mathematics, theology, and philosophy from around the world.

Within a few hundred years, two preeminent institutions, still in existence today, were established: the Al-Azar Mosque and the Dar al-Hikmah in Cairo. The university that now bears the Al-Azar name was founded in the year 972 — only the University of al-Qarawiyyin in Morocco is older, having been in continuous existence since 859. In other parts of the Islamic world, institutions of higher learning called *madaris* spread quickly, with seventy-four of them in Damascus, forty-one in Jerusalem, thirteen in Tripoli, and nine in Mosul.[39]

Because teachers provided certificates, students would travel to any number of locations where scholars of note were teaching, complete a course of study with a chosen teacher, and then move on. Thus, Abu-al Wazim Sulaiman "studied under a thousand professors from Mesopotamia to Egypt, and Tax al-Islam abu Said studied under 400."[40] This internationalization of higher learning was unique not only for the access that it provided to the region's intellectual capital, but also because the power, prestige, and influence of a place of learning rested with the scholars — and not the institution.

In Islamic schools, translations of Plato, Aristotle, Plotinus, Hippocrates, Ptolemy, Galen, Euclid, and Archimedes contributed to a "golden era" of learning in the eleventh century. Islamic scholars developed an experimental-empirical method, encouraged free inquiry, and opened their libraries to the public (at a time when books were hand-copied and therefore very precious); some libraries even accommodated the borrowing of dozens of titles for prolonged research and provided room and board for international scholars.[41] Because of this embrace of educational and cultural assimilation, higher learning flourished in the Islamic world.

As Europe slumbered under the soporific weight of church doctrine and persecuted heterodoxy during the Inquisition, the Islamic Renaissance (which began in the ninth century) gathered momentum. It would go into decline during the fourteenth century — just at the moment that Europe was ready to receive the fruits of centuries of Middle Eastern scholarship that would propel its own reawakening. During its height, the Islamic Renaissance could lay claim almost exclusively to "all that was creative in areas of basic science, particularly physics, astronomy and mathematics; all the important and comprehensive works in philosophy, theology, religion, history, and law; all the important developments in the field of medicine and associated disciplines, to say nothing of art and literature, and music, to which Muslim scholars also made significant contributions."[42]

Although a comprehensive accounting of these scholarly achievements remains beyond the scope of this project, the influence of Islamic learning on the development of universities in Europe (and by consequence on the American university) cannot be overstated. As we noted, Muslim libraries during this golden age became education and research centers that attracted scholars and provided venues for the exchange of ideas, in spaces where the learning of past ages was preserved. The expansion of Islamic enclaves to places like Italy, Sicily, and Spain sped the transmission of Muslim learning throughout Europe.

When Baghdad fell to the Mongols in 1258, bringing the Islamic Renaissance to a close, there were thirty-six libraries in the city and over one hundred booksellers (whose businesses became places of educational exchange as well). Private collections of books could be also quite large. Islamic libraries located further west escaped pillaging by the Mongol hordes, so that the efforts of thousands of translators were not in vain. From the Persian tradition, *One Thousand and One Nights*, Omar Khayyám's *Rubáiyát*, and Ferdowsi's *Book of Kings* were among the most widely read and disseminated in the West, along with works by Euclid.

Greek texts entered European thought largely through Arabic translations before being rendered into Latin, Hebrew, and sometimes Spanish, helping Europe to recover its Greco-Roman educational heritage. European intellectuals engaged "Indo-Persian, Greek, Syriac-Hellenistic, Chinese, and Muslim-Hebrew sciences and philosophies," and that material provided the content for the continent's revival.[43] Emergent European universities in the late twelfth century benefited tremendously from the influx of translations and commentaries in the fields of medicine, science and technology, philosophy and religion, history, and law, among others subjects.

This exchange of ideas and inflow of new information created an even greater thirst for learning that anticipated the Renaissance. Important medical textbooks that first identified the contagious nature of diseases like smallpox were made available — an important contribution as bubonic plague re-emerged in the late Middle Ages and killed countless numbers of people, irrespective of geographical borders or demarcations of caste. All these Islamic contributions make Will Durant conclude, "nowhere else in those eighth, ninth, tenth, eleventh centuries of our era was there so great a passion for books," unless it was in China.[44] His observation is a good reminder of the long tradition of higher learning in China, as we trace its history and development vis-à-vis those of the West.

The First Universities in Europe

As the twelfth century came to a close, just five European universities were in existence. One was a medical school in Salerno, and the others were law schools located in Bologna, Paris, Montpelier, and Oxford. The University of Cambridge, an offshoot of Oxford, was founded in 1209; following its lead, literally hundreds of institutions of higher learning in Europe sprung into being during the thirteenth century, including those at Padua in 1222, Naples in 1224, Toulouse in 1230, Siena in 1264, Lisbon in 1290, and so on.[45]

In terms of the curriculum, the preeminent theologian Thomas Aquinas (1225–1274) brought Aristotle firmly into the Christian fold. He balanced faith with reason by using primary source material from the Islamic world (to which his predecessors did not have access). His *Summa Theologica* asserted that there could be no basic contradiction between theology and Aristotelian philosophy, "between truth as revealed and truth as discovered by reason since, in the final analysis, all truth comes from God."[46] Though imperfect, humankind could move from ignorance to knowledge through learning, but revelation and grace required faith.

With the integration of Aristotle into the curriculum (and the gradual embrace of classical learning that more generally followed), the European university burst onto the world stage, replete with a curriculum that included "lost" learning carefully preserved and augmented by Islamic scholars. Yet, the principle focus of these institutions remained the occupational training of clerics, lawyers, and doctors. The University of Paris was the most prominent institution in thirteenth-century Europe, and it was free from oversight by a king, pope, or even chancellor. The corporate body of the faculty was affirmed as a legal entity; it "could set its own curriculum, issue the license to teach, and confer degrees and appoint its own members." Therefore, the Western university in its original form "was the corporate existence of the faculty empowered with a right to run its own affairs without any responsibility to any administrative officers or any kind of board of control outside of its own membership."[47]

As one might guess, civil and religious authorities continually challenged this ideal of university autonomy and sought to regulate higher learning as a means of civic or theological indoctrination. University governing boards have their genesis in the fourteenth century on the Italian peninsula, and they spread widely during the following century. An important point to note, as we look forward to the genesis of higher education in the United States, is that this ideal of faculty autonomy would persist—and reach its apex in the American university between the Second World War and 1980.

Early European universities developed academic programs of study in the liberal arts and offered independent scholarship opportunities in the scholastic disciplines. Not only was this development a reversal of the prior professional emphasis in higher education, but it also coincided with an increasing willingness to balance the interests of faith and reason, and it laid the groundwork for the complete recovery of the classical tradition. That inheritance was now augmented by Indian, Chinese, Middle Eastern, and Northern African contributions—all of which were collected, translated, and transmitted from the Orient to the West.

The rise of the university, one of the most important intellectual achievements of the late Middle Ages, therefore owes a tremendous debt of gratitude to the Islamic world. This acknowledgment brings to mind Mehdi Nakosteen's conclusion concerning the Islamic origins of Western education. As we move toward the development of higher education during the European Renaissance, it deserves quoting at some length:

> In the universities of the twelfth and thirteenth centuries scholarship was based almost entirely on the writings of the Muslim and Greek authors as translated from Arabic or Greek sources. Muslim Aristotelian science remained the core of the curriculum of the University of Paris until the sixteenth century. Roger Bacon and Albertus Magnus lectured on Muslim sciences and acknowledged their debt to them, particularly to al-Hazin and Jabir. Not until the middle of the sixteenth century and the advent of Copernicus in astronomy, Paracelsus in medicine, and Vesalius in anatomy did Muslim-Hellenistic science give way to the new concepts of man and his world and bring about the decline of the medieval period.[48]

As such, it was classical humanism preserved in the Islamic world that gave the Renaissance its guiding light, and the ensuing shift from a focus on God to humankind is an important one for many reasons. In terms of this study, it speaks to a shared humanistic tradition with China, and it marks a point of early historical convergence of the Ming-Qing era in the East with the European Renaissance in the West.

The gradual nature of reawakening in the late medieval period means that the term *Renaissance* is misleading, insofar as it might suggest a sudden cultural shift. Many of that period's main developments, including humanism, germinated in the Middle Ages, came to fruition on the Italian peninsula, and then spread throughout Europe. The expansion of international commerce, the growth of a new merchant class, the institution of parliaments, the onset of corporate liberties, and the development of early forms of constitutional governments (all coupled with technological advances) meant that the late feudal order of the Middle Ages provided the structure for the cultural transformations that took place later.[49] There was a new spirit of inquiry in the air, and it was individualistic, energetic, transgressive, highly creative, and above all skeptical of the medieval worldview.

The cultural transition away from God during the Renaissance, and toward human beings and their experiences in the world, occurred as the plagues ravaged Europe, extended wars were being fought on the continent, and the terrors of the Inquisition spread fear during the twelfth to sixteenth centuries. All these events challenged the dominant God-centered and earth-centric point of view. The social inequalities of the medieval Age of Faith—with its feudal hierarchies and the exploitation of the masses—that preceded the Renaissance drove the unabating winds of change. As more classical writers were recovered and the canon expanded internationally, the focus of higher education moved from theological and professional training to the potential for personal development.

The writer Petrarch (1304–1374) rebelled against the narrowness of medievalism by insisting on the full recovery of the genius of classical thought (not just Aristotle). He combed church-houses and monasteries across the Italian peninsula "for surviving scraps of text authored by such classical luminaries as Cicero, Virgil, Horace, Livy, Plato, and Homer." Using this approach, he and others, including Giovanni Boccaccio (1313–1375), inspired an immense effort to collate, edit, correct, and translate an entire literary heritage that was largely lost to Europeans up to that point.[50] Within a hundred years, classical learning was well established in Florence (under the patronage of the Medici family), as well as in Ravenna, Venice, Naples, and Rome. From there, Italian humanism spread northward through

Europe, where it would take on distinctive cultural characteristics during the process of its diffusion between the fifteenth and seventeenth centuries.

Like medieval universities that educated the nobility and gentry and existed alongside feudal training for knights and courtiers, the universities of the Renaissance, particularly in France and England, added "polite learning" (cultural education) to their curricula.[51] Renaissance education, "which had a very great effect on Europe, and later on America, was largely for the elite and stressed classical literary humanism and the consequent development of the gentlemanly graces."[52] Thereafter, the humanities took their place alongside divinity studies as a legitimate end of scholarly inquiry. The humanist ideal of the well-rounded person (one who spoke many languages, appreciated art and music, possessed a certain social sophistication, and was equally at ease on the dance floor or on horseback bearing weapons) gained in stature, as well.

What emerged from this potpourri of feudal, classical, and religious influences was an ideal of the educated Christian gentleman who read widely and was well mannered. In the Book of the Courtier, Baldassare Castiglione (1478–1529) contrasted the feudal emphasis on valor and bravery with the new learning and suggested the possibility of their synthesis:

> If I were speaking to [those feudalistic Frenchmen], or with others who had an opinion different from mine, I should strive to show them how useful and necessary letters are to our life and dignity, having indeed been granted by God to men as a crowning gift. Nor should I lack instances of many excellent commanders of antiquity, who all added the ornament of letters to the valour of their arms.[53]

The increasing use of vernacular languages (in place of Latin) and the change from art in service of the church to the celebration of the human form was also in keeping with this humanist impulse.

The liberal arts curriculum would gradually grow to include Latin, Greek, logic, ethics, rhetoric, classical literature (in its full glory), medicine, law, theology, mathematics, and astronomy. The pursuit of individual self-betterment by way of life-long learning was generally seen as a way to foster social amelioration during the Renaissance. Yet, it would be wrong to suggest that all institutions of higher learning eagerly embraced Renaissance humanism. The University of Paris stubbornly clung to its scholasticism and to Aristotelian philosophy as the new learning raged around it. On the other hand, the Oxford reformers welcomed it. Stimulated by the writing of Desiderius Erasmus (1466–1536), Oxford created five Regius professorships (in Divinity, Hebrew, Greek, Physic, and Civil Law), all of which are still in existence.[54]

Erasmus believed that education should have a social function, insofar as it should assist a student in becoming a useful member of the community and engender a devotion to God. The Italian-trained scholars Thomas Linacre (1460–1524) and William Grocyn (c. 1446–1514) first introduced Greek learning at Oxford, and soon they were joined by the likes of John Colet (1466–1519), Thomas More (1478–1535), and other leading English scholars and academicians.[55] Since the higher educational traditions of England and Germany had the most profound influence on the development of colleges and universities in the United States, they warrant further attention.

Outside of the prominent institutions of Oxford and Cambridge, humanistic studies failed to make much headway until King Henry VIII (1491–1547) endorsed a literary revival at court (in order to cultivate a more literate and academically minded gentry or to court women).[56] Following the adoption of what we call the liberal arts curriculum by Oxford and Cambridge, a spirit of free inquiry and an ideological move toward the human experience gave rise to the Protestant Reformation (1517–1648). There were manifold causes for the Protestant revolt: abuses by the Roman Catholic Church (such as the selling of indulgences), the commodification of lucrative ecclesiastical positions, and the schism of rival popes. A general intensification of nationalism, skepticism, and secularism that accompanied Italian humanism also incited the revolution.[57]

Rising up in protest against the authority of the Catholic Church, Martin Luther (1483–1546) instigated the Protestant Reformation when he posted ninety-five theses against that institution to the door of Castle Church in Wittenberg. The authority of the pope to remit guilt by granting pardons and indulgences, the lust and avarice of indulgence preachers, and the false remission of souls in purgatory were among the abuses Luther outlined in that groundbreaking document. Translated into vernacular German from Latin, copies of Luther's theses spread across the country and earned him excommunication (for not withdrawing his attacks on the Church).

Soon thereafter, rebellion stirred elsewhere in Europe. The sectarian leader John Calvin (1509–1569) founded a theology of reform in France and Switzerland that bears his name to this day. John Knox (1505–1572) began the Presbyterian movement in Scotland, and Ulrich Zwingli (1484–1531) helped to spread the Reformation to Switzerland. As they always do, changes in higher education followed these social reforms. The spirit of the Protestant Reformation infused universities with their own version of Christian piety mixed with classical learning. Vernacular languages were embraced as vehicles of scholarship for the first time, the Bible was translated so that ordinary people could read it, and the advent of movable-type printing made the dissemination of new ideas easier than ever before.

The Academy of Geneva, founded by John Calvin, conferred no degrees, but it attracted Protestant scholars from many countries and pioneered a model of institutional governance that was shared between several lay members of the city council and seven professors. The rector (chief academic officer) oversaw these two groups, and in turn the chief officer of the city kept watch on him. The founders of the first colleges in the American colonies drew their models not from Luther's middle Europe, but from Swiss, Dutch, Scottish, Irish, and English institutions that had come under the influence of John Calvin. Calvin's Academy became so prestigious that more than two hundred years later Thomas Jefferson considered "inviting the entire Geneva faculty to join him in the United States" to run his university in Virginia.[58]

When Henry VIII of England severed all ties with the Roman Church, the newly established English Church assumed its functions, now ceding ultimate authority to the reigning English monarch. The greatest change to higher education in England and other Protestant countries was the abolition of church canon and the elimination of degrees in canonical law (in favor of secular civil law). The resulting swing away from the university as a place for training clergy (who tended to become canon lawyers or monastic leaders) to one where academic studies became a means for "confirming one's social status and class, or of moving toward higher social rank"[59] was part of that break with Catholic tradition.

As the student body at the English university began to look less clerical and more secular, the urban bourgeoisie and landed gentry sought out higher learning as a sort of finishing school for their children. Fewer than one-third of those enrolled in Oxford or Cambridge, for example, came from the lower socio-economic classes — indicating that higher education still remained out of reach for those of modest means. Like others before them, Protestants were reluctant to embrace humanism because of its pagan origins, but even Luther allowed some elements of liberal learning to persist (by merging it with Christian truth to create pious and lettered individuals). The intermediating role between the individual and salvation insisted upon by the Roman Church was also eliminated.

In the Catholic world, the Jesuit order founded by Ignatius Loyola (1491–1556) produced preachers, missionaries, teachers, and school founders who embraced humanistic learning and spread its message in lands lost to the Protestants, as well as places much further flung, like India and China. The Jesuits were, at the height of their power, the most successful educators in Europe, and they built permanent schools that were almost exclusively secondary and tertiary institutions. Because they were supported by donation, instruction at Jesuit schools was free, but contributions were often obtained from parents.[60] The Jesuits were successful not for their innovations to the curriculum (which were few) but for their organization, discipline, and zeal to spread higher learning.

The rise of science and empiricism are the final innovations of the early modern European university that underpin the formation of colleges and universities in the United States. On the threshold of the modern age, English universities fell under the influence of Francis Bacon (1561–1626) and Isaac Newton (1642–1727), and they began to explore the physical and biological sciences without limitation. Newton's contemporary, John Locke (1632–1704), advocated for a constitutional government composed of citizens, and he even outlined the legislative, judiciary, and executive functions that are still in use in the

United States. This critical spirit that infused scientific inquiry survived many efforts at reform and emerged with a new orientation toward understanding the physical universe, for humanism had helped to remove the taint of sin that surrounded empirical studies in earlier periods.

However, to suggest that during the early modern period Europe experienced consistent incremental growth and an evolving commitment to science and greater access to higher educational opportunities would be an oversimplification. Rather, what we find are centuries of "fluctuations and alternations, advances and declines, institutional openings and closings, periodic curricular reforms followed by intervals of degeneration and decay, expansions and constrictions." After the mid-eighteenth century, European higher education would increasingly be tied to national systems of public education. In the New World, by contrast, educational experimentation and innovation were "destined to yield quite different types of higher education institutions."[61]

From the Colonial College to the American University

Nine colleges were founded in the United States before the American Revolution in 1776: Harvard College, College of William and Mary, Collegiate School (now Yale University), College of New Jersey (Princeton University), College of Philadelphia (University of Pennsylvania), King's College (Columbia University), Rhode Island College (Brown University), Queen's College (Rutgers University), and Dartmouth College. Seven out of nine of these institutions (together with Cornell) make up the Ivy League,[62] so named after the athletic conference, but now synonymous with elite American institutions of higher education.

Strictly speaking, no agreement exists concerning the founding dates for some colonial colleges, since it depends at what point in the process of establishment one begins counting. The College of William and Mary, for example, sometimes claims a connection to Henricus College, founded in 1619, but that institution was destroyed in 1622 during an "Indian uprising." Either of those dates would make William and Mary older than Harvard College (created by the Massachusetts General Court in 1636), except for the fact that operations never resumed at Henricus until it was officially chartered by King William III and Queen Mary II of England as a "perpetual College of Divinity, Philosophy, Languages, and other good Arts and Sciences" in 1693.[63]

Although Cambridge University produced "the largest number of college educated settlers in the Massachusetts Bay Colony in the 1630s," the bicameral governance model of Trinity College in Dublin was introduced at William and Mary and at Harvard."[64] The one hundred or so individuals educated at Cambridge and around thirty or more from Oxford, who emigrated to New England before 1646, became founders of Harvard College (or fathers of the first generation of students). These individuals very much intended to "re-create a little bit of old England in America."[65] To that end, they dressed formally for dinner as was the tradition at dining clubs back home, kept alive the Puritan (English Protestant) tradition, and renamed Newtowne, where the college was located, to Cambridge—naturally.

In terms of their worldview, these émigrés emphasized leading pure lives, full of work and service, and they felt a uniquely keen responsibility to the future. English Puritanism reinforced to them the necessity of having a learned clergy and a lettered public, and therefore Harvard College initially trained "the school masters, the divines, the rulers, the cultured ornaments of society—the men who would spell the difference between civilization and barbarism."[66] William and Mary also supplied the colonies with clergymen and trained public servants. Yale and Princeton carried on much in the same vein, and together these institutions helped to define the central mission of the colonial colleges.

Many early European settlers to the New World braved the grueling journey across the Atlantic Ocean in pursuit of spiritual freedom. Their religious fervor gave colonial colleges a decidedly denominational orientation that would continue after the independence of the United States (but which gave way to an ideal of secular public higher education in later centuries). The Presbyterians had the College of New Jersey at Princeton (chartered in 1746) put emphasis on "a religion of conversion, on individual experience" following the First Great Awakening (c. 1731–1755). Not to be denied, the Baptists founded the College of Rhode Island at Providence in 1765; the next year, a Dutch Reformed group, which developed during the Protestant Revolution, established Queen's College.[67]

In sum, the orientation of the American colonial college was religious, but denominational diversity promoted tolerance despite rivalries and the strong lure of self-interest. Like their Greek, Roman, and European predecessors, American colonial colleges were not popular institutions. They were shaped by aristocratic traditions and served a male upper class that was being subjected to the stresses of New World conditions. Out of that adversity, the American trope of the rugged individualist, the self-made (self-educated) man in the mold of Benjamin Franklin and Patrick Henry emerged and combined with an ever-present focus on individual religious experience.

On the eve of the American Revolution (1775–1783), provisions for public elementary and secondary education were rare, and college attendance remained quite low. Those who did enroll in one of the handful of colonial colleges in the New World would have studied Latin, Greek, Hebrew, logic, and rhetoric in their first year; to that mix was added natural philosophy in the second. Metaphysics and moral philosophy dominated the third year of study, while the fourth was spent reviewing classical languages, logic, and physics. Women in the American colonies had little or no access to formal higher education for generations—although Salem College and Moravian College both have roots in girls' schools established during the colonial period.

During this early phase in the development of the colonial college, the English university remained "a fountain of inspiration and influence." Colonial colleges borrowed the residential campus model and class designations (freshman, sophomore, etc.) from England[68] and kept abreast of mathematical and scientific advances during the Enlightenment (or Age of Reason, c. 1650–1800). The secularism that these empirical studies engendered would gradually sever the religious roots of American colleges and universities so completely that many of those institutions still in existence no longer affiliate with their founding denominations in any meaningful way.

With a vast frontier beckoning, most middle- and lower-class families saw higher education as something that could wait, so in 1776 there were just three thousand living graduates of American colleges.[69] Between the Revolution and the turn of the century in 1800,

these colleges continued to build upon a synthesis of clerical training and Renaissance humanism to create the basis for a uniquely
American model of higher learning. German higher education, which
Americans feverishly imitated in the late nineteenth century, exerted
an influence on the development of American institutions of higher
learning second only to that of the English university. However, colleges in the United States differed from both English and German
universities in that they were bursting with democratic aspirations as
a result of the successful revolution.

The Rise of the American University

After achieving independence, attention quickly turned to repairing
college campuses damaged during the war, discarding outmoded
courses of study, and instituting more democratic curricular and organizational reforms. New state legislatures in the fledgling nation
began to provide fiscal support to existing colleges and sponsor the
creation of new ones. As the United States transformed itself from
an agrarian society into an industrial one, higher education became
an important vehicle for economic transformation (as it is today in
China). Between 1784 and 1802, nineteen new colleges were chartered
that are still in operation, twice as many as in the previous 150 years.
Inspired by a zeal for democratization, the American public became
hostile to denominational higher education, and even "Harvard, Yale,
and William and Mary adjusted to increased state representation on
their governing boards."[70]

When the French Revolution began in 1789, it set ablaze the
American enthusiasm for freedom and democracy all over again.
The French language began to enter the curriculum, and with it came
French philosophy that included deistic and atheistic thought. At the
same time as colonial religious patterns were breaking down, a belief
in free thought began to permeate all ranks of American society. The
William and Mary–educated Virginian Thomas Jefferson (1743–1826)
forcefully advocated for liberal reform, the development of practical
fields of inquiry, and a more utilitarian focus at the collegiate level. To
that call, George Washington (1731–1799) would add his own plea:
that education would inculcate patriotism in the citizens of the young

nation.[71] In many ways, the conflict between these opposing ideals (education for practical purposes or ideological indoctrination) would be worked out in the following century with the speedy propagation of public colleges and the rise of the first research universities.

The United States does not have a national university, and one reason for that curious feature of American higher education is a tradition of state support for colleges and universities that dates to this period. Today, the federal government funds student loan programs as well as academic research, but it does not create national higher education policy, nor does it have the power of accreditation (which at the moment still remains largely regional and educator driven). Higher education in the United States has "never been forced to conform to any one uniform pattern of organization, administration, or support," and in the nineteenth and twentieth centuries it became increasingly heterogeneous.[72]

Many scholars have found it convenient to symbolically divide American higher education in the nineteenth century into antebellum and postbellum periods. To some degree, it is a sensible division. In the antebellum period between the turn of the century and the American Civil War (1861–1865), institutions of higher learning in the United States suffered from a general "intellectual vacuity."[73] Efforts at reform only bore fruit after the Civil War. Generally speaking, antebellum colleges devoted most of their time to "controlling unruly students" and instilling right thinking in their young adult minds. They employed a "narrow academic curriculum focused on rote learning of classical languages and literature, rhetoric, some rather simple mathematics, and, of course, the 'capstone' course in moral philosophy."[74] Their emphasis on rote learning and "right thinking" has correlates in traditional and modern higher education in China, but colleges in the United States would abandon that narrow curricular focus on indoctrination in the postbellum period. The seeds of that change were sown in antebellum America.

For example, having attempted to tackle public education reform as governor of Virginia from 1779 to 1781, and after leaving the presidency, Thomas Jefferson founded the University of Virginia as a public institution. When it opened in 1825, the university featured an expanded curriculum, offered elective courses, and made the library the center of campus. Up to that point, the library remained somewhat tangential to the mission of the American college. By the late 1830s, a mere seventy thousand books constituted the entire library holdings of Harvard, Yale, and Princeton combined (compared with the four hundred thousand volumes held individually at the Paris, Munich, and Vatican libraries).[75] The typically narrow antebellum curricula did not require rigorous research, and faculty members were not expected to publish (but to focus on teaching).

State universities became increasingly common before the American Civil War, due to the doctrine of the separation of church and state enshrined in the U.S. Constitution. When the New Hampshire state legislature tried to depose the president of Dartmouth College in 1816 and transfer the power to appoint college board members to the state governor (in order to convert it from a private institution into a public one), Dartmouth sued. Citing its 1769 charter granted by the King of England (which stipulated a certain structure of governance), the case went all the way to the U.S. Supreme Court, which upheld Dartmouth's right to continue as a private institution based on contract law. It was an important decision because it protected business charters from undue state influence, and it is generally credited with encouraging investment and growth in an emerging American business sector. The Dartmouth College case also advanced a pluralistic trend in American higher education that was just getting under way, and it legalized "a great private sector in American higher education" and made it immune from governmental interference.[76]

Many of the colleges founded in the antebellum period in the United States took on new forms. For instance, the advent of technical colleges was a response to the utilitarian spirit of education championed by Benjamin Franklin and others. The Rensselaer School in upstate New York became Rensselaer Institute in 1833, and then Rensselaer Polytechnic Institute in 1861. According to its founding document, the school was to focus on "the application of science to the common purposes of life." Its benefactor desired an institution that would "prepare teachers who would instruct the sons and daughters of local farmers and mechanics in the art of applying science to husbandry, manufactures, and domestic economy."[77] As engineering and technology made its way into the curriculum at technical institutions like

Rensselaer, even proud liberal arts colleges would begin integrating the "practical sciences" as well.

The first women's colleges arose in the southern part of the country and would further diversify the landscape of higher education in the United States in the antebellum period. The Georgia Female College (now Wesleyan) was chartered in 1836, followed by Judson Female Institute in 1838 in Alabama. Oberlin College, founded in 1833, was the first institution to offer regular admission to women and blacks in the United States, making it an early adopter of coeducation and an innovator in progressive causes such as emancipation and suffrage.

Although denominationalism re-emerged as a trend around 1800, the state college movement preceded it, thereby impeding the spread of religious higher education. This movement was so strong that some colleges founded as private denominational institutions became public ones, such as William and Mary. When denominationalism re-emerged to counter this secularization of American higher education, hundreds of liberal arts colleges were established and "affiliated one way or another with a parent church."[78] Founders of these "hill top" colleges include the Quakers, Lutherans, Episcopalians, Universalists, and Roman Catholics. Nevertheless, they could not diminish the enthusiasm for public secular higher learning.

The University of Georgia traces its charter to 1785, the University of North Carolina was founded in 1789, and the University of Vermont can trace its founding back to 1791. The state college movement grew further during the first half of the nineteenth century as institutions of higher learning were established in the western territories and the nation expanded toward the Pacific Ocean. All told, more than twenty state universities would be founded in the United States by the time the University of California was established in 1868.

The first Morrill Act, passed by the U.S. Congress in 1862, transformed American higher education even more profoundly by granting each state in the union land to sell in order to establish institutions of higher learning, and it accelerated the trend toward state and federal funding for higher education (which continued until the Reagan presidency from 1981 to 1989). Despite the grave destruction inflicted on the country during the American Civil War, twenty-five years after the first Morrill Act a college of agriculture existed in every state, which helped to satisfy the nation's growing demand for industrial and technical advancement. More importantly, the first Morrill Act made the professional and vocational aspects of higher education accessible to all.

As the state college movement gathered momentum in postbellum America, "there arose a popular demand for a type of higher education that would be more directly responsible to the needs of a new day."[79] The second Morrill Act of 1890 heeded that call by providing for the creation of separate land grant institutions for people of color. Four such colleges were set up under the 1862 Act, followed by another fourteen in 1890. These land grant colleges "universalized utilitarian higher education, helped further the development of agriculture and industry, promoted adult education, and contributed to the general welfare."[80] They were also instrumental in shaping the distinctive American university that would emerge later out of this synthesis of secular/public and religious/private support for higher education.

From a historical point of view, the Land Grant College Acts help to highlight the egalitarian American innovation of offering both academic and technical education in the same institution,[81] and they aided in severing American higher education from its elite Greco-Roman and European roots. Moreover, the Morrill Land Grant Acts contributed to a new ideal of specialization by helping the United States to create a system of higher education that could adapt quickly to the country's needs. One prominent example would be the explosion of "normal colleges" in the late nineteenth century to prepare more teachers for service in the nation's primary and secondary schools.

Yet, when Mark Pattison, Rector of Lincoln College at Oxford, quipped, "America has no universities" in 1865, he was simply giving voice to a common sentiment held both in the United States and abroad. There was no common definition of the university in use at the time, it is true, but more importantly, American "universities" lacked two elements that we associate with their modern counterparts: a commitment to research and graduate studies.[82] For generations, American students seeking graduate degrees went to Germany. As a result, German universities had their greatest impact on higher education in the United States between the Civil War and World War I.

At the heart of the German university system was the notion that true higher learning required "the workshop of free scientific research." To create such a space, German professors championed absolute freedom in teaching and learning and the disinterested pursuit of truth through original investigation. In the latter part of the nineteenth century, a growing preoccupation with pushing the boundaries of knowledge led to new methods of instruction (seminars, laboratory work, and specialized lectures among them). More than ten thousand American students took courses at German universities between 1815 and 1914,[83] and they brought back with them a desire to achieve higher standards in their own institutions of higher learning.

The establishment of Johns Hopkins University in 1876 marks another important milestone in the development of American higher education, for it is the first time that undergraduate instruction was integrated with graduate research and technical training using new pedagogies imported from Germany. President Woodrow Wilson (1856–1924) lauded his *alma mater* as "a new and higher university ideal, whose essential feature was not stately edifices, nor yet the mere association of pupils with learned and eminent teachers, but rather the education of trained and vigorous young minds through the search for truth under the guidance and with the co-operation of master investigators."[84] Following its lead, many traditional liberal arts undergraduate colleges reorganized themselves into full-blown universities (Columbia University, University of Chicago, Cornell University, and Harvard University, as well as the flagship campuses of systems such as the University of Michigan and the University of California).

As science and technology began to be seen as the basis of all practical knowledge, and social Darwinism and laissez-faire economics increasingly justified competition, large socio-economic gaps between the wealthiest and the poorest Americans began to appear. Fabulously rich magnates of industry donated enormous sums of money to endow research universities. Andrew Carnegie (1835–1919) founded Carnegie Mellon University in 1900, and the following year John D. Rockefeller established Rockefeller University. Business tycoons like Carnegie and Rockefeller gave American universities their focus on science education as industrialization became increasingly dependent on invention and innovation.[85] Ever since that time,

American businesses have worked hand in hand with higher education, sometimes unduly influencing curricula and faculty hiring decisions. The rise of faculty governance models in the mid-twentieth century helped to temper that trajectory.

Simply put, the difference in administering a higher education venture versus a business enterprise "lies in the authority and responsibility placed in the faculty, as a body, by tradition, by custom, or by formal bylaw or regulation. A second difference lies in the freedom of speech and of thought accorded the faculty member as an individual." Thomas Jefferson offered provisions that granted faculty members at the University of Virginia the freedom to make decisions about educational programs and the makeup of the faculty, and that move has influenced the governance of American colleges and universities ever since.[86] As chapter four will show, this American tradition of faculty governance is now under siege and is therefore at the center of the current crisis in the academy.

By the end of the First World War in 1918, American research universities were poised to claim the mantle of leadership in global higher education from Germany (because the war disrupted the international flow of students and faculty to and from Germany). Between the world wars, the Great Depression of 1929 wreaked havoc on higher education funding, and in response the American government later poured over $93 million into emergency assistance for students between 1935 and 1943.[87]

When Hitler came to power, many German academics and writers responded by emigrating to the United States, thereby adding important intellectual heft to the American academy. On the eve of the Second World War, 18 percent of the U.S. population was enrolled in four-year postsecondary education. The growth of junior colleges (community or two-year colleges), driven by increasing demand for access to higher education, was another innovation that helped to create something of a "golden era" of American higher education between 1945 and 1980. Two-year colleges privileged the vocational focus in their missions, and they developed academic tracks for students interested in transferring credits to four-year universities. In this manner, an additional defining feature of the American higher education system was put in place.

Another important innovation occurred in 1940 when the American Association of University Professors (AAUP) issued its *Statement of Principles of Academic Freedom and Tenure*, which would set important ethical standards in higher education for generations to come. One of its main principles, which American colleges and universities have regrettably lost sight of today, is that institutions of higher education are "conducted for the common good and not to further the interest of either the individual teacher or the institution as a whole." AAUP calls academic freedom "fundamental to the advancement of truth" and insists that tenure is the best way to protect it.[88] For this reason, the freedom of faculty members to follow individual research agendas and to speak freely inside the classroom (and outside of it) became fundamental to the international success of American higher education from the middle twentieth century onward.

During the Second World War, male student populations in the United States were disrupted again, institutions of higher learning developed courses in defense topics, war industry workers took short courses in engineering and foreign languages, and thousands of students participated in military training on campuses across the nation.[89] When the war effort wound down, the American economy could not accommodate the influx of returning soldiers, so the Servicemen's Readjustment Act of 1944 (better known as the G.I. Bill) provided tuition and living expenses to millions of veterans. In doing so, the G.I. Bill drove an unprecedented expansion in higher education in the United States — one that took place *after* enrollments had already grown steadily throughout the first half of the twentieth century.

In 1900, for example, less than thirty thousand college degrees were awarded in the United States, whereas by 1950, there were five hundred thousand. The number of doctoral degrees granted by American institutions was doubling every eleven years, as well. Just two years after the Second World War came to a close, almost two-and-a-half million students were enrolled in eighteen hundred American colleges and universities — and for the first time they were evenly divided between private and public institutions.[90] This pattern of increased funding and enrollment continued into the early 1960s, when a new generation of "baby boomers" swelled enrollments in American colleges and universities even further. All told, by the mid- to late twentieth century, the United States had succeeded in creating the first complete ladder-system of schools (from preschool to university) exclusive of arbitrary barriers or restrictions.

During the 1960's and 1970s, public institutions of higher learning that were established during the late nineteenth and early twentieth centuries (such as normal schools) started converting themselves into comprehensive state colleges or even universities by expanding programs of study and offering graduate degrees to fill burgeoning demand. American community colleges, comprehensive colleges, and universities all grew in size and number (with some estimates suggesting that a community college opened once a week during the entire 1960s). The 1963 Vocational Educational Act, the Higher Education Facilities Act, and the Health Professions Act all combined with 1965 civil rights legislation to create a new rationale for massive increases in support for higher education.[91] These were also protest years on American campuses across the nation, when proponents of civil rights, women's rights, and the Free Speech movement and those against American involvement in Vietnam gathered to challenge the social and political status quo.

An economic downturn in the 1970s seriously challenged funding priorities for American higher education, but arguably investments made during the 1950s and 1960s sustained it through this period of protracted recession and budget cutting. In fact, the number of higher education institutions continued to grow (from twenty-five hundred in 1970 to thirty-two hundred in 1980).[92] However, business support for higher education dropped by 9 percent in 1971 alone, compounding cuts by federal and state governments. This loss of funding is eerily similar to that faced more recently by American higher education in the wake of the 2008 Great Recession — except that behind institutions of higher learning in the 1970s were decades of private and public investment. Moreover, even in the face of these fiscal challenges, collective bargaining for faculty and other academic professionals increased during the 1970s.

By the end of that decade, however, two energy crises and the Iranian Revolution in 1979 put American citizens in a more conservative — and much less generous — mood. In the presidential election of 1980, voters embraced a form of conservatism (in the figure of

Ronald Reagan) that for generations would eviscerate higher education funding. During the 1980s and 1990s pitiless budget cutting put
tenure under scrutiny, and contingent faculty (lacking tenure protections) began to displace fulltime professors at an alarming rate. With
the benefit of hindsight that a historical overview of American higher
education like this one provides, we see that the period from 1945
to 1980 constitutes an apex in the development of American higher
education. With the election of President Reagan, higher learning in
the United States began its well-documented decline — just as new
international competitors began to appear on the eastern horizon.

During the late twentieth century, American higher education
dominated the international landscape for a variety of reasons, among
them its "sustained focus on the benefits of liberal education; the
identification of the PhD degree as a research degree; the more or
less peaceful coexistence of public and private liberal arts colleges, research universities, and community colleges; and the incorporation of
professional schools into the university." These American innovations
all grew out of a cultural preference for meritocracy, a commitment to
bettering the national welfare, a desire to rapidly industrialize during
the twentieth century, and an orientation around private markets.[93]

Before moving on to a sustained treatment of the causes and
symptoms of the decline in the quality and reputation of American
higher education in chapter four, let us first return to China and consider that country's rapid pace of development from 1980 to the present day. After the modern histories of Chinese and American higher
education are analyzed in detail, the rest of this study will put the great
convergence in international education during the late twentieth and
early twenty-first centuries into a global context.

· · · · · · · · · · · · · · · ·

CHAPTER THREE

The Chinese Moment

TWO YEARS AFTER the death of Chairman Mao in 1976, China began another period of profound social and economic transformation. This time, however, it would be followed by generations of unprecedented economic growth (and not countrywide famine). It is a narrative of renovation that defies belief, yet from 1980 to 2015 the central government transformed Chinese higher education from the dilapidated state of disrepair in which Mao Zedong left it—into one of the most important systems of higher education delivery in the world. Furthermore, forward-looking Chinese leaders plan to continue investing so as to create and sustain top-tier world-class universities and a comprehensive system of higher education that rival those found in the United States and other leading countries.

As we saw in chapter one, the Chinese tradition of higher education dates back to at least the first millennium BCE. The sage Confucius, whose teachings became influential throughout East Asia, emphasized lifelong learning, moral self-cultivation, propriety, humanity (human heartedness), and obedience to authority (both familial and institutional). An intensive system of civil service examinations arose out of that Confucian tradition that alienated a large number of intellectuals who could never pass provincial or metropolitan exams. Due to foreign invasion, a growing technology gap with the West, and a certain "backwardness" of thinking (ridiculed by writers like Lu Xun), China in 1911 was in turmoil, largely impoverished, and divided.

From 1911 to 1976, a democratically inclined Republican government rose and fell, and a civil war between Communists and nationalists raged across China. When the communists won control in 1949,

ary, and tertiary education to a halt from 1966 to 1970. When schools
began to reopen, most of them (including the nation's colleges and
universities) were converted into propaganda machines that spread
Maoist thought. After Mao died, Deng Xiaoping (1904–1997) emerged
as China's new leader. As Mao had anticipated in 1966, a "capitalist
restoration" was soon underway. Deng's 1978 "Open Door" policy
encouraged outside business investment in China, allowed student
exchanges, and permitted the re-emergence of a repressed Chinese
entrepreneurial spirit through market reforms.

Starting in the 1960s, Chinese higher education followed Russian
curricular models (even though political relations between the countries had lapsed). Soon thereafter, a set of "canonized disciplines and
professional specializations" was linked forever to the structure of the
bureaucracy. Thus, the Soviet Five-Year Plan provided an effective tool
for the maintenance of a hierarchical sociopolitical order,[1] and it was
used repeatedly to chart the future course of Chinese higher education
into the twenty-first century. Similar multiyear strategic planning cy-
cles are now part of the "best practices" duplicated mindlessly by campus administrators across the United States. Regrettably, the irony of
the widespread use of authoritarian Soviet-style planning apparatuses
remains lost on many intellectuals in the American academy today.

When he took office, Deng Xiaoping clamped down on the Democracy Wall Movement that sputtered along from 1978–80 by arresting its prominent leaders and using the death penalty to deal with
radical elements left over from the Cultural Revolution. In addition to
their call "for democratic reforms, a socialist legal system, and human
rights," student protestors demanded the freedom to travel, noted the
need for a "modernization of lifestyles," and pointed to the necessity of "learning from other countries." The students referenced the
human rights policies of American president Jimmy Carter (b. 1924)
and put up wall posters that ridiculed Maoist thought as "ideologically absurd."[2] Even after such brazen displays of bravado, the Chinese
intelligentsia refused to join with the students, in part because they
"never really overcame the shocks of the first Anti-Rightist Movement
in 1957" nor those that followed in later years. Moreover, they felt that

Deng Xiaoping might provide them with a means of reacquiring the social prestige that was lost to them during the years of the Cultural Revolution (in the form of a restructured system of higher education).[3]

As Deng moved to put down this student democracy movement and close Democracy Wall where protestors posted their placards, he placated the intelligentsia with promises of economic development for China. Ten years later, when much larger student demonstrations began in Tiananmen Square, Deng again cut short that democratic impulse (first felt by Sun Yat-sen and others at the beginning of the century). Yet, even though he acted the tyrant with the students, Deng Xiaoping initiated pragmatic educational reforms that set the stage for the remarkable development of Chinese higher learning in the decades that followed.

In a speech delivered before the National Education Work Conference in 1978, Deng reiterated a long-held Chinese belief in the power of education to transform the nation (social amelioration was the ideal outcome of the Confucian project and remains ingrained in the Chinese mind despite decades of Communist propaganda). Deng spoke of the need to "master and advance modern science and culture and the new techniques and technologies of all trades and professions,"[4] and he granted the Ministry of Education the power to create nationally standardized lesson plans, teaching outlines, and textbooks.

The phenomenon of specialization, which mirrored what took place in American universities decades earlier, began to emerge in China during the Deng era. A new emphasis on research followed quickly, as university presidents were given more internal institutional control and science and technology became intimately tied to the political, social, and economic goals of the Communist Party following the death of Mao Zedong and the elimination of the Gang of Four (who had purged Deng in an unsuccessful attempt to continue the Cultural Revolution).

As a result of these policy directives, the number of higher education institutions in China grew from just over six hundred to around one thousand between 1980 and 1985. One hundred and forty of these new institutions were "vocational universities with short-cycle programs administered by city governments." Teacher-training institutes also grew from 172 in 1980 to 253 in 1985. The number of specializations, a manifestation of the Russian educational influence, was reduced as the redefinition of knowledge areas started in earnest.[5] In accordance with the 6th Five-Year Plan,[6] nearly forty thousand Chinese students studied abroad (just a fraction of the current numbers).

Beginning in the early to mid-1980s, curricular reforms in China were combined with a less hierarchical structuring of knowledge. The party leadership held firmly to power as the Open Door policy facilitated the flow of information and goods, raised the standard of living for millions of its citizens, and prompted a resurgence of Chinese power and influence on the world stage. Because the quality of Chinese higher education had been so badly damaged during the Cultural Revolution, the 7th Five-Year Plan (1986–1990) called attention to the urgent need to tap the potential of China's colleges and universities and encourage them to "reinforce their ties with production and scientific research and other sectors of society." The goal was to increase the number of people with an undergraduate degree by 70 percent and a graduate degree by more than 400 percent.[7]

University entrance examinations were reinstated in the early 1980s, and academic degree programs were made to follow the American model (that is, BA, MA, and PhD). By the middle of that decade, postdoctoral programs took shape in China, and urban colleges and universities began to open branch institutions in rural locations (a trend which accelerated in the 1990s and 2000s). Finally, the creation of special economic zones in cities such as Shenzhen benefited local institutions of higher education by "utilizing foreign capital, introducing foreign technology, and expanding educational and technological exchanges with foreign countries."[8] Chinese GDP growth rose dramatically as a result of these and other reform efforts (from a GDP of US$200 billion in 1980 to US$11 trillion in 2016). China currently boasts an economy that is second in size only to that of the United States, but all serious predictions suggest that ordering will be inverted in a few years' time.

As we can see, the acceleration in convergence with the higher education outcomes of global leaders like the United States and Britain started in the 1980s. The stated goal of the "Decision to Reform the Educational System," proposed by the Central Committee of the Chinese Communist Party (CCCCP) in 1985, was to "help narrow that gap between China and the other developed countries of the world," which meant raising the living standard of woefully underpaid teachers and making nine years of education compulsory for every Chinese citizen.

The 7th Five-Year Plan included measures to "gradually enhance the competence, raise the social status and increase the material benefits of scientists, engineers, teachers, and other specialized personnel and to provide them with better working, studying, and living conditions."[9] As demand for adult education rose through the mid-1980s, the Chinese government started a Radio and Television University, ran worker and peasant colleges (to improve productivity), established cadre colleges (to train party members in management), offered continuing adult education for primary and secondary educators, and administered correspondence universities.[10]

Since adult education was considered pivotal to the country's modernization, reforms to this sector in 1987 emphasized job skills, basic education for those who had not completed secondary schooling, and technical training.[11] These types of programs filled important gaps in adult learning since so many Chinese people had missed the opportunity for formal education during the Cultural Revolution. Due to the fact that its system of colleges and universities was still relatively small in the 1980s compared to the nation's population, alternate avenues such as these relieved some demand for better access to higher education, and they contributed to China's economic development by nurturing a well-trained workforce.

The particularly tiered nature of its expanding higher education system meant that Chinese students who were most successful academically at the secondary level went on to college or university, while others had to seek different options for continuing education. As it transitioned from a planned economy to a market economy throughout the 1980s and Deng's reforms took hold, China's thirst for natural resources became unquenchable. However, the country remained incapable of meeting its own needs for grain, copper, steel, electricity, and oil and gas through domestic production, which meant China had no choice but to increase its level of international engagement. This shift marks a significant transformation ideologically, for during the Mao years emphasis had been put on self-sufficiency, inwardness, and independence from the world community.

As China's population passed the one billion mark in the early 1980s, tremendous pressure was put on food resources and other commodities. Some scholars believe that the rising cost of food contributed to the student protests in Tiananmen Square in 1989.[12] More students became politically active as prices rose faster than incomes, and some even called for more democratic methods of university administration (for there is no tradition of faculty or student governance in China). Direct control of higher education by the Chinese Communist Party gradually eased through the 1980s, and a deliberate process of decentralization gave campuses more control over curricula and teaching methods. The Educational Reform Document of 1985 contained many innovations, among them that enrollments would not be set by the state exclusively. Universities could suddenly contract with private students and enterprises (who would pay their own way), relax strict job assignments, and retain more financial institutional autonomy.[13] Political education became less dogmatic as well (although it was still present in the curriculum when I was teaching in China in the late 1990s).

Even so, the Chinese Communist Party continued to exert considerable control over student life, and that unpleasant reality spurred dissident behavior. Although student organizations were closely monitored and usually disbanded promptly, groups at Beijing University and Beijing Normal University emerged independently in 1989 (suggesting a failure of economic growth to translate into meaningful democratic reform). On April 15, just two days after the death of General Secretary Hu Yaobang (1915–1989), who had supported political liberalization, students from several institutions of higher education in Beijing began to march on Tiananmen Square.

Initially, no clear leader or organization came to the forefront to lead the protests. The first few days at Tiananmen were spontaneous and haphazard. By April 19, however, Beijing University (Beida) students managed to organize despite the real fear of swift punishment from the authorities. Nine leaders were selected from among the speakers that day, but student groups like this one suffered from continual infighting during the three-week protest. At Beijing Normal University, three students (Wu'er Kaixi, Zhang Jun, and Liang Er) formed an autonomous faction and bravely signed their names to a big-character poster announcing the formation of the group. Theirs proved to be more stable than the Beida group,[14] and as more individuals became involved in the protests each day, students began to look to the Chinese Communist Party for recognition of their demands.

On April 27, more than one hundred thousand students defied blockages and calls of condemnation to rally, after an article in the *China Daily* accused the protesters of being traitors to the party and government. On May 4, the anniversary of antigovernment student protests in 1919 against the Treaty of Versailles that ended the First World War for Germany, more than one million students filled Tiananmen Square. When CCP leaders remained intransigent, the students went on hunger strike, taking up vigil at the Monument to the People's Heroes in Tiananmen on May 13. Thereafter, the crisis escalated quickly, and Premier Li Peng (b. 1928) declared martial law nine days later. After a few more weeks of protest, the army entered Tiananmen Square on June 7, and those who resisted the soldiers or their equipment "were forcefully moved — or shot."[15]

The exact number of citizens massacred by the Chinese government that day remains unknown, but it is estimated to be between two hundred and two thousand souls. All hopes held by Chinese students that the country would adopt a Western-style democracy were summarily crushed. Today, the Chinese Communist Party maintains control of the country and its mass media by trading the generational economic growth it has generated in return for civil liberties. This formula has worked until the present day, yet one cannot help but wonder what will happen when three decades of 10 percent growth gives way to the transition from an industrial to postindustrial economy (with its lower growth rates) in the coming years.

In sum, the Tiananmen Square protests, while ultimately unsuccessful, demonstrated that the political loosening that gave birth to the student movement in China could be tightened again at will — and that the regime was convinced that economic liberalization could, and must, take place without political liberalization.[16] As I indicated in the introduction, students currently attending Chinese colleges and universities are largely unaware of the carnage that took place in 1989 — such is the power of the central government to rewrite history. Furthermore, the protests and their subsequent erasure from public consciousness help to illustrate how an authoritarian regime may quickly initiate widespread systemic change in higher education and in other sectors of the economy (such as in healthcare delivery during the Severe Acute Respiratory Syndrome outbreak in 2002). By contrast, the number of independent players and complexities of policy change in the United States make rapid and categorical reforms to higher education difficult, if not impossible, especially given the limits of federal government involvement.

After effectively putting the student protests at Tiananmen Square behind it, the Chinese Communist Party announced Project 211 in 1993 to improve higher education delivery, encourage scientific research, and streamline institutional management. Specific universities and colleges were targeted for investment by the government, and an over-arching goal was met to double the number of students attending its tertiary institutions in the 1990s. In addition, Project 211 mandated the flagging of one hundred institutions of higher learning that could be made into universities of "world standard" status. *This surge in financial support for Chinese higher education corresponds to equally dramatic declines in funding for American colleges and universities during the same period.* Therefore, the years from 1980 to 2015 mark an important period of quickening in the pace and scope of global convergence in higher education.

Cheng Kai-ming observes that Project 211 stirred intense competition among Chinese institutions for the coveted "world-standard" designation, and sometimes prestigious universities were combined "to increase their competition capacity" on the world stage. For example, five universities were merged in Hangzhou Province and eight in Jiangsu province. However, because of corruption in the selection process, some of these mergers were more about winning Project 211 accreditation than an honest effort to improve excellence or efficiency.[17] Two other trends in the early to mid-1990s warrant noting as well: the introduction of student fees and the localization of institutions of higher learning.

Overall, competition for tertiary education remained stiff through 1995, as almost three million students enrolled in formal higher education institutions and another two-and-a-half million more did so in the nonformal sector. Still, formal institutions of higher learning in China admitted only half of all secondary graduates.[18] In terms of rising student costs (tuition and fees) and localization, the Chinese government paid for 96 percent of all education expenses with public funds in 1978. Gradually through the 1980s and 1990s, institutions of higher learning gained the right to "retain part or most of their incomes and to decide their own spending plans." The more revenue they could generate, the more they could earn.

Soon thereafter, the government formally encouraged institutions of higher learning to seek out diversified sources of funding, which included university-run enterprises, services, commissioned training, endowment donations, and the aforementioned student fees.[19] These educational trends in China mirrored broader shifts to a market-based economy, privatization, growing entrepreneurial competition, and a gradual dismantling of the "iron rice bowl" (that once insured cradle-to-grave social welfare according to the Communist ideal).

The "foreign expert" program, initiated in 1995, encouraged the exchange of scholars and the creation of international partnerships by bringing foreign teachers, administrators, scientists, and professionals from all disciplines to China for long and short stays. This designation was bestowed on me when I taught at Fudan University from early 1998 to late 1999 (although it remains difficult to see any benefit brought to those of us teaching university courses in the humanities). The program persists to this day, albeit in modified form—and with a scientific and technological focus.

Project 985 was the final important development in Chinese higher education during the 1990s. Announced in 1998, it targeted elite universities for generous infusions of cash, specifically to increase Chinese global competitiveness in scientific research. Nine Chinese universities received funding that exceeded one billion RMB (or *renminbi*, the Chinese currency) per institution for developing infrastructure, purchasing equipment, funding faculty members to attend international conferences, bringing scholars in from abroad, and so on. The nine universities funded by the initial phase of Project 985 (Fudan, Nanjing, Beijing, Shanghai Jiaotong, Tsinghua, Xi'an Jiaotong, Zhejiang, Harbin Institute of Technology, and the University of Science and Technology of China) dubbed themselves the "C9 League" as a deliberately provocative correlate to the eight institutions that make up the American "Ivy League."

All told, at the end of the 1990s, more than two hundred universities and institutions of adult higher learning were transferred from state and ministry control to local education bureaus as a consequence of restructuring.[20] To imagine the scale of the expansion of higher education in China over that twenty-year period, one need only consider the one million students enrolled in institutions of higher learning in 1980—a figure that grew to thirteen million in 2001 and then to thirty million in 2010! The massification of Chinese higher education took place during these years, but as enrollments grew, the government's share of the costs of the expansion of higher education actually dropped to 47 percent (from nearly 100 percent) as a consequence of the introduction of tuition and a process of privatization that encouraged finding alternate revenue streams.[21]

The next decade witnessed equally impressive gains in the higher education sector. China joined the World Trade Organization (WTO) in 2001, and the government officially promoted private education in 2002 (for the first time since Mao declared the creation of the People's Republic). Transnational higher education and joint venture programs were formally sanctioned in 2003, and the next year Project 985 was expanded to include funding infusions for nearly forty institutions in its second phase. All of these developments had a profound influence on the advancement of Chinese higher education. Broadly speaking, higher education policies before 1997 favored steady and moderate student enrollment increases because of financial constraints and institutional limitations. However, leading up to entry in the WTO, with an economy clocking 10 percent GDP growth per year, policies were put in place to significantly expand access to higher education in the country.

If we look past the official Party line from 1999 to 2003, we find other motivations for aiming to double the size of student enrollment in higher education in China. An economist with the Asian Development ment Bank Mission in China, Min Tang, wrote to Premier Zhu Rongji (b. 1928) proposing enrollment expansion, for "Tang believed that doubling higher education enrollment in the next three years would not only encourage families to spend their huge savings on higher education but also stimulate investment in service, construction and other related industries and would eventually increase consumption by about one hundred billion RMB, which amounts to 0.5% of the GDP."[22]

Because ordinary people were afforded little or no social welfare in imperial China, their only means to stave off starvation during times of conflict was to save money. As such, this habit remains deeply engrained in the Chinese psyche. Saving rates during the early 1990s in China were above 40 percent (compared to around 15 percent in the United States). So, in order to further stimulate economic growth, Chinese leaders had to discover ways to loosen the pocketbooks of their citizenry to create domestic demand. Because the Chinese people traditionally value education, as both a source of social prestige and upward income potential, Min Tang and others believed that the public would finance the expansion of Chinese higher education out of their savings. As the rest of the region shook off the lingering effects of the Asian financial crisis in 1997, China launched into another unprecedented effort to grow its higher education sector.

As a result of adopting Min Tang's recommendations, the savings rate in China dropped below 40 percent from 1999 to 2002 (in part due to increased domestic expenditures on education by private households, as predicted). Data suggest that government spending on social services in China hovered around 10 percent of GDP from 1996 to 2001, while it was less than 2 percent in the United States.[23] When we consider the causes of the decline of American higher education from 1980 to the present in the subsequent chapter, dwindling governmental support for education ranks among the foremost.

In fact, the demand for higher education has always been high in China, due in part to the emphasis that Confucius placed on it thousands of years ago. So, rather than object to increased costs, the Chinese public welcomed the move to double college and university enrollments, since they saw education as a means for individual and national socio-economic advancement. This advantageous overlapping of public and private interests in East Asian culture has led to an enduring belief that "individuals with better educations tend to achieve greater success in the labor market."[24]

Correlating with the idea that "economies with higher enrollment rates and years of schooling appear to be more dynamic, competitive in global markets, and successful in terms of higher income per capita," East Asia experienced faster growth per year than did Latin America from 1991 to 1995. There emerged simultaneously a general consensus among the Chinese leadership concerning the importance of creating "a well-developed system for science and technology" as a means for the country to achieve its aspirations for greater economic power and influence in the world. The commonly held view was that cultivating its nascent knowledge economy would allow the country to compete in an increasingly globalized and integrated world.[25]

The expansion of tertiary enrollments in the early part of the twenty-first century had the additional positive effects of postponing student employment after high school and easing the national labor market. Increasing educational spending stimulated domestic consumption, which in turn promoted growth in related industries. Finally, the expansion of Chinese higher education during the early 1990s also reduced pressures on high schools, discouraged teaching to the test (i.e., the university entrance examination), and encouraged broad education.[26]

Despite these reform and expansion efforts, competitiveness among Chinese high school students for access to the nation's institutions of higher learning remained fierce. Because of that fact, a typical week of study still includes a full school day (from roughly eight in the morning until four in the afternoon), a short break for supper, and then outside courses at private academies, examination preparation and private tutoring, or classes to improve test-taking skills (similar to SAT prep courses in the United States). Weekends bring little reprieve to these modern-day would-be Mandarins, as the study load faced by most college-bound Chinese students hardly lightens at all on Saturday and Sunday.

The "one child" policy, first instituted in 1979 to control population growth, means that the typical Han Chinese student is now an only child, which adds to the pressure for higher education attainment. In a real sense, the imperial civil service examinations that we learned about in chapter one have a new guise in the twenty-first century in the form of the university entrance examination. Today's adolescents in China exhibit many of the same anxieties associated with test preparation as did their peers in centuries past. Rising rates of suicide are also of great concern, for according to China's Center for Disease Control and Prevention, suicide remains the top cause of death among Chinese youth.[27]

Another reason to note these historical connections between the imperial civil service examination and the modern university entrance examination in China, from an American point of view, is to consider the real cost of implementing more standardized testing in our primary and secondary schools (under propagandist slogans like "No Child Left Behind," "Race to the Top," and the "Common Core") — as well as the rush to do the same at the university level by way of mandates for "student learning outcomes" and "value-added assessments." Standardized testing is another symptom of the neoliberal ideology that continues to erode the quality of the American educational system. In China, we have a prime example of the limitations of test-based learning to ponder.

Following China's entry into the World Trade Organization, new international demands were placed on its higher education sector. In response to them, the Chinese government adopted transnational education as an official policy tool to spur economic development. It revised its education legislation to allow overseas institutions to offer programs in China in accord with WTO regulations.[28] The Chinese government also gave its consent to the General Agreement on Trade in Services (GATS), which includes provisions for transnational education. This new preoccupation with internationalization and globalization in China is stunning in the context of the Mao era that preceded it from 1949 to 1976.

In 2003, the State Council issued its regulations on "Chinese-Foreign Cooperation in Running Schools," which encouraged "local universities to cooperate with renowned overseas higher education institutions" to launch new academic programs, remove restrictions on overseas institutions making a profit, and adopt a state-guided market-oriented system characterized by heavy regulation as part of a transitional economy.[29] Due to the eagerness of Chinese leaders to turn their manufacturing economy into a knowledge economy, foreign universities began to establish a foothold inside China for the first time since the Republican period (1911–1949).

The Johns Hopkins–Nanjing Center was the first American institution of higher learning to establish a physical presence in China (in 1984), but it could only offer certificate programs (that restriction has since been lifted, and now the center offers a two-year joint master's degree in international studies). The State Council regulations of 2003 made it possible for foreign universities to operate more freely and offer different degree options to Chinese students in the country. Lured by the promise of steadily increasing enrollments and a new foreign revenue stream, the University of Nottingham Ningbo China (UNNC) was the first Sino-foreign joint-venture university to open, and it has offered degree programs taught in English since 2004.

The University of Michigan–Shanghai Jiao Tong University (UM-SJTU) Joint Institute, established in 2006, grants degrees in China as well—and in 2013 it could boast of fifteen hundred students paying 50,000 RMB per year in tuition. Despite that high cost of admission, joint-venture programs are attractive to Chinese students because of the name recognition offered by both institutions, and in this case because of the high acceptance rate for UM-SJTU graduates seeking admission to the University of Michigan. More recently, New York University built a campus in the Pudong area of Shanghai, and it offers a variety of bachelor degrees to two thousand students per year. The mere existence of these joint higher education ventures offers proof of the great changes in China's tertiary system of education since 1978.

Collaborative higher education ventures like these are of several distinct types: joint curriculum and foreign degree, joint curriculum and double degree, and foreign curriculum and foreign degree; some-times these options come with certificates, as well.[30] Most popular with Chinese students are 2+2 and 3+1 programs, because they are more affordable (since part of one's studies are undertaken in China) and include the opportunity to study abroad. These 2+2 and 3+1 programs also ease visa application processes, provide students with language skills and cultural literacy before departing, and introduce foreign pedagogies (which are often quite different from the direct instruction and rote memorization traditionally practiced in Chinese classrooms).

One unwelcome consequence of China's internationalization and higher education reform during the last two decades is the number of Chinese students who now skip provincial, national, and joint-venture colleges and universities altogether and go directly abroad to study. In 2006 alone, more than 130,000 Chinese students studied abroad, and they made up nearly 12 percent of the total number of foreign students in the United States.[31] Beginning in 2010, China claimed from India the distinction of sending the most foreign students to American colleges and universities (with nearly 275,000 Chinese citizens studying in the United States during the 2013–14 academic year). Underlying this exodus is a supposition among Chinese students that attending only the most elite Chinese institutions of higher learning would be preferable to earning foreign degrees, which are often perceived as having more gravitas, particularly at the graduate level. Students in other East Asian countries, such as Taiwan and South Korea, hold similar perceptions, and this pattern of seeking higher education abroad applies to them as well.

The flight of students from China can also be attributed to the persistence of ideological indoctrination in the standardized curriculum. Although Chinese colleges and universities experienced internationalization throughout the 2000s, new high school textbooks rolled out region by region for students in the eleventh and twelfth grades. Their subject matter came directly from the national college-entrance examination (*gaokao*). Recently, a group of international scholars studied the goals of curriculum reforms, as articulated by the Ministry of Education and the State Council, and attributed them directly to changes in textbook content. They identified the following objectives (which read like student learning outcomes found on American undergraduate and graduate syllabi these days): students should be able to learn about Chinese democracy, understand the importance of the rule of law for legitimizing the Chinese government, know the "Three Represents" (三个代表) ideology expounded by former president Jiang Zemin (b. 1926), appreciate traditional Chinese ethnic heritage, comprehend the virtues of state-owned enterprises, and be conscious of environmental issues.[32]

An analysis of the results of these curricular changes suggests that "around 20% of students who would not have held the government's desired views in the absence of exposure to the new curriculum were persuaded by it." As such, schoolbooks proved a more effective tool of persuasion than other means of "oblique" transmission of beliefs, such as advertising or mass media.[33] Historically speaking, we recall that the imperial civil service examinations were also a tool for political indoctrination and a mechanism for eliminating heterodoxy.

Chinese students who failed to return to China after graduating from colleges and universities abroad also contributed to the phenomenon of "brain drain." Throughout the 1990s, the worst offenders were Chinese nationals who completed doctoral work in American universities and remained in the United States afterward. However, brain drain is a common occurrence in international education and is not specific to China; it is experienced by many developing countries. Obviously, when China was closed to the outside world during the Mao years, academic flight was impossible. Following the Open Door policies of Deng Xiaoping, "brain drain," "brain circulation," and "brain regionalism," which are all features of the globalized economy that China signed up for in 2001, increased along with student mobility.

Most estimates suggest that out of the nearly one-and-a-half million Chinese students who have studied abroad, just under four hundred thousand have returned to China.[34] Upward economic mobility among an emergent middle class in China has only just started to reverse that trend. In recent years, the return rate has been rising, but brain drain continues to pose serious challenges to China's system of higher education (since so many Chinese nationals could return home to improve Chinese universities but choose not to, often for good reasons). On the other hand, as we approach global convergence in higher education, the flow of educational services is beginning to expand in the other direction.

Consider the fact that China hosted 85,000 students from more than 175 countries in 2002. By 2004, 110,000 students studied abroad in the Middle Kingdom, and that figure grew to nearly a quarter of a million by 2008. The trend is obvious, and China's generous scholarships help to attract foreign students. For example, the Chinese government provided funding for nearly six thousand students from around the world in 2001.[35] By 2007, China had become the fifth-ranked destination for international students (behind the United States, the United Kingdom, France, and Germany) as a result of its educational reforms and increasing interest in Chinese language and culture worldwide.

All told, the number of American students studying in China increased more than five fold between 2000 and 2010, and they account for about 7 percent of all foreign students in China.[36] China's growing economic and political clout, combined with an increasing number of foreign companies operating in the country, suggest that these trends will keep accelerating in the near term. Undeniably, China is exercising more "soft power" than ever before by subsidizing the study of Chinese language and culture around the world. In light of the unparalleled economic growth in the country since 1980, students from across the globe (and particularly from neighboring East Asian countries) are learning Chinese in the hopes that it will improve their employment prospects in the international marketplace. More South Korean students now study Chinese than English as a second language, and even in the United States, Mandarin Chinese is quickly replacing Japanese at the primary, secondary, and tertiary levels.

In late 2004, the Chinese government began to open "Confucius Institutes" to teach Chinese language, culture, and history across the world. An enterprise similar to the Alliance Française, which the French government uses to support the spread of its language and culture abroad, these institutes have proven extremely popular outside of China. Confucius Institutes and Confucius Classrooms offered nine thousand Chinese courses around the globe by 2009, with total enrollments exceeding a quarter of a million students. Of the more than three hundred Confucius Institutes in existence in 2010 (in ninety-six countries and territories), the greatest number were located in the United States, accounting for nearly 22 percent of the global total.[37]

In addition to language teaching for primary and secondary students, Confucius Institutes offer training for teachers of Chinese, administer language exams, arrange tutors, and provide commercial information about China. Jointly managed by the foreign host and one of seventeen Chinese universities, the primary operational funding for Confucius Institutes comes directly from the China National Office for Teaching Chinese as a Foreign Language (Hanban), while contributions from the host institution generally include providing physical facilities for instruction.[38] Because of this funding model, and the fact that Confucius Institutes in the United States tend to be situated on American college and university campuses, the American Association of University Professors recently issued a report calling on "American universities to cease their involvement with Confucius Institutes unless they can renegotiate their agreements to ensure they have 'unilateral control' over all academic matters — including recruitment of instructors, determination of the curriculum and selection of texts — and academic freedom for the Confucius Institute instructors."[39] While it is difficult to predict what the effect of this and other challenges to Confucius Institutes will mean for them going forward, their existence should be understood in the context of China's attempt to expand its cultural influence abroad and exercise its growing soft power.

One final innovation in the Chinese experiment with higher education in the post-Mao era deserves acknowledgement: the privatization of higher education. So far, we have explored the explosive growth in demand for higher education in China during the last thirty to forty years, and we have seen how the Chinese government twice doubled the size of higher education delivery in just a few decades. Yet, even such herculean efforts could not accommodate every Chinese citizen who wanted access to higher education, so in the 1990s, the Chinese government first implemented "Provisional Stipulations for the Establishment of *Minban* Higher Education Institutions." *Minban* institutions are nonstate-run universities (called private institutions in international nomenclature) that generally offer bachelor's degrees, or lower, in China. *Minban* proliferated throughout the late 1990s and 2000s, "financed by tuition fees, donations, and income generated by training programs, consultation, and technical services."[40] A 2002 law gave private universities in China the same legal status as public institutions and guaranteed their autonomy.

Generally, "privatization" refers to the shift of assets from the public to private sector, and because of the fear that it will undermine the legitimacy of the Communist regime, euphemisms such as denationalization (*feiguo youhua*) and marketization (*shi chang hua*) are used in China instead.[41] In her recent study of private education in modern China, Li Wang identifies several models for institutions that operate on a cost-recovery basis according to market principles. Some of them, like the Dalian University of Foreign Language, are called *guo you minban* because they were transformed from public institutions into private ones. In this particular case, the Liaoning provincial government retains ownership of the university, but it was freed from the obligation of subsidizing it with public funds.

Other higher education institutions in China, such as Zhejiang Wan Li University, were privatized when they were taken over by corporate entities. Although the provincial government holds ownership of Zhejiang Wan Li University, the company that bought it oversees all administrative, financial, and academic concerns.[42] In many such cases, retaining the state affiliation benefits these "transformed" institutions by giving them enrollment priority and more leeway in awarding undergraduate degrees.

While these two examples of *minban* are essentially quasi-private, since they were turned from public entities into privately operated ones, institutions of higher learning that start out independently can now be owned and operated by nonstate entities (such as businesses and nonprofits). In some cases, private companies with considerable capital will build campuses, hire faculty, and finance the entire institution (as in the case of Beijing Geely University), while other institutions are established by a group of founders who share responsibility for day-to-day operations.[43] In reality, *minban* colleges and universities in China constitute a second-tier system for those who do not gain entry to more prestigious public institutions or self-finance their studies abroad.

Private higher education institutions in China mostly focus on offering courses at the undergraduate level or below, and many are not permitted to grant bachelor's degrees at all. For example, of the more than three hundred independent colleges in China in 2010, only forty-eight *minban* institutions were allowed to offer undergraduate degrees (and most of those were transformed from public to private entities). Therefore, the majority of *minban* award lower degrees, certificates, or offer services such as test preparation only.[44] It should be noted that this privatization of higher education in China is a market-based reform effort, which implies that the application of Western capitalist strategies diversified its higher education delivery. In fact, global "ideological convergence" around neoliberalism has transformed the style of governance in many countries, and it definitely manifested itself in education policy and university governance in China.[45]

China's 12th Five-Year Plan, covering the years 2010 to 2015, emphasized higher-quality growth, addressed wealth disparities, slowed GDP to 7 percent per year, developed the remote western regions of the country, tackled pollution, and increased enrollments in high schools to 87 percent. The ambitious and longer range "State Guidelines for Medium-to-Long-Term Education Reform and Development Plan between 2010 and 2020," known simply as the Development Plan, suggests more about the future direction of Chinese higher education.

In the Development Plan's opening lines, we glean the importance that the Chinese Communist Party continues to place on higher education: "A nation's enduring future hinges on education. Education is the cornerstone of national rejuvenation and social progress, and a fundamental way to improve citizens' quality and promote their all-round development, bearing the hope of millions of families for a better life. Education must be enhanced if a nation is to prosper."[46] Such a proposition is clearly rooted in the nation's Confucian past, as well as in its current focus on expedited economic transformation through market reforms and internationalization.

The second paragraph of the Development Plan, which warrants direct quotation, reminds its readers of the significant changes to higher education made under the leadership of the Chinese Communist Party. It begins by asserting a continuity of leadership under which those profound changes took place:

> Since the founding of the People's Republic of China, the entire Party and society, working hard under the leadership of the Party's three generations of central collective leadership with Comrades Mao Zedong, Deng Xiaoping and Jiang Zemin at the core, and the Party's Central Committee with Comrade Hu Jintao as General Secretary, have blazed a road to develop socialist education with Chinese characteristics, established the world's largest education system, and guaranteed the right to education for billions of Chinese.[47]

Despite the obvious propagandist flair, Deng Xiaoping deserves credit for instituting lasting educational reform in China. Mao's inclusion above simply serves the ideological needs of the socialist state (since he was responsible for bringing higher education to a halt during the Cultural Revolution).

The text of the Development Plan continues in much the same vein as its introduction, and it lists a set of accomplishments that correspond to genuine progress made in the country. As such, it neatly summarizes recent developments in Chinese higher education:

> Since the beginning of the 21st century, free compulsory education has become the norm in urban and rural areas, while vocational education has made headway fast. In the meantime, higher education reached a new stage of popularization, as rural education grew in strength. Remarkable progress has also been made in achieving education equity. Education development has vastly enhanced the quality of the entire nation, and stimulated innovation in science, technology and cultural prosperity, thereby making irreplaceable and significant contributions to China's economic growth, social progress, and the betterment of people's livelihood.[48]

Although it may pain some pundits to admit it, these claims are largely accurate (although they are framed in the best possible light and lack nuance).

Nonetheless, as the best indicator we have of the general direction that higher education in China will take between 2015 and 2020, from a policy point of view, the central goals of the Development Plan warrant brief summation. First and foremost is a commitment to raise the quality of higher education generally, so as "to produce high-caliber professionals and top-notch innovators." The need for better research at leading universities is cited as essential to innovation in knowledge, technology, and national defense industries. To that end, support will shift from well-established coastal universities to those in the central and western regions of China. The Development Plan emphasizes the need to accelerate the "building of first-class universities and faculties" between 2010 and 2020, and it recommits to Project 985 as the basis for "innovation in advantageous disciplines."[49]

The Development Plan also includes a tacit recognition that traditional Chinese pedagogies, such as direct instruction and rote memorization, create mental rigidity. Moving forward, China hopes to make teaching more "heuristic, exploratory, discussion-based, and participatory," and it intends to find ways to assess the effects of those pedagogical shifts. Efforts will also be made to "terminate the practice that a single round of examinations decides the destiny of a student" and to enhance and diversify enrollment mechanisms. It is a curious fact of global convergence that just as China is attempting to develop new methods of teaching and learning and deregulate its universities, American institutions of higher learning are introducing policies that centralize administration, standardize learning outcomes, and ensure that part-time professors do most of the teaching on campus.

While clearly Chinese leaders intend to create "a modern college system with Chinese characteristics," it remains uncertain what that really means, especially as international norms and Western models of higher education steal into China, along with the influence of neo-liberal market-based thinking. In a real sense, the dramatic gains in the size and quality of Chinese higher education since 1978 mask serious challenges that lie ahead. For example, China continues to invest heavily in higher education, but the CCP still largely sees it as a means of ideological indoctrination, worker specialization, and a force for the growth of a postindustrial economy.

Simon Marginson argues that a unique "Confucian model" of higher education is emerging in East Asia generally and China most specifically. It is characterized by close national supervision, blistering growth in tertiary participation beyond 50 percent and toward universal levels, "one chance" national examination systems that mediate social competition for educational access, and high investment in science research and the formation of leading science universities.[50] All this is true, but notice that Confucian humanism, with its emphasis on moral self-cultivation and social obligation, is absent from what Marginson calls the "Confucian model." Marginson also overlooks the role of socialist ideology in his paradigm, particularly in regard to how it makes the case of China (the birthplace of Confucianism) different from more democratic East Asian countries such as Korea, Japan, and Taiwan.

Nevertheless, the preeminence of science and technology in Chinese higher education has meant the eclipse of the humanities (an indigenous tradition) at a time when the country desperately needs creative and innovative thinkers. In addition to this loss of humanistic learning, which defined so much of the history of higher education in imperial China, the country faces a predicament concerning the quality of its graduate education programs. Chinese master's degree programs are often ill-defined as to whether they train researchers or professionals, and the promulgation of part-time doctoral programs to serve government officials and businessmen has essentially turned Chinese doctoral studies into quasi Executive Master of Business Administration programs.[51] Over the years, in various teaching capacities at universities in China and South Korea, I have witnessed this phenomenon firsthand. It is a significant problem at a time when Chinese faculty members are expected to earn doctoral degrees, and it helps to explain why terminal degrees from American, European, and Australian universities generally carry more prestige in China (and other parts of East Asia).

As part of efforts to improve the international standing of its colleges and universities, China must curtail government intervention in the higher education sector, find ways to bring the best students back home after their studies abroad, and continue the expansion of the sector at a slower pace that puts emphasis on quality over quantity. Moreover, there exists an important question about the viability of the Chinese Communist Party and the single-party system in China more generally. Since 1978, tens of millions of Chinese people have been lifted out of poverty, and a country on the brink of collapse after the Cultural Revolution is suddenly a world player once again. But, at what point will an increasingly educated Chinese populace balk at CCP censorship and control of the media? When will Chinese university students once again demand democratic reforms in their country, as well as the right to elect their leaders? Student protests in Hong Kong during the fall of 2014 serve as a compelling reminder of the formidable appeal of democracy in East Asia.

The continued ability of the Chinese Communist Party to direct education reform in an authoritarian manner has kept the country on course in terms of internationalizing its system of higher education and creating several world-class universities (using one five-year plan after another). In this regard, China currently enjoys an advantage over Western democracies in effecting change from such a position of uncontested authority. However, any prolonged period of political instability in the country (like the Tiananmen Square protests in 1989 or the more recent ones in Hong Kong) might quickly erase these gains, as our survey of the historical development of Chinese higher education in chapter one affirms.

Nonetheless, for all of these shortcomings and more, the near term looks much better for Chinese higher education than it does for tertiary education in the United States. That the Development Plan was a collective effort, with "23,000 people involved in consultations, and 2.1 million pieces of feedback and suggestions" collected from "consultations and from other mechanisms or channels"[52] bodes well for a gradual process of democratization in the country. It may be hard for some to admit, but as we review the accomplishments of China's higher education reform efforts from 1978 to the present day and contemplate its ongoing challenges, there is little question that the massification of higher education in China has been highly effective.

China's complex policy-making processes have resulted in a uniquely bold approach that simultaneously seeks to expand higher education enrollment, institute a new governance structure, and nurture world-class universities.[53] However, since internationalization and reform of higher education in China have been "borrowed from Western models and the American higher education system in particular," tensions still exist between deep-rooted Chinese traditions resistant to foreign higher educational practices (such as tenure and freedom of speech) on the one hand and the growing embrace of Western-style pedagogies on the other.

In this chapter, we have seen that universities in China are now competing directly with those in the United States and other parts of the world to attract the best faculty and recruit the most foreign students. The Chinese leadership has been proactive in developing a series of overseas talent recruitment schemes to bolster the quality of its teaching faculty. Since its inception, the Hundred Talents Program has brought more than one thousand scholars to the country, and it seeks to bring up to three thousand more to work for periods in excess of six months. The 211 Project complements this endeavor to create "world-class" universities by recruiting top scholars (including Nobel laureates) into the nation's top institutions.[54] As Rui Yang aptly notes, one of the most striking features of the Chinese situation is the "strong commitment by both institutions and governments to the quest for world-class universities, something rarely found in most Western societies."[55]

At the present moment, forty-five hundred colleges and universities in the United States serve more than twenty-eight million students. It is an enormously influential system internationally, and we saw that it emerged out of an ideal of higher education for everyone, for the greater benefit of society. Regrettably, America's colleges and universities are in a state of neglect and disrepair—like much of the country's infrastructure. The symptoms and causes of that decline are the subject of the next chapter, which should be read against the backdrop of the Chinese advancements in higher education charted above.

CHAPTER FOUR

. . . .

Crisis in the American Academy

IN THE LATTER PART of chapter two, we followed American higher learning from its genesis in colonial colleges serving the elite class during the seventeenth and eighteenth centuries, through its phases of religious denominationalism that eventually yielded to the public school movement, so that by the mid-twentieth century the country's preeminent institutions of higher learning attracted the best students and faculty from around the world — as Germany and Britain had done before it. The federally funded G. I. Bill combined with generous state government support to create a sustained period of expansion and innovation between 1949 and 1980. During these years, the United States invested in primary, secondary, and tertiary education for the benefit of the commonweal and the advancement of its economic goals.

In this chapter, we examine the damaging educational policies that commenced in the late 1970s, accelerated during the Reagan era from 1981 to 1989, and continue unabated until the present day. The fact is that the United States no longer enjoys the privileged status of unrivaled leader in global higher education. Such a claim might sound overstated to some readers, particularly those sympathetic to a neoliberal point of view. These individuals might reference "measures of quality" such as research spending, patents, invention, and global rankings and would see little imminent threat of crisis in the academy. After all, the United States remains the destination of choice for international students and scholars — and it still boasts of more world-class universities than any other country. Indeed. But for how much longer?

This is a difficult question to answer with certainty, for the erosion of the preeminence of American higher learning is the result of transformations in the public's attitude about the role of education in society more generally. Many of the problems that American higher education institutions (and primary and secondary educational entities as well) face today are byproducts of these shifting public values, and therefore they can theoretically be undone. So, while the following critique foresees higher education in the United States as imperiled, the American public may choose to shift away from the neoliberal values that have turned its colleges and universities into businesses with bottom lines and its students into paying customers (who purchase commodities branded by market research firms).

As the Chinese and American higher education systems converge around a global model of the world-class university, China progresses but the United States regresses. We need only to consider the restoration of Chinese higher education as an example of what can be done with determination and vision. From 1980 to 2015, higher education in China made giant leaps through coordinated and sustained investment, while the United States chronically underfunded its own system. This chapter puts that well-documented decline in a global context by recognizing that other higher education systems, including those in Scandinavian and Western European countries, are already testing American hegemony in this sector of the world economy.

The American public commonly believes that while its primary and secondary schooling is notoriously poor, higher education has always been of a superior quality. Lamentably, while stellar institutions of higher education still exist in the country, the assurance of quality across the board no longer holds. We saw earlier that symptoms of that decline are not limited to administrative bloat, or to steadily rising tuitions, or to the loss of faculty governance, or to models of business management. They also include the exploitation of adjunct and contingent faculty, corporatization and the commodification of the products of the university, generational budget cuts at the state and federal levels, the proliferation of meaningless assessment regimes, and a rhetoric of continual "strategic planning" that is better suited to Soviet-era authoritarianism than to a palace of the mind. Moreover, the ills that plague less prestigious colleges and universities in the United States are insinuating themselves into the country's top-ranked institutions, which were once immune to the endless mimicry of "best practices" that make universities look increasingly alike.

David Mihalyfy argues that the University of Chicago "serves as a window into the fully corporatized future of education, where an unquestioned goal is profit for top staff" and the checks and balances of the trustee system no longer function. He locates the cause of that dysfunction in the disappearance of the ideal of administrative public service throughout the academy. In order to hide this deficiency, the university news office increasingly resembles a propaganda machine for the administration. Moreover, the extremely high executive salaries at the University of Chicago (President Robert Zimmer brought home more than $3 million in 2011), combined with ongoing campus infrastructure development projects, mean that the university has now taken on "debt equal to more than half of its endowment."[1] If the University of Chicago serves as a window into the future of American higher education, it offers a gloomy spectacle.

The growth of corporate models of governance in American colleges and universities is just one outcome of the expansion of its functions into services of all sorts, such as running hospitals and state-of-the-art research laboratories. Still, there is a strong case to be made that the transference of corporate business practices into the academy is poorly suited to the traditional nonprofit orientation of higher education. More than thirty years ago, Bruce Wilshire drew attention to the fact that the American university had adopted the structure of a managed organization in order to integrate all its functions with its bureaucracies. As a consequence of the ballooning number of bureaucrats needed to manage more complex university operations, academics (who often get far too caught up in their specialized disciplines) no longer comprehend the workings of the whole institution.[2] The fracturing that results among disparate fields of inquiry (often referred to as "silo-fication") mirrors that of the rupture between faculty members and the administration. Where once that relationship was civil and respectful, it is now increasingly marred by animosity and antagonism.

During the apex of American higher education between 1945 and 1980, the two main functions of the university were knowledge creation (through research) and knowledge dissemination (through teaching). Because their mission is hybridized between the public good and the individual interests of its students, American institutions of higher learning differed significantly from for-profit corporations: shared governance was more cumbersome, universities and colleges had stronger incentives to be selective in choosing their students, and they were not beholden to small groups of stakeholders who expected a monetary return on their investment.[3] In spite of these crucial distinctions, American institutions of higher learning continue to adopt corporate models of governance that are turning campus administrators into highly paid executives — and professors into dispensable knowledge workers.

Jennifer Washburn observes that this new commercial ethos is "changing the priorities of universities in ways that raise disturbing questions about what parents and students are getting in return for the increasingly steep tuitions that they pay."[4] No place in the American academy exemplifies the deleterious effects of business logic (applied to an enterprise whose mission lies firmly outside the motivations of profit) more glaringly than the utilization of part-time adjunct and contingent faculty members, who now make up the majority of the professoriate on campuses across the nation.

The phrase "contingent faculty" may require some unpacking. As the word suggests, college and university administrators consider these professors nonessential. They hold temporary positions that are "liable to chance and change"[5] and are often denied the same protections of free speech as their tenured and tenure-track colleagues. Contingent faculty members who are fulltime employees, usually called instructors or lecturers, generally work on one-to-three-year renewable contracts that provide basic medical coverage and a modest living wage. When contingent faculty members are employed on a part-time basis, they are referred to as "adjunct professors."

In the caste-based hierarchies of today's American academy, adjunct faculty members are the untouchables. They are paid by the class, work on semester-by-semester contracts, and serve at the whim of department chairs or deans. Because many are forced, gypsy-like, to travel from campus to campus, the work of adjunct faculty members can be essentially invisible to their peers. Yet, they perform essential instructional duties that sustain the institution, including teaching large introductory and developmental courses that full-time faculty members sometimes avoid. Graduate teaching fellows, who instruct their courses independently, as well as teaching assistants who work with tenured faculty or alone, also fall into the contingent category.

All told, across the nation in 2014, more than 73 percent of faculty members on American campuses worked on a contingent basis. This eye-popping figure represents an inversion of the situation during the 1960s, when tenurable professors made up three-quarters of the faculty. That is to say, fifty years ago, American college and university students had a three-out-of-four chance of learning from a fulltime professor who was invested in the institution, possessed the appropriate credentials, enjoyed the protections of free speech and inquiry that came with tenure (after a probationary period of several years in duration), and was guaranteed due process before his or her employment could be terminated.

By contrast, in our current post–Great Recession era, "low wage migrant professors teach repetitive courses they did not design to students who travel through on a kind of conveyor belt, only to be spit out, indebted and desperate into a jobless economy." No doubt, the entire professoriate is negatively impacted by the casualization of intellectual labor that contingency represents, due to its profoundly deprofessionalizing effect. In 2013, adjunct faculty members made less than $3,000 per sixteen-week course (before taxes) on average across the nation—frequently without benefits.[6] In addition to having to cobble together enough courses to sustain themselves and their families, adjunct faculty members frequently lack the office space needed to meet students, rarely qualify for faculty development funds, and teach all year round (making research, publication, and conference attendance nearly impossible).

Contingent faculty exploitation on such a massive scale (as it now exists) only serves the "on-demand" needs of bottom-line-minded administrators, who are too often more interested in finding new "revenue streams" than providing full-time professors for their students. According to one critic, the "only people immediately benefitting inside this system are the administrative class—whores to the corporatized colonizers, earning money in this system in order to oversee this travesty."[7] While this individual certainly expresses an acerbic point of view, it is one increasingly held by faculty members across the country who find themselves marginalized (and in the case of adjuncts, impoverished) by the institutions that once charged them with providing institutional governance.

As we compare the state of American higher education during its zenith between 1945 and 1980 to the palace of ashes that it is today, the disappearance of the tenured teaching faculty must count as a primary cause for that clear and ongoing deterioration. Before the 1980s, college management was largely faculty driven, and it was the tenured professors who took temporary positions as chairs, deans, and even provosts—but they returned to their teaching duties after serving. Many of them also taught at least one course per semester in addition to their managerial responsibilities. In this way, the administrative prerogatives of the institution never strayed too far from the classroom and the best interests of the students.

Moreover, not only were administrative positions in the American academy once filled by faculty members who "returned to the ranks" after serving, the financial incentives of taking such posts did not exist in the same exaggerated manner as they do today. As a result, a mode of governance emerged that privileged the faculty in all curricular matters, and administrative overreach was prevented—or at least made preventable. When the majority of faculty members were tenure eligible, the professoriate could more effectively assert that teaching and research should be the primary functions of institutions of higher learning.

By contrast, it is now rare for deans, associate provosts, and presidents to teach. Some of them might have once taught, but most quickly become divorced from the day-to-day realities of the classroom, the ongoing research agendas of the faculty, and the needs of their students. In addition, an increasing number of executives and administrators in the modern American academy are products of doctoral programs in management or business—or worse still, institutional assessment and advancement—and have never taught at all.

Yet, most parents and students who are always paying more for higher education remain oblivious to what they are getting—or not getting—for their tuition dollars. While many part-time professors are capable scholar-teachers and might be among the most popular instructors with their students, they lack the safeguards needed to effectively challenge administrative agendas, express heterodox notions, and speak freely in the classroom. Most worryingly, when less than one-third of all professors at American colleges and universities possess the tenure protections established by the American Association of University Professors (AAUP), as is the case today, the university's role as a guardian of American civil liberty and democracy is gravely imperiled.

In order to counter the exploitative practice of using contingent labor, students (and their parents) should choose institutions of higher learning that invest in students by investing in the faculty. A few years ago, two economics professors from Louisiana State University at Baton Rouge parsed federal data from more than one hundred and thirty public research institutions between the years 1987 and 2008, and they concluded that the most cost-effective ratio of tenurable faculty to administrators is three to one. Indeed, three fulltime professors to do the important business of teaching and research—and one to manage administrative affairs—sounds reasonable enough. Shockingly, the current numbers are inverted at more than two administrators for every faculty member.[8]

As a result, Robert E. Martin and R. Carter Hill concluded that administrative bloat (not faculty remuneration) accounts for the skyrocketing cost of American higher education and that the hiring of adjunct professors at low wages has simply been a tool to offset much higher administrative salaries. Citing the American Institutes for Research and other sources, Jon Marcus states the case in the starkest terms: from 1987 until 2012, American "universities and colleges collectively added 517,636 administrators and professional employees, or an average of 87 every working day."[9] Furthermore, while more than half of all faculty members in American colleges and universities work part-time making a few thousand dollars per course, the average pay for a CEO of a higher education institution is $274,300.

In stark contrast to the plight of contingent faculty members, life on American campuses looks pretty good for the ubiquitous administrator—for these heady salaries are not limited to presidents, chancellors, and CEOs. The College and University Professional Association for Human Resources salary survey for 2012–13 shows that the average dean of arts and humanities pulled in $145,356; a dean of business made out even better at $169,428. The chief budget officer swept up a sweet $108,269 per year, while the head information-technology administrator brought home $99,425. In spite of that kind of salary inflation for administrators and managers over the last thirty years, deans and provosts continue to hire assistant and associate deans (who in the arts and humanities make $100,492, and in business averaged $131,425). An associate provost must settle for a comparatively paltry annual salary of $123,146.

How can it be that the president or CEO of any institution of higher learning earns an average of seventeen times more than the lowest paid contingent faculty member on their campuses (who does the primary work of teaching)? At private institutions, one hundred and fifty presidents were paid more than half a million dollars, and thirty-six brought home in excess of $1 million in 2012 alone. Clearly, corporate remuneration practices are wrongly applied to the higher education sector—and we need only to consider the crisis in healthcare to gauge the effects of business logic on traditionally nonprofit enterprises like education. Simply put, we have lost the humanistic foundation upon which American higher education was built, one that oriented institutions of higher learning toward the public good and not the individual "consumer" who has the means to pay. It is unconscionable that boards of trustees across the United States have sanctioned these exorbitant salaries for administrators at the expense of faculty members and the students whom they teach. Understandably, many board members come from the business community and bring mercantile values with them to their appointments, but higher education is managed best when the quality of teaching is kept foremost in mind.

The exorbitant cost of this glut of highly paid executives and administrators is being passed on to students in the form of tuition, fees, and student loans. Based on data from the U.S. Department of Labor, college tuition and fees in the United States have surged 1,120 percent since records began in 1978 (outpacing both inflation and the cost of healthcare delivery).[10] Meanwhile, student loan debt has surpassed $1 trillion per year, so that the average American undergraduate leaves school with just under $30,000 of debt. Such debt levels hinder not only the economic prospects of students but also those of the nation, as default rates rise. Curiously, the U.S. federal government collected a jaw-dropping $66 billion between 2007 and 2012 as the originator and guarantor of student loans, despite those growing default rates.

In chapter three, we saw how systematic, targeted, and sustained investment in higher education by the Chinese government began in the late 1970s and continues to the present day. While the interests of the Chinese Communist Party in higher education are manifold and informed by a long-standing cultural tradition (handed down from Confucius) of emphasizing education as a positive force for social amelioration, behind this massive influx of funds lies a motivation to train workers for its fledgling knowledge economy. We would do well to remember that China is just one of many countries around the world investing in higher education as a means of social and economic development.

In contrast, spending per student on American higher education dropped more than 30 percent on average, when adjusted for inflation, between 2008 and 2012 alone. The state governments of Arizona and New Hampshire led the way with 50 percent cuts in spending per student. Not surprisingly, tuitions have increased 78 percent in Arizona and 36 percent in New Hampshire.[11] The *Chronicle of Higher Education* recently published data that tracks declines in both state funding and federal subsidies in the United States between 1987 and 2012 by institution and region. If we take the nation's intensive public research universities for the sake of example, state funding for the University of Illinois at Chicago dropped from 53 percent to 17 percent, University of California at Riverside and Davis both went from funding levels in excess of 60 percent to just over 30 percent—as happened at the University of Massachusetts at Amherst.[12] This tier of research institutions once drove the innovation that made the United States into a superpower following the Second World War.

The colleges and universities occupying lower rungs of the proverbial ladder, such as public master's granting institutions, have fared even worse under the axe of defunding. The University of Illinois at Springfield, for instance, saw its state support drop from 83 percent of its budget in 1987 to just 27 percent in 2012. Carolina Coastal University went from 54 percent state support to a meager 13 percent during the same period.[13] In fact, baccalaureate colleges across the United

States have been struck by similar rates of decline in public support.

During the 1950s and 1960s, American colleges not only had "a thriving professoriate," but their "students were given access to a variety of subject areas, and the possibility of broad learning" that included courses in literature, philosophy, sociology, history, and foreign languages and cultures.[14] Whereas professional specialization at the undergraduate level encourages the fragmentation of knowledge, the study of literature, history, philosophy, and the arts provides a vocabulary for formulating ultimate questions of unique import to young people seeking an understanding of the world and a path in life. As Andrew Delbanco asserts, "the humanities may have the most to offer to students who do not know that they need them—which is one reason it is scandalous to withhold them."[15]

In this respect, the United States seems determined to ignore the shortcomings of Chinese higher education, which is grappling with its own lack of creativity and innovation among students due to the displacement of humanistic learning by business, science, and engineering. Although marginalized and ornamentalized in today's American academy, humanistic studies (the liberal arts) help to supplement narrow scientific worldviews, provide a hedge against utilitarian values, and at their best fulfill the classical notion of higher education as a vehicle for self-knowledge (something that is not easily quantified).

The radical notion that higher education should be a common good open to everyone and should cultivate in students a sense of civic responsibility was an American innovation. It took shape in American colleges following the Revolutionary War and is perhaps best exemplified in Jefferson's vision for the University of Virginia. Nevertheless, in our time, an individualistic and utilitarian instinct seems to be driving higher education policy to our detriment. We risk abandoning the true spirit of higher education that the founder of the University of Pennsylvania, Benjamin Franklin, clarified: to make the inclination and ability to serve "Mankind, one's Country, Friends, and Family" the "great Aim and End of all learning."[16] The declines in funding for, and enrollments in, humanistic disciplines such as English, history, philosophy, and classical studies all witness to a loss of that spirit.

As we saw in chapter two, American colonial colleges were places where the elite sent their children, but the gentry class eventually turned them into finishing schools (rather than spaces for serious academic inquiry). This fact might lead one to mistakenly conclude that the current trend toward vocational and professional training as an individual commodity marks a return to the notion of higher education as a means to inclusion in a particular social class. In point of fact, American universities occupied an unchallenged position of global preeminence following the Second World War as a result of "high rates of educational attainment, vigorous governmental support of scientific research, and a massive influx of scholars from Europe seeking refuge."[17] In the twenty-first century, China is applying the same formula of investment and access that the United States used to overtake Europe as the global leader in higher education during the previous century.

In other words, there is little reason "to believe that American colleges are, on average, the best in the world" any longer. After decades of substandard primary and secondary education, college graduates in the United States are now performing below average on (admittedly problematic) measures of literacy and critical thinking like the Program for the International Assessment of Adult Competencies (PIAAC). Today, the wide disparities of knowledge and skills present among American schoolchildren are not ameliorated by higher education, but rather they are magnified. This new reality should alarm anyone who believes "America's long-term prosperity rests in substantial part on its store of human capital."[18]

To understand how American higher education fell into such a state of disrepair, we must return to the 1950s and 1960s, when research universities rose to the technological challenge that the success of the Russian Sputnik satellite represented. Access to higher education grew dramatically. In that expansion, the academic job market presented unprecedented opportunities to those who would enter its halls. The United States soon assumed a leading international position in the sciences, including medical research, and "a new synergy between the American research university and high-technology industries came into being."[19] However, some of the effects of that partnership were unforeseen and unwanted, as the divide between the humanities and sciences that emerged in the late nineteenth and early twentieth century only widened.

From the mid-1960s through the 1970s, the culture wars between free speech, civil rights, and anti-war activists on one side and more conservative social forces that represented an entrenched status quo on the other, grew in intensity. A public distrust of what were portrayed as radical impulses coming from campuses across the nation, particularly around the issue of the Vietnam War, became hardened. Thereafter, educational policy began to shift in favor of the noncontroversial subjects of science, technology, and engineering (among others). In response, the social sciences took a more empirical turn, learning to quantify more than qualify knowledge, thereby leaving the arts and humanities isolated. Unfortunately for the American academy, these conservative cultural warriors failed to appreciate the historical role that the humanities played as "critics of social values and of societal practices and policies."[20]

At one time, scholars in humanistic disciplines saw it as their job to "challenge the commodified, uncontroversial, and codified certainties thrown at the public by the prevailing political powers and the unguided and unthinking media."[21] The anti-establishment sentiment that permeated college campuses in the 1960s and 1970s arose out of broader calls for a more open and tolerant society—and outrage over what was widely viewed as an unjust war in South Asia. In the early 1980s, cries for fiscal austerity raised by conservative politicians finally found the ear of the public after years of "stagflation" and high unemployment.

In his scathing critique of Reagan-era higher education policies, University of California at Los Angeles professor Peter Lunenfeld calls attention to the change from a culture of "us" in the United States to a culture of "me, myself, and I." In the excerpt below, he summarizes the tools Reaganites used to make sure the protests that rocked campuses across the nation would never take place again:

> During Reagan's two terms as president, dedicated funding for outright grants-in-aid decreased, federal guidelines pushed individual loans, and private bill collectors were brought in to ensure that the hardest kind of debt to escape was whatever you took on for your education. Even more important was the shift in tone and expectation. Public goods became private services, and by the end of the 1980s, the anti-tax, infra-structure-starving, neoliberal

Weltanschauung meant that as states cut their budgets, support for higher education was thrown into a cage match with every other necessary public good.[22]

This excerpt is, sadly, a highly accurate summary of the profound and lasting impact that conservative policies have had on the American college and university. Perhaps it will come as no surprise that as governor of California years earlier, Ronald Reagan initiated the privatization of that state's sprawling higher education delivery system — once the envy of the nation.

When he later ran for the presidency of the United States, the former actor did so on a platform of supply-side economics (the lowering of tax rates to encourage savings and growth). After he won office, the mounting costs of pensions, welfare, and healthcare delivery became effective justifications for conservatives across the nation to employ the same rhetoric of austerity to help them gain control of government and to leverage economic policy in order to defund higher education.

As the Reagan tax cuts, which benefitted the wealthy most, were emptying federal coffers, military spending during his presidency far exceeded the reductions he oversaw to education and other public services. All told, President Reagan increased the federal budget deficit by roughly $150 million per year during the first six years of the 1980s. A small portion of that deficit spending managed to "trickle down" to select institutions of higher learning. The Department of Defense, for instance, became the fastest growing source of support for American research universities. With so much military money up for grabs, new research parks and other business incubators on campus promoted the "formation of new firms with venture capital and equity stakes."[23] Inside the American academy, such initiatives were often coupled with a desire to ramp up state governance of education and centralize the administrations within them.

The Bayh-Dole Act of 1980 cemented the relationship between corporate America and the nations' colleges and universities. Intellectual patents for research supported by the federal government were transferred to universities — who in turn licensed them to industry. The idea was to find new ways to transfer relevant innovations of the academy to the marketplace as quickly, and as profitably, as possible.

Thus, intellectual property became an important revenue stream for the first time, particularly at research universities. The corporatization of American higher education was under way in earnest.

The biggest beneficiaries of this new arrangement with corporate America were elite institutions (e.g., the Massachusetts Institute of Technology) that were able to capitalize on patents that were actually profitable (many are not). As patents became potential sources of university revenue, academic programs in computer science and biological engineering received greater financial support, while humanities departments, already seen as unprofitable, were filled with critical voices that administrators would rather not encounter. The Bayh-Dole Act also opened opportunities for trading education, consulting services, and scientific innovation for cash in the marketplace, an arrangement that became increasingly attractive to university administrators facing budget cuts. Bok reports that by 2000, just twenty years later, the volume of university patents had increased ten times, and institutions of higher education earned more than $1 billion a year in royalties and fees.[24] However, something of incalculable value was lost in that commercialization of higher education: the emphasis on broad liberal learning that we owe to our classical heritage.

From the vantage point of 2015, we can see that the humanist response to the culture wars of the 1980s and 1990s and to the neoliberalism creeping into the university was diffuse, unorganized, and inadequate. Humanities scholars never successfully made the case that "wrestling with questions of competing values, morality, and ethics, and thinking critically about these subjects" was essential to good citizenry — or that knowledge and understanding of "other cultures, languages, and literatures were essential for the nation's welfare and security."[25] During the Reagan administration, support for the arts and humanities, never robust to begin with, slowed to a trickle. As American universities became more utilitarian in focus, the liberal arts were further marginalized.

Between 1968 and 1986, student enrollments in the humanities, social sciences, mathematics, physical sciences, and psychology dropped from 47 percent to just 26 percent, establishing another trend that continues to the present day: an increased demand for technical training and professional education. With the introduction of a new business-minded culture starting in the 1980s, student interests changed in such a way that "developing a meaningful philosophy of life" in college was replaced in mass by a principle concern with being "financially well off."[26] Not surprisingly, hundreds of tuition-dependent small liberal arts colleges would close their doors during the 1980s, unable to withstand the neoliberal forces that were moving the focus of higher education away from the policies that made American institutions global leaders just a generation or two before.

Following economic recession during the early to mid-1980s, higher education enrollments increased across the United States, but those gains followed additional state cuts to college and university budgets. For the nation's twelve million enrollees, higher education tuitions increased by 106 percent between 1981 and 1987. Such pricing practices resulted in another "innovation" of the 1980s: marketing and strategic planning.[27] In an unprecedented manner, one after the other, college and university leaders adopted practices from the private sector to create brands with which its customers could identify.

Next, "twenty-seven states undertook major reviews and evaluations of their higher education systems" between 1985 and 1990, and some of them resulted in the establishment of statewide multicampus governing boards (for example, in Massachusetts and Maryland). Changes such as these did not augur well for faculty governance, since they evidenced a greater centralization at the state level and the growing influence of state governors (who sought to appoint officials to governing boards).[28] In terms of enrollment patterns, attendance at two-year colleges increased only slightly during the 1980s. The number of women attending American colleges and universities grew steadily, whereas male attendance rates dropped sharply at the end of the Vietnam War. Black women enrolled in greater numbers than their male counterparts, while Hispanics trailed behind both groups.[29]

Meanwhile, struggling to keep down rising tuitions, the nation's research universities worked diligently to bolster income from private sources. Small private colleges, ever reliant on donations, had to streamline to survive and could no longer afford to ignore fundraising to cover operating expenses and to grow endowments. Pell Grants increased only modestly, and student loan programs grew to pick up the slack. Over time, the rising costs of higher education were pushed from state and federal governments onto students, who were forced to borrow to pay their tuitions. In China, we recall that the implementation of tuition and fees became an important way for the government to encourage its citizens to spend their savings (but not to go into debt for higher education).

As a result of these trends, many American colleges and universities today are really quasi-corporations where collegial forms of shared governance are seen as obstacles to effective management. Faculty members report that decision making has become "more bureaucratic, top-down, centralized, automatic, and managerial."[30] On the campus where I teach, to take an example, a new dean of the School of Social Science overturned the results of a faculty search last year—despite student and faculty protests. Shortly thereafter, our provost and vice-president for academic affairs made two associate provost appointments without the pretense of national (or even internal) searches. While unilateral actions such as these violate the principle of shared governance, they also speak directly to the corporate-style reward system now in place for those who exhibit unblinking complicity with the managerial prerogatives that erode campus democracy.

Ultimately, however, the responsibility for the increasing corporatization of campuses across the nation must be laid at the feet of university presidents who, intent "upon accumulating money to expand the size and reputation of the institution," have forced the methods of the marketplace on "a reluctant (or indifferent) faculty."[31] This process of commercialization can be seen in other aspects of American culture as well, including the formation of charter schools, the charging of admission to public museums, private contracting for the operation of utilities, and "outsourcing" to external providers.

When George H. W. Bush (b. 1924) became president of the United States in 1989, he inherited massive budget deficits that resulted from Reagan's penchant for military spending and tax cutting for the wealthy. When President Bush had to break his election-season promise that there would be "no new taxes," he made way for an insurgent southern Democrat from Arkansas named Bill Clinton (b. 1946). While in office, Clinton governed as a fiscally conservative centrist, and he managed to turn the deficits that dogged George Bush into record surpluses by the time he left office in 2001.

Nevertheless, American higher education suffered further set-backs during the 1990s. The ongoing culture wars meant the con-tinuance of a conservative strategy of eroding the social and cultural foundations for "a growing middle class that was racially diverse and politically powerful, while keeping their technical capacities intact." By 2000, it was clear that the conservatives had succeeded, as four-fifths of the overall American workforce had experienced no real wage growth since the late 1970s—while the top 10 percent of earn-ers enjoyed income growth equal to, or above, the average rate of eco-nomic growth.[32]

We see in these transformations that the very fabric of American society is despoiled by the loss of the ideal of the university as Jeffer-son, Franklin, Dewey, and others envisioned it. In its place, a seem-ingly unstoppable profit-minded approach to college and university governance has taken firm hold. It is a cruel blow to the ideal of the university as a place for the free exchange of ideas when it traffics in vocational and professional training in support of the corporate interests that increasingly fund its operations. By the year 2000, the pattern of private subsidies for higher education (in place of public funding), combined with a continued embrace of corporatization, resulted in visible signs of decay that persisted over the next fifteen years. Inside the academy, canonical wars raged over the inclusion of texts by minorities and underrepresented groups (such as homo-sexuals), and they increasingly became fodder for those on the right who complained of liberal indoctrination and a pervasive leftism in the academy—neither of which was true.

Yet, this lingering suspicion by those on the right that the Ameri-can university was a bastion of liberalism created the ideological jus-tification for unrelenting cuts to public higher education, which made the way ready for corporate players (with agendas and strings attached to their educational investments). As an example, industry funding for academic research grew from a mere quarter of a million dollars in 1980 to $2 billion in 2001. Duke University now draws 31 percent of its research and development budget from industry, while Georgia Institute of Technology takes 21 percent, and MIT 20 percent in to-tal.[33] These startling figures should raise red flags about the integrity, intent, and direction of higher education in the United States.

The senseless assessment regimes that now pervade the academy also date from the late 1990s and early 2000s, and they represent another business practice imported thoughtlessly into higher education. Politicians, accrediting bodies, university presidents, and even some shortsighted professors now scream for more "accountability" and for "student learning outcomes" (SLOs) to be added to every syllabus. In fact, professors have been evaluating student progress using grading systems (that vary from institution to institution and from instructor to instructor) for hundreds of years without issue. Therefore, we should see assessment as merely another way to exert more control over faculty, who traditionally enjoyed a good deal of autonomy in carrying out their duties—including the evaluation of their own students' progress.

Those who advocate for the assessment of higher education outcomes often fail to ask the most basic of questions, such as What does it mean to learn something? How do we know when learning has taken place? In what ways does learning happen? Can learning be quantified so that large groups of students can be compared to each other? Does learning always take place immediately (in the classroom) or can it happen over time? When we look at the questions objectively, we see that the art of teaching, and the act of learning, are incredibly complex phenomena that defy easy quantification.

Faculty members should not be fooled by administrative assertions that accreditation requires ongoing assessment. Rather they should understand that for generations, college and university administrators have "been aware of the potential value of externally mandated performance criteria as instruments through which to wrest control of the curriculum from faculty." At many institutions this is already a fait accompli, as faculty senates become advisory bodies to the administration but have no real power. Like strategic planning and the deprofessionalization of intellectual labor, value-added assessments have no place in a nonprofit sector such as higher education—whose main task is to critique society and not capitulate to its imperatives.

Since assessment is another attempt to gain control of testing and "relocate that authority" from the faculty,[34] it should be particularly offensive to the professorate, whose tenured ranks have been devastated.

Unfortunately, too many members of the faculty remain mute regarding the dramatic changes taking place in the academy because they are focused on their own teaching and research — and because progressively heavier workloads stifle dissent. Accountability measures like those currently in vogue did not exist prior to the 1990s, and any suggestion that they must be required today to ensure quality is absurd. If quality were really the goal, then most American faculty members would hold tenurable positions, which they do not. Collegiate assessment, on the scale that it is being practiced, is just another way to reduce college professors to the same subordinate status to which elementary and secondary school teachers have already been relegated.[35]

Moreover, the costs of assessment regimes are rarely audited — and hardly ever is the rational circularity of the process subject to scrutiny (for logical flaws, intentional deceptions, or a reliance on statistically unsound numerical "data"). In the State University of New York (SUNY) system, for example, students currently taking a course with a Western Civilization attribute are expected to "relate the development of Western civilization to that of other regions of the world" by the end of the semester. Those who finish a course with an American History attribute should gain an "understanding of America's evolving relationship with the rest of the world." Simple common sense tells us that these "student learning outcomes" are too overgeneralized to be measured with any statistical validity.

Such overzealous efforts to find another application of the scientific method ignore the fact that data acquisition processes in assessment frequently violate fundamental statistical sampling requirements. In fact, when they attempt to measure complex phenomena (such as whether students across sixty-four SUNY campuses understand "America's evolving relationship with the rest of the world"), statisticians recognize a limitation known as reasonable aggregation. Before statistical analysis can begin, one must conjecture which, out of an essentially infinite combination of quantities, are drivers of a suspected cause-and-effect relationship or correlation relationship — and how to measure such drivers. If one's reasoning is not valid at any stage in this process, then everything else that follows will be flawed as well; the more complex the relationships being measured, the less precise the results.

Ignoring the requirements of statistical sampling and the limits of statistical quantification, the current neoliberal penchant for making education reducible to easily digestible numbers for lazy bureaucrats is changing the way we think about teaching and learning. Standardized assessment, college rankings, "value-added" indicators, and "student learning outcomes" are just some of the buzzwords associated with this misplaced faith in quantification. These terms obfuscate, mislead, and color public perceptions about the quality of higher education delivery in the United States. Nevertheless, they are increasingly required on course syllabi, and accreditation bodies are demanding evaluation of them. Moreover, imposing administrative machineries have emerged in the last decade to collect and analyze data and then quantify the performance of academic units, including the faculty, vis-à-vis stated outcomes. This flow of corporate audit culture into the academy is having a deleterious effect on teaching and research.

In *The Last Professors* (2008), Frank Donoghue argues that the modern American university, by virtue of its conservative inertia following the culture wars, has become a hostile place for pursuing the truth.[36] Increasing centralization, the loss of tenure and rise of the part-time professor, the influx of business audit practices (and the daft assessment regimes that go with them) mean that anyone taking a hard look at American higher education should expect it to continue to lose stature on the world stage.

American faculty members have unintentionally contributed to their own demise by being so slow to understand the threat that neoliberalism represents to the academy. What academics can, and should, do now is write in ways that engage the general public, so as to raise social awareness of these ominous trends before American higher education becomes a palace of ashes beyond restoration. We do well to remember that between 1975 and 2005 the total number of administrators on American campuses increased 85 percent and professionals 240 percent, according to federal government categories for executive, administrative, and managerial employees.[37]

Toby Miller, in *Blow Up the Humanities* (2012), argues that this expansion of administrative and management positions in American colleges and universities means more obedience, external review, and metrification of tasks, as well as less autonomy and time to research. The mantra of "change" that comes with a strategic planning and assessment culture really translates into the managerial mistrust of academics and speaks to "a new type of conformity to national and international governmentalization and commodification in which faculty devote vast amounts of time to filling out forms describing what they have done, are doing, and intend to do" for a new class of unaccountable evaluators.[38]

Furthermore, there is no end in sight to the phenomenon of adjunctification since contingent teachers are "much cheaper than tenure-track or tenured faculty," as well as being more fully subject to administrative supervision. Unhappily, there is every reason to believe "adjuncts will continue to replace fulltime faculty at most of America's colleges and universities," so that within a few decades "only a very small percentage of faculty members, mainly at elite schools, will hold tenured or tenure track appointments."[39] By the year 2000, contingent teaching professionals made up a massive 70 percent of the American faculty—fifteen years later that figure was closer to 74 percent, suggesting that the bottom has yet to be reached.

All told, in just over thirty years, the American faculty has been stripped of a role in shared governance, had their autonomy (once sacrosanct) circumscribed by assessment regimes, and been transformed into a part-time workforce by a group of managers and administrators. It defies comprehension that the American public, to say nothing of parents and students who have funded this expansion of administration with unprecedented tuition hikes, would tolerate the situation for this long. Yet it has, and it continues to, while countries around the world (such as China) are challenging American preeminence in higher learning.

College and university administrators have been aided in their efforts to marginalize the teaching faculty (and bolster their own ranks) by an academic job market overflowing with eager and qualified PhDs who compete for the precious few remaining tenure-track positions (which provide the livable wages and benefits that most contingent positions lack). Some people blame doctoral programs for continuing to produce graduates for whom there are no full-time academic positions (save for the select few whom fate has favored—sometimes inexplicably). Even so, because doctoral candidates provide another source of cheap intellectual labor (when they work as teaching assistants and graduate fellows), it matters little to program administrators that *40 percent of humanities PhDs find no work in their field after graduation.* Moreover, the majority of science doctoral candidates in the United States are foreign-born, and they face legal obstacles to finding employment after graduation.[40]

Before moving on to the central claims of this study concerning convergence in global higher education, we should review several developments between 2000 and 2015 contributing to the decline of higher learning in the United States. We recall that the AAUP defended intellectual freedom, made tenure the principle means to protect it, and set forth codes of shared governance. Commenting on the dire situation facing American higher education today, the AAUP asserts that the United States has "completely squandered" the historic advantage it once enjoyed as its college graduation rates and higher education attainment levels fell below "many high-income countries and behind some medium-income countries" between 1980 and 2010.[41]

If wreaking havoc on the tenure system and assaulting the principles of academic freedom were not enough, hundreds of American colleges and universities have put so-called civility codes in place. These codes restrict "forms of speech and conduct that might have been seen as offensive or hostile by particular groups or designed to intimidate or harass individuals based on their racial, religious, social, gender, or other characteristics."[42] Because most campus administrators are anxious to avoid vocal dissent from faculty and staff, these codes are sometimes justified on the grounds that they protect the institution from lawsuits or that they are considered a "best practice."

In fact, the U.S. Department of Education warns against adopting antiharassment codes, as they may infringe upon constitutionally guaranteed First Amendment rights and protections. Nevertheless, when enacted, administrators can use them to bully or silence their critics, especially at private institutions, which offer broader leeway.[43] On the other hand, civility codes have not held up well in court, and given the administrative dislike for public criticism, writing and speaking out may be the best hope for any restoration of the professoriate to its once central position in the university mission. Those with the protections of tenure are under a special obligation *to use them* for the benefit of their colleagues and their students alike.

In 2006, U.S. Secretary of Education Margaret Spellings formed the Commission on the Future of Higher Education, which released a document entitled, "A Test of Leadership: Charting the Future of U.S. Higher Education" (more widely known as the Spellings Report). In its preamble, we find a startling acknowledgement: "We may still have more than our share of the world's best universities. But a lot of other countries have followed our lead, and **they are now educating more of their citizens to more advanced levels than we are.** Worse, they are passing us by at a time when education is more important to our collective prosperity than ever."[44] The Spellings Report cites the rising cost of American higher education as increasingly prohibiting entry, an unfortunate need for remedial math and English due to poor high school preparation, and declining literacy rates among college graduates.[45]

Although the commission's evaluation of the state of American higher education was accurate, the changes that the Spellings Commission recommended were woefully misguided. For example, consider its first stated goal: "We want a world-class higher-education system that creates new knowledge, contributes to economic prosperity and global competitiveness, and empowers citizens."[46] The global race to create hubs of "world-class" higher education is well under way, and the next chapter examines them in more detail. However, the unfortunate transformations outlined in this chapter mean that many institutions in the United States are ill prepared for the new period of global competition that lies ahead—despite a lingering misperception concerning the superiority of American higher education among some members of the world community.

The language of business and commerce, which permeates the Spellings Report, is a direct reflection of its neo-liberal agenda. The Spellings Commission writes,

> What we have learned over the last year makes clear that American higher education has become what, in the business world, would be called a mature enterprise: increasingly risk-averse, at times self-satisfied, and unduly expensive. It is an enterprise that has yet

to address the fundamental issues of how academic programs and institutions must be transformed to serve the changing educational needs of a knowledge economy. It has yet to successfully confront the impact of globalization, evolving technologies, an increasingly diverse and aging population, and an evolving marketplace characterized by new needs and new paradigms.[47]

If one scrutinizes the membership of the Spellings Commission, one discovers a few academics and university administrators, along with a vice president for the Boeing Company, an executive vice president for the IBM Corporation, a vice president from Microsoft Corporation, the chairman of Kapla (an incorporated test preparation company), and a senior vice president of the U.S. Chamber of Commerce.

Their market-oriented approach, repeatedly touted as such in the Spellings Report, employs dubious educational practices to create a landscape that "includes new providers and new paradigms, from for-profit universities to distance learning." Their emphasis on for-profit higher education is particularly troubling for many reasons. The members of the Spellings Commission claimed to understand that as other nations rapidly improve their higher education systems, there exists increasing "evidence that the quality of student learning at U.S. colleges and universities is inadequate and, in some cases, declining."[48] Yet, its emphasis on growing the for-profit sector encourages the same socioeconomic disparities found with increasing frequency in American higher education.

As alluded to earlier, higher education in the United States now resembles a caste system whereby the college that a student attends affects his or her chances of graduating—and determines the level of debt that he or she finishes with. At the top of this caste system are elite colleges and universities, whose high tuition rates are discounted by half for most students. At the bottom are for-profit institutions that market themselves to "low-income students and veterans" and the like, who aspire to better their lot, yet might be especially vulnerable to deceptive marketing practices that lure underprepared students with promises of gainful employment and a prosperous future.[49] For example, in February 2014, the Consumer Financial Protection Bureau (CFPB) filed a lawsuit against ITT Educational Services for allegedly encouraging students to borrow beyond their capacity, usually by way of high-interest loans. In fact, an associate's degree at many for-profit institutions costs more than an equivalent degree from a state-funded community college or four-year institution.

Steven Salzberg at the Johns Hopkins University School of Medicine has studied for-profit colleges in the United States, and he concludes that "they offer low-quality, almost worthless degrees. They have virtually no academic standards. They will accept anyone who can pay, and they seem to care primarily about the bottom line."[50] Salzberg argues that degrees from for-profit colleges "are not highly regarded by employers, who are right to view them with suspicion." He compares diplomas from many of them to the Yugo, a famously inferior automobile made by the Yugoslav/Serbian Zastava Corporation.[51]

In keeping with its corporate zeitgeist, the Spellings Report recommended more accountability mechanisms and "value-added" assessments. The commission asserted that the generous state funding for higher education of bygone days would never return enough "to support enrollment demand without higher education addressing issues of efficiency, productivity, transparency, and accountability clearly and successfully." Such accountability regimes are the new rigor, but rather than resulting in improved quality, they mean better jobs for an army of well-paid educrats and technocrats who just add to the top-heavy mechanism afflicting the American university.

The Spellings Commission argued that the "federal government should provide incentives for states, higher education associations, university systems, and institutions to develop inter-operable outcomes-focused accountability systems designed to be accessible and useful for students, policymakers, and the public, as well as for internal management and institutional improvement."[52] In other words, there should be more standardized assessment for bureaucrats in the university and in the federal government to interpret, because professors cannot be trusted to teach their own students effectively without oversight or without using "core-curriculum" content that has been pre-approved. Such a position flies in the face of the long history of state funding for American higher education as well as the established tradition of intellectual freedom that once made American colleges and universities an inspiration to the global community.

In sum, while the Spellings Commission correctly identifies the potential of the American system of higher education to surrender its leadership role on the world stage, its recommendations are informed by neoliberal ideology, which the present study (like many before it) has attempted to refute as a poor fit for effective higher education delivery. The Spellings Report asks that accrediting bodies make "performance outcomes, including completion rates and student learning, the core of their assessment as a priority over inputs or processes," so that institutions can be ranked against each other more easily (read standardization). All in all, the Spellings Report is a dreadful document that did very little to address the causes for the American plummet into the abyss of outcome-driven instruction; rather, it advocated many of the policies that contribute to the structural deficiencies it identified.

The Higher Education Opportunity Act of 2008 (which reauthorized its 1965 predecessor) included amendments that required all American institutions participating in Title IV student aid programs to post institutional data to a net price calculator (called Integrated Postsecondary Education Data System, or IPEDS) for prospective students. Provisions were also made for increasing the maximum size of Pell Grants, putting caps on subsidized student loan rates, and increasing institutional transparency by way of the College Navigator website. When Barack Obama (b. 1961) became president of the United States in 2009 during the Great Recession, he appointed Arne Duncan (b. 1964) as Secretary of Education, a position that, lamentably, Duncan has held ever since. I am generally supportive of President Obama and even wrote a book about tropes in his campaign rhetoric,[53] but the selection of Duncan (perhaps more for his skills on the basketball court than his vision as a leader in education) is one that can only be understood in the context of the president as a conservative-centrist democrat (rather than a left-leaning liberal).

Instead of eliminating the much-maligned No Child Left Behind program that he inherited from the Republican Bush administration, Arne Duncan created a similar one known by the equally propagandistic moniker of "Race to the Top." It granted more federal funding to primary and secondary schools — so long as they adopted preferred educational policies that tied them to numerical scores on selection criteria. Race to the Top also insisted on performance-based standards for primary and secondary teachers and their principals. In other words, it meant more standardization through the adoption of common learning measures and assessments.

Once a professor of law at the University of Chicago, President Obama seems to have lost touch with those of us who have dedicated our lives to the college classroom. In September 2013, he made a call for "performance-based" higher education funding, which threatens to tighten the neoliberal stranglehold on American higher education. Under his plan, colleges will be rated on affordability, graduation rates, and graduate earnings. As soon as he announced performance-based funding for higher education, "Arne Duncan jumped in to lay the groundwork for the demonization of public university faculty, the same way that he tried to demonize public school teachers." We want to see "good actors be rewarded," asserted Duncan.[54] Rudy Fichtenbaum and Hank Reichman, from the AAUP, counter that the "solution to the crisis in higher education, characterized by rising tuition and student debt, is not a report card based on poorly defined metrics."[55] These policies encourage colleges and universities to compete among each other for what remains of public funding — and to do more with less. As a matter of fact, educational policies like these do precious little to address the growing gap in quality among American institutions of higher learning and those in other parts of the world.

Although President Obama's 2015 education budget increases individual Pell Grants by $1,000, at the same time it spends money to "publish a new college ratings system that will identify colleges that provide the best value to students and encourage all colleges to improve." The U.S. Department of Education cites the "potential for breakthroughs on cost and quality through State reforms — such as performance-based funding and strong alignment among the K–12, post-secondary, and workforce systems — and institutional innovations, such as accelerated degrees and competency-based education" as part of the future direction of tertiary education in the United States.[56] Taken together, No Child Left Behind and Race to the Top represent more than fifteen years of stunningly misguided educational policy in the United States. Everyone agrees that the United States is falling behind other key players in the world, yet we keep instituting the same senseless policies that ensure such trends continue.

In this chapter, we have traced the arc of decline in American higher education from 1980 to the present day. The twin energy crises of the 1970s, the culture wars of the next decade, deficit reduction efforts by the Clinton administration, and the assessment regimes of the second Bush and Obama administrations all took place in an environment of decreasing state and federal funding for higher education, the deprofessionalization of the faculty, the growth of highly paid administrators, and skyrocketing tuitions to sustain it all. Moreover, these declines were all happening against a larger backdrop of the loss of American hegemony in the world more generally and the rise of Asia more specifically. As Jonathan Cole asserts, "Asian nations, particularly Japan, Korea, and China, have come to realize the enormous social and economic returns that come from a highly trained workforce and from a set of universities that produce world-class research."[57]

Over the past forty years, Michael Lind observes, the American manufacturing sector has been "decimated by subsidized imports from China, Japan and other mercantilist countries" and by the decisions of many American multinationals to "shut down American factories in order to exploit cheap labor and take government subsidies in other lands. America's infrastructure is spottily decrepit, but Congress cannot even agree about how to fund the aging interstate highway system, much less invest in twenty-first-century transportation and communications systems. In addition, most of the jobs being created in the United States are in the low-wage, nonunion, no-benefit service sector where millions are trapped in the status of the working poor."[58] It is, in short, a lamentable state of affairs.

In the next chapter, we confront the phenomena of globalization, the loss of American influence in the world, and the rise of neoliberalism concurrently. The final chapter of this book reflects upon the cost of paradigm shift in American higher education at a time of increasing internationalization, global competition among international institutions of higher learning for students and faculty, and the convergence around a standardized model of the world-class university.

. . . .

CHAPTER FIVE

Global Convergence and Competition

IN 2011, MARTIN WOLF observed that during the nineteenth and early twentieth centuries, western Europe (and most of its success- ful colonies) gained an enormous financial advantage over the rest of the world, resulting in widely divergent and uneven global economic growth. By the mid-twentieth century and onward, convergence emerged and accelerated as developing peripheral and semiperiph- eral countries moved toward equal purchasing power parity with the United States. We can illustrate that trajectory clearly in the case of China's per capita income (purchasing power parity), which was just 5 percent of that of the United States in the 1950s. A mere sixty years later, that figure ballooned to 19 percent, and it continues to grow steadily. Of course, in the 1950s Japan industrialized rapidly as well (followed by South Korea during the next decade), moving from 10 percent per capita income to 64 percent of American levels in 2008.[1] However, during its ascension, the pace of China's economic growth exceeded that of either of its East Asian neighbors.

The economic convergence currently under way promises to sig- nificantly transform the balance of power in the world over the next few decades, particularly in terms of natural resource allocation. There are roughly 350 million people in the United States, compared to nearly one-and-a-half billion in China, all of whom will need to be fed, clothed, housed, and so on, at advanced income levels. Nobel laureate Michael Spence argues that by 2050, 75 percent of the world population will enjoy a living standard similar to those in today's high-income countries.[2] In point of fact, the middle class in these emerging nations (which make up more than 85 percent of the global population) has already started to "accept many of the values and aspirations of the Western middle classes."[3]

This prediction about the future is predicated on continually increasing access to information technology, which brings people together and eliminates knowledge gaps among countries at different levels of economic development. In 1950, 750 million people lived in the so-called developed world, which left 4 billion individuals behind. To gain a sense of how quickly some nations are advancing, we might consider that while countries like China, Japan, and South Korea were able to sustain growth rates well in excess of 7 percent as they grew, during the "first 200 years of the Industrial Revolution" growth would have only been between "2 and 2.5 percent."[4]

Singaporean diplomat and scholar Kishore Mahbubani sees a new world civilization taking shape as a result of global convergence, one in which the geographical, cultural, and linguistic barriers in place for millennia are gradually transcended. As evidence to support his prognostication, he cites the relatively few wars and combat deaths by historical standards, the disappearance of absolute poverty, an increasingly educated global population, an expanding middle class, the spread of free-market economies, social contracts that are more democratic, and the rise of multilateralism. These and other contributing factors to the phenomenon of global convergence all point to a process of international social amelioration that has almost utopian implications. "For millennia," Mahbubani asserts, "humanity as a whole has been divided by geography, history, religion, culture, verbal language, and body language," but now "we are converging on a certain set of norms on how to create better societies."[5] This "new global civilization" promises important advances that humanity has been anticipating for centuries, such as the elimination of dire poverty and the expansion of a global middle class.

Yet, for policy makers in America and other advanced countries, convergence means scrutinizing this emergent global economy to "figure out which sectors of it the US can now compete in."[6] Manufacturing jobs lost to China, for instance, will not be brought back without considerable effort, but the American information technology sector may be ripe for investment and further growth and innovation. Because it was assumed that "they would be the biggest beneficiaries of them," America and Europe once supported global institutions and global liberalization. However, current shifts in the global status quo mean what they fear most now is that all the benefits will go to China and India.[7] This is a legitimate concern, for as global economic development accelerates, Europe and the United States will have to share the chief offices of major international institutions like the International Monetary Fund, World Bank, and World Trade Organization.

In chapters three and four, we followed the astonishing developments of Chinese higher education following the Open Door reforms of the 1980s and the corresponding decline that has characterized American higher education since the Reagan era. Now, we look ahead to the great convergence of the two largest systems of higher learning in the world and consider what the future holds for the American university. In doing so, this study augments the work of Spence, Mahbubani, and others by extending their socioeconomic and political analyses to global higher education.

By facilitating the flow of information, knowledge, people, values, ideas, and goods and services across national borders, globalization has had a profound impact on higher education. What is generally termed "internationalization" in higher education studies has been accelerating for centuries. We recall the itinerant scholars in the Islamic world during the tenth and eleventh centuries, who almost always took their manuscripts, textbooks, teaching materials, pedagogies, and curricula with them wherever they went, thereby helping to widen the diffusion of higher learning. During the last two hundred years in the West, we witnessed similar transmissions, through the British, the French, and the German models of higher education, and then by way of the widespread export of the American model to other countries.[8] The convergence of higher education due to globalization will mean continued growth in the international exchange of students and faculty during the twenty-first century.

For example, in 1950 there were just 110,000 foreign students worldwide; by 2006 the number of students studying outside their own countries reached more than two-and-a-half million. The United States, Australia, United Kingdom, France, and Germany received more than half of those students, while the leading countries of origin continue to be China and India (together supplying 20 percent of all foreign students worldwide). Although this situation has stood for some years now, traditional countries of origin are transforming themselves into host countries (including Malaysia, Singapore, Thailand, South Africa, Qatar, and Dubai).[9] China, as we saw earlier, is already a major host country.

The Great Recession of 2008 sent shockwaves across the globe. In responding to it, Western governments, together with the financial sector, "imposed fiscal austerity from one side of Europe and North America to the other," thereby reducing resource allocations to primary, secondary, and tertiary education. Christopher Newfield and others (like myself) believe that these dramatic and sustained cuts inevitably have a "devolutionary impact on the economic and social capabilities of high-income countries."[10] Our case study of China and the United States supports such a supposition, for there were more than 17,000 institutions of higher learning in 184 countries, all competing in the global economy in 2010 alone.

For generations, the United States has enjoyed preeminence in the transnational market for higher education, but its influence is in decline (along with American hegemony more generally). Most jobs in today's knowledge economy require tertiary education, and the demand for international higher learning continues to grow as students everywhere become more mobile. Kemal Gürüz observes that this surging demand has coincided with the rise of market forces, which globally have resulted in institutional resource diversification, a greater number of private institutions worldwide, and the spread of lay governance (combined with strengthened administrations). As global institutions of higher learning become more business minded, a long-standing distinction between public and private is being replaced with a "new non-profit—for-profit divide" as the formation of a global higher education market shifts into high gear.[11]

Perhaps because of the number of world-class universities that it can still claim and the number of foreign students it attracts every year, the United States has remained largely complacent in the face of increasing global competition in higher education. In contrast, recognizing the enormous soft power of higher education delivery internationally, China has made economic advancement through higher learning a national priority. After becoming the world's second-largest economy and building the fastest supercomputer in 2010, the following year it opened the most expansive underground laboratory in the world in Sichuan province, which enables Chinese physicists to potentially play leading roles in the search for dark matter and the study of neutrinos.[12]

In their new study of higher education in the Middle Kingdom, Robert Rhoads and his colleagues note that pride in accomplishments such as those above have caused Chinese leaders to expect that their universities will "assume standing among the elite universities of the world — the Harvards, Oxfords, and Stanfords — and at the same time, they hold them accountable for assisting in China's economic and social transformation."[13] To that end, a diversity of funding sources are now in place to support academic science in China, including government research grant opportunities (at the national, provincial, and municipal levels) and the ability to petition foreign and international funding agencies. Moreover, there is now a greater emphasis in China on connecting research to the needs of industry, introducing institutional development strategies to expand philanthropic activity, and implementing faculty promotion and reward policies that put emphasis on funded research and grant writing.[14]

While the American university provides the basic template for the "world-class" institution currently in vogue, we noted that global convergence allows for minor variations based on cultural preferences. That is to say, China may aspire to American-style higher education, but its cultural traditions and single-party political system mean it inevitably takes on Chinese characteristics. Modern universities are foreign transplants to China, after all, and indigenous Chinese higher learning institutions share only superficial resemblances to medieval European universities. As it stands, "the central purpose of China's modern higher education is to combine Chinese and Western elements" in such a way as to ensure the fulfillment of its global ambitions.[15] While it strives to create more elite universities, some of which already spar with up-and-coming regional competitors like the Russian Federation and South Korea, China will continue to adapt the American model of the world-class university to suit its cultural traditions and political realities.

The extraordinary (by American standards) financial commitment that the Chinese leadership makes to higher education in order
to transition to a knowledge-based economy means that China will
keep a sharp focus on the country's colleges and universities; there
exists a sustained determination that institutions of higher learning
will receive ample support from the government in the near-to-mid
term. Although significant challenges remain, "building universities
capable of competing in a global marketplace seems like a reasonable
concern and a wise investment" for the Chinese government.[16]

Developed and developing nations alike now "look to the U.S.
research university as part of a broad effort to elevate their own universities' research capacities and move toward the development of
world-class universities capable of contributing to economic development, in what has been described alternatively as a new knowledge
economy, an information age, and a technology and computer-based
network society."[17] This situation is infusing internationalization into
the teaching, research, and service responsibilities of global higher
education institutions.

However, one measure of this internationalizing competition is
the propagation of dubious ranking schemes that attempt to measure
institutional excellence comparatively. In China, these "world university league tables are taken as symbolic indicators of the standard of
universities in the globalized education marketplace," and as a result,
they are viewed seriously by many governments and universities in
East Asia, and their influence is growing in the region.[18] In spite of
the media scrutiny that university ranking systems rightly receive for
their suspect rubrics of evaluation, poor data collection, facile comparisons among institutions, privileging of institutions with large
endowments, and overlooking of the unique features of each institution, these rankings remain powerful shapers of global public opinion — and they reinforce the ideal of the world-class university.

Prominent examples of global university ranking systems include
but are not limited to the following: the QS (Quacquarelli Symonds)
World University Rankings, the Academic Ranking of World Universities compiled by Shanghai Jiao Tong University, and the *Times
Higher Education* World University Rankings. These systems tend to
grade institutions based on their research, teaching and learning

environments, internationalization of campuses, industry income, and rate of citation for institutional publications. At the time of writing, in a large image splashed across its webpage, the QS ranking sensationally posits the question "Who Rules?" On their 2013 list, MIT, Harvard, and Cambridge dominate the top three spots, respectively (following selection criteria that bases 50 percent of a score on academic reputation and employer reputation as judged by an annual survey of over sixty thousand people). QS cites their "survey software, survey design, effectiveness of communication and database management" as proof of statistical validity.[19]

The Shanghai Jiao Tong academic ranking lists Harvard first, Cambridge second, and MIT third—meaning there is little difference between its evaluation and the analysis of QS in the top tier, despite differing evaluation criteria. Shaking things up a bit, the *Times Higher Education* table puts Caltech in the top slot, followed by Harvard and Oxford, by using what it calls "carefully calibrated performance indicators to provide the most comprehensive and balanced comparisons."[20] In this case, learning environment and volume of research constitute 60 percent of the final score. If we parse the results a bit further, the *Times Higher Education* locates seven of the top ten world universities in the United States (and the remaining three in the United Kingdom), Shanghai Jiao Tong gives eight of the top slots to American universities and two to the United Kingdom, and QS varies slightly in awarding only six positions in the top ten to the United States and four to Great Britain.

Conspicuously missing from the top ten on any of these rankings are Chinese universities—although CCP leadership would like to see that change in the coming decades. At the moment, Beijing University is the only Chinese institution that ranks in the top fifty according to QS, while the *Times Higher Education* list adds Tsinghua University. By contrast, and probably more realistically, the Shanghai Jiao Tong index does not rank even one Chinese university among its top one hundred.

More importantly, rankings systems like these negatively impact the structure and organization of teaching and research at institutions of higher learning around the world—due to the standard performance indicators that are used to determine final scores. The leading markers of global "super research universities" include a diversified financial base, team-based research focused on practical problems, innovative relationships with governments and corporations, world-wide recruitment, technological infrastructure, and partnerships with international organizations that validate international stature.[21] Ranking systems therefore are another force behind an international move toward standardization in keeping with the phenomenon of global convergence—and the accompanying entrepreneurial focus of the world-class university that goes with it.

In essence, the global trend toward convergence in institutional governance, organization, and entrepreneurialism means that the world is adopting a single "universal university model."[22] In chapter two, we charted the historical development of American higher education to its apogee between 1949 and 1980, and we complicated that analysis in chapter four by noting the trends leading to its decline. Indeed, it is a strange moment in history when the world looks to the United States to provide a template for a universal university model when its own system of higher learning is in a state of crisis.

As a result of its downward slide, the idealized image of the American university, imprinted on the universal model and exported to other countries, is one that most institutions of higher learning no longer live up to (because of the pernicious influence of neoliberalism in the academy). And yet, neoliberalism itself is a global—and not just American—phenomenon. It is embedded in the universal university model, as well. In this sense, the world-class paradigm taking hold in international education is a hybridized one, for it draws from the American university during its zenith and adds elements of a global business culture dominated by neoliberal ideology. That model in turn takes on unique cultural features in every region of the world (for example, a world-class university with "Chinese characteristics") and thereby allows for some variation, as noted earlier.

Going forward, however, global convergence on a single dominant model threatens to erase all but the most superficial of distinctions among global institutions. To be sure, there are some benefits to the standardization that is occurring. It is a glib analogy, but if one likes a certain dish at a chain restaurant, that person might be gladdened to have it look and taste exactly the same in some far-flung part of the world. Therefore, the flattening effect of globalization may be positive or negative, depending on one's perspective and socio-economic position. Convergence around a standard universal model of the university is positive, insofar as it encourages investment in education and social reform, moving countries like China in a positive direction. For the United States, however, convergence is having adverse effects on its higher education system.

In recent decades, global higher education has been reconceived as a tradable and purchasable good, a troubling trend that is shaping all aspects of higher education worldwide.[23] The international commodification of education means that student-teacher relationships are altered by the transactional nature of this paradigm (which has its roots in corporate practices and not in traditional American models of college and university organization and governance). Nevertheless, global convergence on a dominant model of the "universal university" means that international forces are remolding smaller American colleges and universities, as well.

If we take the globalization of the American automotive industry as an analogy for a moment, we understand that the poor quality of many American automobiles from the early 1970s through the mid-1980s allowed Japanese competitors to eventually overtake American production levels by manufacturing more reliable and efficient vehicles. In 2014, the Japanese company Toyota produced more vehicles than any other company in the world. Korean manufactures, such as Kia and Hyundai, have improved their designs and are becoming more desirable brands. Although China has yet to manufacture an automobile that can pass American emission and safety standards or make a university that truly competes toe-to-toe with one of the oft-cited top ten, one suspects it is only a matter of time before China arises to the challenge.

We find the same pattern in steel production, textile manufacturing, and furniture making (to name but a few sectors of the American economy fundamentally altered by the forces of globalization over just a few generations). From this point of view, China is simply following in the footsteps of its East Asian neighbors. However, it occupies a much larger geographical area, has a more sizable population, and enjoys a generous share of the region's natural resources (including rare-earth minerals). Should the United States not take sufficient heed of these examples and invest in — rather than defund — higher education, then hubs of higher learning in other parts of the world will converge on, and eventually surpass, American colleges and universities as the first choice for international students and faculty. In its entirety, that process may take several decades, perhaps more — but as the Chinese proverb has it, "the beast with a thousand legs is a long time dying, 百足之虫死而不僵."

The reader will recall that American colleges and universities were forced to diversify their revenue streams from the 1980s onward, as state and federal funding dwindled away and left research institutions hostage to corporate interests that desire trained workers and not intellectuals who challenge the status quo. As a result, the United States slowly ceded ground to its international competitors by embracing a corporate orientation that displaced traditional (postcolonial) American notions of learning as a public good and vehicle for shared economic prosperity. Rising tuitions, reliance on part-time faculty, and administrative bloat on American campuses give countries like China another advantage in the global marketplace. In this context, the further American higher education retreats from the traditional values of the academy, the more unpromising the future.

As we have seen, there is nothing mysterious about what constitutes a world-class university or about how ranking systems reinforce their desirability and shape their organizational structures. To make nation-states more competitive in the global marketplace, colleges and universities around the world have been under tremendous pressure from governments and the general public "to restructure/reinvent themselves in order to adapt to the ever-changing socio-economic and socio-political environments." Heavy weight is being attached to the buzzwords "efficiency and quality," which means institutions of higher learning are being subjected to unprecedented levels of external scrutiny.[24] The global trend toward restructuring that is market oriented, corporatized, and privatized means increasing international standardization will make institutions of higher learning more easily, and less meaningfully, comparable.

Important distinctions between cultural traditions of higher learning in the Western world are collapsing as well. The Bologna Process in Europe, for example, created the first European Higher

Education Area in 2010. This major reform effort included forty-six countries and, according to the European University Association, one of its main goals was the adoption of a three-cycle degree program for undergraduate bachelor degrees and graduate master's and PhD degrees (to match the system in the United States).

The Bologna restructuring made international academic credit transfers between European colleges and universities and institutions around the globe much easier, and it facilitated the transfer of credits within Europe as well. These changes were instituted to increase the competitiveness of European higher education in the global marketplace. Accompanying the Bologna reform effort is a standardized assessment regime disguised rhetorically as "quality assurance." The European Quality Assurance Register for Higher Education was born in 2008 to manage various agencies charged with carrying out that task.

European higher education institutions did not initiate the Bologna Process, Gürüz rightly notes, but rather the process "was a subtle imposition on them by politicians"[25] who used legislation to enforce a preferred educational policy. Their ideological emphasis on mobility, employability, competitiveness, and attractiveness is anathema to the European tradition of higher education.[26] Anne Corbett calls the decision to force "the great university systems of Europe" to adopt the features of the American university a "not so hidden agenda." Another intention of the Bologna Process was to counter brain drain to the United States and to do more to attract bright students to the European Union.[27] The long-enduring European view of education as a public good, which ensured low tuitions, high subsidies for education, and fewer private colleges and universities, is being lost in that process of restructuring.

In fact, the Bologna Process has already resulted in higher tuition, fees, and user charges (which are all still on the rise); the disappearance of grants and scholarships; and more of the financial costs being passed to the individual. Sound familiar? Unfortunately, it should, and similar transformations are taking place around the world, most notably in Australia and New Zealand. As the individualistic and entrepreneurial spirit of neoliberalism gains a foothold, the interests of the commonweal (the happiness, health, and safety of all people) are invariably lost.

Other regrettable developments that accompany the adoption of the universal university model include several forms of cultural imperialism. Rarely is "internationalization viewed from Chinese perspectives, with its powerful, long-standing philosophies of Confucianism, Buddhism, Daoism, and Islam, which are now mixed with almost sixty years of Communist ideology and nearly thirty years of a developing market economy."[28] For China, internationalization means a commitment to English as the language of instruction as opposed to Mandarin, as well as a push to have faculty publish books and peer-reviewed journal articles in English — a second language for most Chinese professors. In this manner, the form of "Western hegemony encapsulated in the contemporary processes of globalization and internationalization" has victimized foreign academics and their institutions.[29] Cultural displacement of this sort is a key feature of the internationalization of higher education.

Resurgent countries (like China) are gaining access to leadership positions in world governing bodies such as the WTO, and yet the power and privilege of leading core nations remain embedded within the policies and procedures that enable globalization. To compete in the twenty-first century, peripheral and semiperipheral nations must therefore surrender "aspects of their cultural values in favor of developing positive relations" with nations such as the United States.[30] Entrenched in the internationalization of higher education lurks a form of neocolonialism that is a byproduct of globalization, and it finds form in the rush to adopt a universal university model that encourages Westernization.

Higher education institutions in China and other parts of East Asia, including South Korea, Taiwan, and Japan, "consciously or subconsciously" equate internationalization with Westernization — particularly Americanization — which has encouraged them to adopt Western pedagogies and a new consumer orientation. Some East Asian faculty members feel that this paradigm shift transforms higher education from an intellectual pursuit into a commercial one and is therefore an undesirable development, although most likely impossible to stop.[31]

The perceptive reader will recognize that the influence of neoliberal doctrine on the internationalization of higher education is taking place around a set of values that differ considerably from those that characterized the American university at the height of its importance. After all, the primary reason for the university is "not to be found in mere knowledge conveyed to the students or in the mere opportunities for research afforded to the members of the faculty." Instead, the justification for its existence (even more so in our digital information age) is that it "preserves the connection between knowledge and the zest of life, by uniting the young and the old in the imaginative consideration of learning."[32]

In its truest form, the American university is a place where disparate strands of learning can be woven into effective instruments of progress. The ideal American university is a palace of the mind where culture is transmitted and the intellect and imagination may be developed. This classical notion of the primary function of higher learning cannot be easily packaged and delivered into today's marketplace—lest the spirit that informs the perpetuation of the arts, sciences, and humanities be obscured. The conventional American belief in democracy and inclusion led to a combination of educational policy and practice that created a space where the art of the utilization of knowledge could be acquired and applied to the empirical world—and to the questioning self.

In this respect, the decline of American higher education since 1980 can be tied directly to a jettisoning of a set of moral obligations that once constituted the chief duty and responsibility of the college and university to society as a whole. When the obligations of ethical teaching, knowledge production, technical training, and community outreach are displaced by a rhetoric of the marketplace and administrators and their staff outnumber teaching faculty two to one, then the very fundamentals of American democracy are imperiled by the sword of profit and the axe of accountability.

As Stanley Aronowitz asserts in the opening lines of his influential book *The Knowledge Factory* (2001), it is increasingly difficult to find colleges and universities in the United States where learning, as opposed to "education" and "training," is the main goal.[33] The classical expectation that higher education helps to create a more democratic society, "enunciated eloquently by Thomas Jefferson, Frederick Douglass, John Dewey, and more recently by civil rights and feminist movements," has regrettably passed from debate, and in that vanishing, a critical citizenry capable of governing itself will gradually shrink from existence along with it.[34]

The vocationalization of American colleges, the patenting of faculty research by universities in return for corporate support, decades of state and federal defunding, the neutering of the faculty by business-minded administrators, and a relentless wave of standardization are sweeping through primary, secondary, and tertiary education alike — and they augur poorly for the future. As countries around the world rush to recreate their own systems of higher learning, they do well to heed the American example and dispose of neoliberal doctrines that have been driving these destructive transformations. Global convergence has meant that governance arrangements at colleges and universities around the world are becoming more centralized, hierarchical, and authoritarian — rather than the bottom-up, decentralized, and democratic organizational structures that once distinguished American higher learning.

Historically speaking, values of the classical humanist tradition, preserved well into the twentieth century, have been replaced by those of commerce in less than half a century. We are witnessing the "insidious acceleration of countervailing developments that, collectively, have had the effect of marginalizing liberal education, moving it off the policy and public radar screen altogether."[35] This displacement of liberal learning is another negative aspect of the universal university model that is currently ascendant, for a grounding in the liberal arts prepares students to live in a complex and quickly changing world by instilling in them the analytical skills, the ability to communicate in writing and speech, the intercultural collaborative proficiencies, and the work preparation that once constituted the well-rounded college education. It was a solid foundation on which a specialty could be built in graduate school or in the workplace.

Another startling example of this shift away from the humanities is the decline of the once central English department, which has lost countless students to more vocationally oriented media and communications departments. Toby Miller suggests that in order to survive at all, what he calls "humanities one" (such as literature, history, and philosophy) and "humanities two" (communications, media studies, sociology) must merge to create a third incarnation of the humanities that combines the best features of both fields into "cultural studies" writ large.[36] Because disciplines like English and philosophy contain important intellectual reserves of antideterminist thinking and should be conserved in some form, the proposal to merge traditional humanistic studies with the social sciences may prevent the liberal arts from going the way of departments of classical studies—and never coming back. This displacement of a humanistic tradition (that produces the skills and qualities demanded by today's employers) by neoliberal values is one of the many paradoxes of convergence.[37] Yet, this important point too often goes unrecognized, as American students and their parents seek (what they perceive to be) direct linkages between higher education and vocation following the Great Recession of 2008.

Since neoliberalism is creating homogenization and corporatization in global higher education and is a primary contributor to the waning of American prominence in that sector, we should briefly extend the definitions that have steadily been put in place since the opening pages of this study. In order to accomplish that task, the remainder of this chapter will be framed around an analysis of the neoliberal university that is quickly replacing the decentralized, faculty-driven model of American higher learning that reached its full flowering in the mid- to late twentieth century.

As Giroux and Giroux explain, the rise of neoliberal ideology has radically changed colleges and universities in the United States, and not for the better:

> The ascendency of neoliberalism and corporate culture in every aspect of American life not only consolidates economic power in the hands of the few; it also aggressively attempts to break the power of unions, decouple income from productivity, subordinate the needs of society to the market, reduce civic education to job training, and render public services and amenities an unconscionable luxury. But it does more. It thrives on a culture of cynicism, insecurity, and despair. Conscripts in a restless campaign for personal responsibility, Americans are now convinced that they have little hope for—or gain from—the government, nonprofit public organizations, democratic associations, public and higher education, or other nongovernmental social agencies.[38]

Moreover, within the neoliberal corporate paradigm, knowledge becomes privileged merely as a form of investment in the economy, even though it appears to have little value in terms of teaching "self-definition, social responsibility, or the capacities of individuals to expand the scope of freedom, justice, and democracy."[39] Neoliberalism transforms such noble ideals as a dedication to the public good into anachronistic inanities that are derided as impractical, economically unsustainable, and even utopian (in its pejorative sense).

Across the United States, institutions of higher learning of all sizes are being turned into what Gaye Tuchman calls "Wannabe Universities." Wannabe universities have thoroughly adopted corporate cultures, eagerly compete with their peer institutions for rankings and resources, and have snatched institutional governance from the faculty. Tuchman's provocative book is a veiled critique of her own institution's attempt to conform to the same corporate culture that other universities are adopting to improve their rankings (although she has publically refused to name the University of Connecticut as such).[40]

A conformist university does what must be done "to elbow its way up the rankings, to survive in and to serve the neo-liberal state. It will increasingly impose an accounting regime. As the decades pass, working at the university will become more and more like working in the corporate world."[41] Meanwhile, administrators will follow the businesslike career paths that give them, according to Tuchman, a professional exemption from corporate auditing practices.[42] These "transformations" are actually devolutionary, and they challenge the autonomy and academic freedom of the faculty, which were once the hallmarks of the American academy.

Arguably, the unreflective adoption of neoliberal ideology is the defining paradigm shift in American higher education thus far into the twenty-first century, and we can even herald the arrival of a "New American University" based on it. *Newsweek* magazine calls it "one of the most radical redesigns in higher learning since the modern research university took shape in 19th-century Germany."[43] Yet, it is not really that either, as innovations by American universities outpaced those of their German counterparts in the mid- to late twentieth century (as chapter two demonstrates). Rather, neoliberal wannabe institutions, such as Arizona State University (ASU), chart their way to the top of the rankings by blindly conforming to selection criteria and abandoning the altruistic values that once informed higher learning in the United States.

The current president of Arizona State University (ASU), Michael Crow, immodestly calls his institution a template for the "New American University" because under his leadership, the budget has been doubled through corporate relationships and a cadre of world-class researchers has been hired, both of which helped to raise the status of Arizona State from a lower-tier university into a more prestigious one. Crow began the "transformation" of Arizona State by eliminating traditional departments and creating what he calls "transdisciplinary institutes" in their place. In some of these institutes, such as Barrett Honors College, very few of the professors are tenure eligible but rather hold contingent positions as "Honors Faculty Fellows." According to the program webpage at the time of writing: "Barrett Honors Faculty Fellows are master teachers and scholars. These core honors faculty are hired through national searches; they hold doctorates from top institutions, and regularly win university-wide commendations as educators."[44] There is, however, scant mention of their lecturer status or the three-year renewable contracts that most Barrett honors faculty members sign. Since nontenurable lecturers constitute the majority of the honors teaching faculty, Barrett differs significantly from the traditional American liberal arts college.

For the sake of example, in addition to that core group of contingent teaching fellows, "Faculty Honors Advisers" (holding tenurable positions in other academic departments) may serve as points of contact for Barrett students in their chosen fields of study. "Disciplinary Honors Faculty" members, again belonging to departments, could teach courses, mentor students, or guide thesis projects as first and second readers. Tenured faculty in academic departments might also apply for the position of "Visiting Honors Professor" at Barrett. The ASU website claims that Barrett faculty include professors from any college "who make sustained contributions" to its programs. Since any faculty member who teaches or mentors students "is considered a member of the Honors faculty," Barrett can astonishingly claim that "1300 faculty teach honors students" through seminars, honors contracts, independent study, thesis work, and creative projects.[45]

To be fair, all college and university websites contain a certain amount of propagandizing—diversity photos often being among the most conspicuous examples. However, the Arizona State University seems especially adept at self-promotion and branding, which contributes to a blurring of the boundary between public and private institutions of higher learning (a bifurcation that was once a traditional feature of the American higher education landscape). The ASU "New American University Resource and Downloads" webpage contains promotional videos, PDF files, press links, and even a "New American University Reader." The press office at ASU, like at a lot of wannabe universities, operates in high gear.

At the Seventh Glion Colloquium in Switzerland in 2009, Michael Crow delivered an address with a telling subtitle: "The Reconceptualization of Arizona State as a Prototype for a New American University." In it, he argues that American research universities should not only produce fundamental or "pure" research but also what he calls obliquely "socially useful outcomes" of scientific and technological research. Notice the language of business and commerce that characterize his speech when he uses the term "academic enterprise" to describe this new model. He declares, "since becoming the president of Arizona State University in July 2002, I have been leading an effort to reconceptualize a large public university as a competitive academic enterprise dedicated to leading the vanguard of innovation while addressing the grand challenges of our era."[46]

Mr. Crow claims to have "undertaken the task of pioneering the foundational model" for the New American University because of a need for an "egalitarian institution committed to the topmost echelons of academic excellence, inclusiveness to a broad demographic, and maximum societal impact." Employing the same inflated rhetoric, Crow lists eight points that he identifies as constituting "a new paradigm for academic institutions, both public and private, that I advocate without reservation." Above all, the New American University enjoins academic communities to

(1) embrace the cultural, socioeconomic, and physical setting of their institutions; (2) become a force for societal transformation; (3) pursue a culture of academic enterprise and knowledge

entrepreneurship; (4) conduct use-inspired research; (5) focus
on the individual in a milieu of intellectual and cultural diversity;
(6) transcend disciplinary limitations in pursuit of intellectual
fusion; (7) socially embed the university, thereby advancing
social enterprise development through direct engagement; and
(8) advance global engagement.[47]

At this point in our own analysis, it should be clear that Mr. Crow is
not offering anything new, but instead he is simply codifying broader
neoliberal trends found in the American university, and in American
culture, more generally today.

That fact does not prevent President Crow from bragging to his
international audience that Arizona State University has "produced
a federation of twenty-three unique interdisciplinary colleges and
schools" and in that process eliminated "traditional academic departments, including biology, sociology, anthropology, and geology."
These departments represent what Crow calls "arbitrary constructs
that may once have served certain social or administrative purposes
but are no longer useful as we prepare to tackle global challenges."[48]
Note how Crow applies a rhetoric of internationalization and globalization and uses it to argue that the entrepreneurial interests of the
"New American University" make traditional distinctions between
disciplines a hindrance to "progress."

Crow attempts to convince those in attendance that "academia
most effectively responds to the demands of the global knowledge
economy through the production of both 'knowledge capital' and
'human capital.'" For that reason, Crow claims, Arizona State University is pioneering the New American University, which embraces
the entrepreneurial impulse unapologetically and abandons with glee
the notion that the American university should defend the interests of
the commonwealth against those economic and political forces that
would undo it.

Not content to claim credit for what is really a thirty-year global
trend, Crow attacks the standard model of American higher education as ossified and failing in "the most obvious dimension of academic enterprise," which is of course "taking innovation from the
research laboratory to the marketplace." Crow asks, "where are all the

engineers our nation requires going to come from, or the scientists or doctors or teachers," if not from his New American University? His focus on STEM fields may remind the reader of the modern Chinese university examined in chapter three.

Bringing his speech to a conclusion, Crow acknowledges that "Princeton and Berkeley are undeniably great institutions, but they epitomize the traditional model of excellence of another era and seemingly cannot respond to what our society needs going forward."[49] For Crow, Princeton and Berkeley simply do not produce the highly skilled and narrowly trained workers required by today's global knowledge economy—as does Arizona State University. In the following chapter, we consider the ultimate price of this neoliberal paradigm shift in American higher education, for which Crow misleadingly claims credit.

CHAPTER SIX

· · · · · · · · · · · · · · · ·

Pricing the Paradigm Shift

IN THE LAST CHAPTER, we noted the neoliberal paradigm shift in the United States that has been turning higher education from a public good into a private commodity over the last thirty years or more. We recall that the focus of its earliest colleges was on educating the colonial elite, and it was only after the Revolutionary War that education became more democratic and inclusive. The continued investment in, and expansion of, higher education by federal and state governments during the nineteenth and twentieth centuries came to an abrupt halt in the 1980s, as neoliberalism began to creep onto the American campus.

Unfortunately, faculty members were slow to recognize its arrival. Before many realized it, the tenured professorate was dramatically reduced in number and could no longer mount a meaningful defense of its own interests. Despite the rhetorical claims of Michael Crow and others, such as John Sexton of New York University and Richard Miller at Olin College, this chapter will show that the neoliberal university is a backward step for American higher education, very much in keeping with the values of the New Gilded Age in which we find ourselves.

As noted in the previous chapter, global convergence in higher education is complicated by the fact that an idealized American model provides a basic template for what international actors have agreed a universal university, or world-class university, should look like. That template is based in part on the American colleges and universities of yesteryear (and in part on neoliberal ideology). As such, the universal university model includes provisions for tenure and free speech, for instance—if for nothing else but an ideal around which creative and innovative thinking has been known to flourish. The Chinese government is not eager to grant their faculty members such free-doms just yet. In that refusal, we observe that the positive values that took shape in the American academy between 1949 and 1980 and help to define the universal university model can be shrewdly amended to each country's political reality. Even so, globalization brings with it a flattening effect whose byproduct is standardization, which discourages all but minor variation on a prevailing paradigm.

That paradigm shift in American higher education reflects broader global trends that are increasingly commercializing traditionally nonprofit sectors. Fortunately, the model of the world-class university currently in fashion is not simply an imitation of what Micheal Crow calls "The New American University." If it were, global international institutions of higher learning that adopted the world-class model would be boosting the numbers of contingent professors, cutting funding, killing departments, increasing tuitions more than inflation every year, hiring hundreds of administrators and paying them enormous salaries, and so on. In the case of China, we saw an authoritarian streak associated with Communist governments that combined with a neoliberal market orientation following Deng Xiaoping's Open Door policies. In spite of this shortcoming, China accelerated funding for higher education and dramatically increased access to it since 1978, an inversion of the situation in the United States.

So, rather than simply imitating the neoliberal policies that are eroding American preeminence in higher education wholesale, developing peripheral and semiperipheral countries might adopt some of the superior practices found in the American university during its prime and combine them with an international orientation in order to develop creative and innovative workforces that can compete with advanced economies. After all, as globalization continues to smash borders and blur cultural distinctions among nations, local academic communities have no choice but to seek out linkages with international ones.

As our historical survey of Chinese and American higher education makes clear, global convergence is an ongoing process that began thousands of years ago at a point of great divergence between East and West; it is only in recent centuries that convergence quickened so appreciably. In order to illustrate this important point, we traced Chinese higher learning back to the Zhou dynasty, surveyed its Confucian moral underpinnings, and showed how a system of civil service examinations ensured political orthodoxy and supplied the nation with scholar-bureaucrats. When the Qing dynasty collapsed in 1911, it ushered in the Republican period, during which time Chinese higher education was profoundly influenced by German, Russian, and American models of tertiary learning (which differed considerably from indigenous ones).

The colleges and universities that proliferated during the Republican era in China were consolidated in the early years of Chinese Communist Party rule. Higher education suffered tremendous setbacks during the Cultural Revolution, before Deng Xiaoping charted a new economic course and made higher education the cornerstone of the country's growth. From the late 1970s onward, the government made significant investments to create an enormous higher education delivery system with upward of thirty million students. Moving forward, the Chinese Communist Party intends to further improve the quality of its institutions of higher learning by taking advantage of the quickening pace of global convergence to overtake other international leaders in the sector.

The history of higher education in the United States differs considerably from that of China, not only in terms of its origin and development, but also most poignantly in terms of its present state. The historical heritage of the United States includes roots in ancient Greece and the rise of democratic city-states of the Peloponnesian peninsula. Institutions of higher learning founded by Plato, Aristotle, Zeno, Epicurus, and others provided a model for higher education in Rome. Western classical learning was preserved (and greatly augmented) by Islamic scholars during the Middle Ages and then transmitted back to Europe as it awoke from a thousand-year slumber at the beginning of the Renaissance. Early European universities of the twelfth and thirteenth century developed academic programs of study in the liberal arts and professional training, which fueled a rise in rationality, logic, and empiricism during the Age of Reason—and fired the idealism that propelled the American Revolutionary War.

Thereafter, American higher education began to differentiate itself from its European forbearers by way of a religious denominationalism arising from the Protestant tradition. Later, it was profoundly changed by democratic impulses (crushed in recent decades by neoliberalism) that led to the massification and universalization of higher education. When American colleges and universities entered their "golden age" following the Second World War, decentralization, shared governance, and liberal humanistic learning were among their defining characteristics. The federal and state budget cuts that followed the culture wars of the 1980s made way for the unprecedented corporatization of higher education, which continues on campuses across the United States.

In adopting such a broad historical point of view that bridges East and West, we gain a much better sense for the processes of internationalization that have brought higher learning in China and the United States together for the first time in their contrasting histories. The question to be addressed now is what these historical patterns portend. In the short term, at any rate, we understand that global convergence benefits rapidly developing countries like China more than advanced industrial ones like the United States — where paradigm shift means a retreat and retrenchment from the values of civic responsibility.

The neoliberalism that is eroding American higher education was first "enacted politically and economically through the leadership of Reagan (Reaganism) and U.K. Prime Minister Margaret Thatcher (Thatcherism)" but has subsequently been "implemented at a global level through non-governmental organizations (NGOs) and intergovernmental organizations (IGOs) such as the WTO, IMF, and World Bank, which more or less establish and promote the basic rules of international trade and development."[1] The influence of neoliberalism is now the most significant factor in the development of the current rendition of the U.S. research university.

A heightening of the entrepreneurial focus on American campuses led to the capitalization of knowledge through the tapping of research for its revenue potential — a situation that turned university presidents into chief executive officers (CEOs). Meanwhile, business-minded managers redeployed professors as knowledge workers, and students were framed either "as consumers, to whom higher education as a product is sold, or as marketable products to be bought by business and industry."[2] In this way, the Germanic ideals of serious intellectual pursuit across a variety of disciplines, including social science and cultural studies, has given way to a narrow-minded and shortsighted version of science that is bereft of any critical reflective capacities.[3] As such, this paradigm shift does not bode well for the United States in the current environment of intense global competition among international colleges and universities of every tier.

So, what is the real cost of paradigm shift in terms of institutional quality and prestige? How much longer can elite institutions of higher learning in the United States lead (undeniably flawed) world rankings? When will Chinese universities overtake American ones as destinations of choice for students and faculty? Such questions defy easy rejoinders since they are predictive—but the implications seen in them are clear. In the final pages of this study, we show that the continuance of budget cuts to higher education, which first started in earnest in the late 1970s and early 1980s, put American preeminence in global higher learning at risk.

Worse than fiscal deficiency, the displacement of the values that once made American institutions better places (though not idyllic ones) following the Second World War were reoriented to the marketplace. The academy forged relationships with industry and the government that impinged on their public missions and set the stage for the current crisis. In making such assertions about the positive features of the American academy of the past, we do not forget that before the 1960s, it largely excluded women, people of color, the poor, and other minority groups such as the LGBT community.[4] Therefore, we look not backward but forward to a new model of the university that is more inclusive and democratic for all of its members.

As it stands, American higher education keeps moving in the wrong direction by welcoming corporate influences. From the point of view of a faculty member or that of a student (or parent) increasingly struggling to pay for tuitions that have outpaced inflation for generations, it is now possible to see a wasteland where once blossomed a garden, a palace of ashes where stood a grand citadel of learning. That citadel is burning, set ablaze by conservative and corporate forces in retaliation for the counter-culture movements of the 1960s and 1970s.

Indeed, the flames of chronic defunding have charred the halls of learning, and the ramparts are covered with the soot of neglect and decay. This state of disrepair is the real cost of the neoliberal paradigm shift. In rehearsing that history, we understand that "critical citizens aren't born, they're made, and unless citizens are critically educated and well-informed, democracy is doomed to failure."[5] Over the last three decades, campus democracy in the United States has been throttled — and if democracy cannot thrive in that space, how long might it endure in American society?

The organization 'Junct Rebellion ("established to raise awareness about the demise of the American university system, through its rampant practice of adjunct faculty labor abuse and its steadily eroding concern about the quality of education provided to students") outlined the five ways that the American university was undone. First, it was defunded. Second, the professors were deprofessionalized and impoverished, and then an insurgent administrative and management class stole governance from the faculty. The welcoming of corporate culture and corporate money into the halls of learning (despite a corrupting influence) was the fourth step. The final blow was making college affordable only to the most affluent and instituting core curricula featuring administration-designed "common syllabi" courses "taught by an army of underpaid, part-time faculty in a model that more closely resembles a factory or the industrial kitchen of a fast-food restaurant than an institution of higher learning."[6]

Lawrence Wittner maintains that unlike professors who have been "reduced to rootless adjuncts" and students who have been saddled with enormous debt (collectively over $1 trillion worth), university and college administrators are thriving. He notes that forty-two American college and university presidents make more than $1 million per year (plus generous perks that include housing, the use of luxury cars, and in extreme cases even "flights on private jets").[7] Another scholar, with a more caustic point of view, sarcastically quips, "generally speaking, a million-dollar president could be kidnapped by aliens and it would be weeks or months before his or her absences from campus were noticed."[8]

Unquestionably, management positions on American colleges and universities have swelled so much that between 1987 and 2012, "the number of administrators at private universities doubled, while their numbers in central university system offices rose by a factor of 34."[9] Depending on how one defines executive, administrative, and management positions on campus, the individuals occupying them can easily outnumber faculty by more than two to one. This proliferation of administration continues to consume larger portions of campus resources across the nation—despite the despicable and immoral exploitation of adjunct professors as a way to "balance the books."

Campus administrators in the United States, like bureaucrats everywhere, tend to multiply quickly, producing assistant/associate deans, associate vice provosts, assistant vice presidents, and so on, all with support staff. As nonprofit organizations, American colleges and universities of the past contained costs by employing a model of faculty governance whereby a professor would take a temporary position in administration but return to the classroom after a few years. In this manner, administrative bloat was avoided, highly paid presidents and their minions were superfluous, and the institution could focus on delivering higher education as a public good.

In pointing out these and other shortcomings, we do not bemoan the loss of a "golden age" in higher education but instead acknowledge that American priorities and values have shifted away from those that favor fully funding higher education (and a host of other social services). Yet, never before in American history has the academy been a place where top-ranking administrators could become wealthy; it was a place where people came to serve. For this reason, faculty and administrative salaries remained considerably lower than those in the private sector—now only faculty salaries continue to be so modest. Former Harvard president Derek Bok argues that commercialization truly threatens the core American education principle of furthering the interests of students and society. For Bok, a profit motive "shifts the focus from providing the best learning experience that available resources will allow toward raising prices and cutting costs as much as possible without losing customers."[10] Commercialization also impairs a college or university's reputation for objective, disinterested teaching and research—once the prime measures of academic integrity.

Another aspect of global convergence, where the United States has ceded ground due to neoliberal paradigm shift, is the erosion of funding for the arts and humanities in favor of STEM fields (science, technology, engineering, and math). Together with the centralization of administration, American colleges and universities increasingly resemble those in China—insofar as they aim primarily to produce highly trained professionals rather than a critically educated citizenry. Indisputably, continued investment in STEM fields remains critical to making American higher education a place for experimentation and invention in the sciences and social sciences. Therefore, in no way should the STEM fields be defunded; but the arts and humanities should be restored and recognized for being engines of cultural creativity and innovation. After all, American literature, music, movies, and other cultural productions contributed significantly to the nation's soft power after the Second World War, through the Cold War years when the principles of capitalism and Communist socialism were contested, and into the present era.

The broadening of access to American higher education after 1945 by way of the G.I. Bill, together with additional military research and high-tech investment during the Cold War, contributed to an expansion in the size and quality of American higher education that persisted until the 1980s. Since then, the rapid growth of academic research in Europe, and especially in East Asia, indicates that a convergence in world science and engineering will translate into a diminished American share.[11] During the last two-and-a-half decades, American research output has slowed and college degree attainment in other developed countries has overtaken that of the United States. Simultaneously, the granting of American doctoral degrees in STEM fields declined in absolute terms.[12] Nor are American researchers (outside of disciplines such as global healthcare or agriculture) collaborating across international borders at rates corresponding to their colleagues' in other countries at a time when "one-quarter of all scientific papers have co-authors from two or more countries."[13]

Lastly, as a result of global convergence and paradigm shift, elite American colleges and universities are creating applications so excessive in their requirements that SATs, GPAs, class ranks, and letters of recommendation all play a part in the admission process, as do applicants' service work, languages, awards, and honors. Consequently, argues former Yale professor William Deresiewicz, admission standards are so warped that "kids who manage to get into elite colleges have, by definition, never experienced anything but success." In fact, what one often finds behind that "façade of seamless well-adjustment" are "toxic levels of fear, anxiety, and depression, of emptiness and aimlessness and isolation" among the student body at elite institutions.[14]

Deresiewicz attributes this situation to students' aversions to risk, which could derail a college application, and to the commonly held notion today that higher education is about getting a return, a monetary reward for completion, rather than "building a self." Even universities like Yale, Harvard, and Princeton (America's best hope to compete in the great convergence) have campus cultures in place that regard students as customers, "people to be pandered to instead of challenged." Building a self, Deresiewicz asserts, is the act of establishing communication between the mind and the heart, the mind and experience, a process through which one becomes "an individual, a unique being — a soul."[15] Such a critique may sound rather metaphysical in our vocation-obsessed culture, but self-knowledge has always been the essential core of the American liberal arts college.

In that traditional humanistic focus, the goal of higher learning was to "create human beings who are integrated and therefore intelligent" rather than the "subservient, mechanical, and deeply thoughtless" students emerging from the present American system. Liberal education does not seek to "produce mere scholars, technicians, and job hunters, but integrated men and women who are free of fear; for only between such human beings can there be enduring peace."[16] Since the 1980s, American higher education has digressed disastrously from this understanding. In its new orientation, the humanities have been made ornamental. We might thank Clark Kerr (1911–2003), the former president of the University of California, for this paradigm shift in higher education delivery, as he popularized the concept of American higher education as a "knowledge industry" that should produce products deemed useful by the marketplace.

Kerr's call for the transference of fiscal resources from the humanities to the applied sciences has been widely emulated at colleges and universities across the country and around the world. Still, undertaking a course of study in liberal arts was conventionally not only

"the premier gateway to the learned professions," but a liberal education also encouraged students to "cultivate a sense of intellectual curiosity, to appreciate debate and diversity, and to make aesthetic choices
and moral judgments."[17] Lest we mistake these observations as some
form of deluded nostalgia, it is worth recalling the illustrious remark
attributed to Gustav Mahler: "tradition is not the worship of ashes,
but the preservation of fire."[18]

As if to reinforce the foregoing analysis, while writing this morning, all faculty members at my college were forwarded an email from
the State University of New York system administration (which oversees sixty-four campuses state-wide) encouraging us to attend a SUNY
Applied Learning Workshop. In defining "applied learning," the associate vice chancellor and vice provost for academic operations writes,

> The most effective way we have been able to capture the variety of
> high quality Applied Learning experiences offered at SUNY is to
> describe "Applied Learning" as an 'umbrella term' where SUNY
> Works, SUNY Serves and SUNY Discovers are used to showcase our
> commitment to career readiness, service and research. We are also
> using these terms as framework for organizing all of the varied
> Applied Learning opportunities on campus, including Internships,
> Cooperative Education, Service-Learning, Community Service,
> Clinical Preparation, Practicum, Research, Entrepreneurship, Field
> Study, Work Study, Civic Engagement and International Applied
> Learning Opportunities.[19]

We recognize in these words, and in the writer's complex title, many
of the hallmarks of the corporate model associated with the neoliberal
takeover of American public colleges and universities. In place of a
long tradition of pursuing liberal learning and scientific understanding to augment human knowledge, we find an emphasis on the values
of the marketplace that are diluting it. When vocational and technical learning trump the quest for self-knowledge and students are not
being taught to think, imagine, criticize, or compare, then a free and
democratic society cannot long abide.

In this respect, the forces of the great convergence, coupled with
misguided education policies, are making American colleges and universities into institutions that are failing to prepare students for the

realities of the twenty-first century. For Europe as well, globalization has meant the introduction of the market to, and the withdrawal of the state from, higher education,[20] as the promotion of free trade and competition became codified from 1999 to 2002 following the introduction of the euro currency.

Historic shifts in global economic growth patterns during the middle of the twentieth century allowed emerging East Asian economies to experience rates of growth surpassed only by China's meteoric rise in recent decades. Under the old system of global economic development, a few powerful countries (such as those in the G7) worked together almost exclusively to avoid global destabilization. Now, they share power with a larger cohort of twenty countries (a mix of advanced and high-growth nations). More than 150 countries are represented in the World Trade Organization, with dozens of observer nations aspiring for a seat at the table. This trend of high-growth economies in the developed world taking a role in the shared governance of world institutions augurs well for the development of and access to higher education worldwide, and it further reinforces the fact that in the global service sector, convergence has brought huge benefits to East Asia in the past few decades.

What makes the case of China so instructive in its relation to American higher education is that the size of the two systems are roughly comparable, and the two countries have the largest economies in the world. By juxtaposing their long and distinctive traditions in higher education, we see that profound cultural differences between Chinese and American higher education have been erased in the twenty-first century as world-class universities compete among each other to attract students and faculty and gather resources. While the United States still draws many Chinese students (who, at public universities, usually pay out-of-state tuitions) to its shores, increasingly this flow of students is moving in the other direction, as American students are beginning to clamber to study abroad in China.

As Michael Spence explains, economically the "implications of this new convergence are profound and extensive." They include rising costs for goods and services (as low-cost laborers are lifted out of poverty worldwide) and more competition for natural resources.[21] Another way to think about it is that by the middle of the twenty-first century—a scant thirty-five years from now—both China and India will be advanced-income countries. Together, they will make up more than 60 percent of the population of the G20 countries and account for the same percentage of G20 economic output.[22] Much has been written on this topic (cf. Spence and Mahbubani), so keeping our focus on higher education, we only make note of the larger political and economic implications of convergence taking place around the world. Globalization is predicated on increasingly open exchange across borders—and knowledge, technology, and innovation are among the many "commodities" now traded internationally.

We learned that when China abandoned its planned economy in 1978 and opened to the rest of the world, it averaged real growth rates in excess of 9 and 10 percent a year for three decades. China also stabilized Asia during the 1997 financial crisis and recovered quickly from the Great Recession of 2008.[23] By contrast, the same period, from 1978 to 2008, corresponds precisely to an era of defunding in U.S. higher education as Americans increasingly came to regard college as a highly priced luxury good for personal consumption—and not one to be funded from public coffers.

To those skeptical of public funding for American higher education, who ask why college education should be funded with their tax dollars, we answer that the ideal of education for the common good translated into unprecedented economic expansion following the Second World War. Federal monies to encourage economic competitiveness combined with state support to help transform the United States into a superpower. China, the world's next superpower, has adopted many strategies that proved successful in creating exceptional American colleges and universities.

The Chinese Communist Party has invested heavily in higher education in order to spur economic growth and to enhance China's standing and influence in the world. Chinese universities now outperform their Indian counterparts by most measures, due in part to the improvement and expansion of campus infrastructure across the country. What China seeks now, but which it cannot buy, is the "intellectual atmosphere that has developed over centuries in European and American campuses" that conventionally values free inquiry above political or economic interests.[24] A long tradition of humanistic learning that predates Confucius may perhaps yet be recovered and brought forward to generate such exchange and inquiry.

At China's top universities, continued improvement can be expected in each of the following eight areas: "infrastructure for research and teaching, research capacity, scholarly productivity, university-industry connections, internationalization, academic quality, faculty promotion processes, and faculty recruitment practices."[25] In terms of infrastructure, additions to Chinese lecture halls that enhance technical capacity, larger and more comfortable classrooms, better access to important discipline-specific databases, and higher quality textbooks should lead to more empowered teaching and learning in due course. Project 985 provides generous government funding to expand the research capacities of thirty-nine Chinese universities, but along with this money comes the expectation that faculty will publish in top-tier international journals and with prestigious academic presses.[26]

The history of scholarly output provides another gauge of China's current rate of development. Chinese academics published little in the 1980s, and in the 1990s, they managed about twenty-five thousand publications in total. By 2011, however, Chinese scholars produced over 150,000 publications, as connections among Chinese institutions of higher education and industry provided a way for professors to supplement their modest incomes and develop networks that might help their students after graduation.[27] Faculty promotion processes were also formalized to encourage better teaching and to emphasize the need for even more scholarly output.

China continues to build ultra-modern campuses, attract and retain world-class scholars, and lure foreign students to its shores with generous scholarships. Brain drain in the country has been checked, and Western-trained Chinese academics are returning home. The ongoing effort to move from authoritarian top-down paradigms to more decentralized campus governance models also bodes well for China in the short-to-medium term. In making such a claim, I wish to recognize the cultural and authoritarian assumptions that continue to undermine mandates initiated from on high by the central government (such as the *guanxi* connection system and the corruption it engenders). Nor should we forget that in the Confucian view of knowledge, cultural influence rests primarily with the teacher, which tends to reinforce the authority of university professors and at times undermines more democratic and participatory views of learning.

Although Chinese higher education continues to improve in many ways, we should remember that the country still has plenty of room for betterment. When I first taught in the country during the late 1990s, most Chinese professors lectured in large classrooms full of bright, but bored, students. Some instructors simply stood at the podium and read directly from their textbooks. These days, "American style" teaching is more valued than in the past, and one sees the first stirrings of more collaborative learning, fieldwork, discussion, and other nontraditional pedagogies in Chinese college and university classrooms. Perhaps, the throngs of foreigners who teach in China have made Western pedagogies more familiar to Chinese faculty members.[28] In any case, these advancements are laudable, even if their derivations are suspect.

The Chinese government is trying to engineer "a much more broadly educated public, one that more closely resembles the multifaceted labor forces of the United States and Europe." Two-hundred-and-fifty billion dollars a year is a considerable investment in the human capital of the country—especially when compared to the paltry funding levels for American higher education. To the extent that China succeeds in attaining its goal, such educational leaps could have profound implications in a globalized economy as its millions of college graduates seek employment opportunities elsewhere, including in the United States.[29] At the moment, China's 2,400 institutions of higher learning produce eight million graduates per year, about five million more than do American colleges and universities.

However, for elite Chinese universities to seriously compete head-to-head with those in the United States and the United Kingdom, far more than fiscal investment is required. The country faces immense challenges in its quest to forge a new society through higher education. Many of those obstacles are endemic to its culture, for example, the corruptive force of the *guanxi* system of connections noted earlier or the emphasis on vocationally oriented rote learning. Other culturally embedded issues include the accepted practice of junior scholars putting their senior colleagues' names on their own research (regardless of any contributions to it), the lack of true blind peer review in the country, and nebulous standards for holding office hours and meeting with students outside of the classroom.

Moreover, Chinese university students, while excellent in many ways, are still apt to plagiarize work—and unfortunately the same propensity can be witnessed among the faculty as pressure increases for them to "publish or perish." Scandals resulting from the discovery of plagiarism are not just a Chinese problem but are common in other East Asian countries as well. For example, the ongoing cases of Haruko Obokata, Ryoji Noyori, and Shinya Yamanaka in Japan all follow a drive "to publish in high-impact journals rather than to focus on generating good science."[30] Such is the force of academic competition in the age of global convergence.

While China has successfully lured its Western-trained scholars home to take leadership positions to improve the nation's standing in global higher education, many Chinese academics working abroad still prefer their teaching or research positions in the United States and the United Kingdom. There are manifold reasons for their reluctance to return, and they are not usually financial. Many individuals cite environmental degradation in urban and rural areas of China, the terrible traffic and noise in its major cities, the scarcity of equivalent research facilities, the lack of intellectual and political freedom or democratic processes, a fledgling legal system, and corruption resulting from the one-party system.

One might add to this list the absence of an established tenure system that protects intellectual freedom and freedom of speech, tight media controls by Chinese authorities, and censorship by the General Administration of Press and Publication (新闻出版总署), which reviews all books before they can be released into the fairly robust Chinese book market. We saw earlier that Chinese colleges and universities have become more decentralized in recent decades, particularly in giving campus leaders more autonomy. Nonetheless, they generally remain hierarchical and authoritarian. The will of a president, university party secretary (党委书记), or similar authority figure is rarely publicly challenged, and administrative restrictions can hinder scholarship, particularly in political science, law, and the arts and humanities.

As observed in chapter five, Chinese universities also suffer from the neoliberalism that is spreading through global higher education. Its origins in China can be traced to the market reforms of Deng Xiaoping in the 1980s. During the earlier Mao years, universities tended to be highly centralized and authoritarian spaces, but following Mao's death, they took on the added entrepreneurial features that manifested themselves in growing social inequality and the unacknowledged reinstatement of capitalist class power in modern China. In our review of contemporary Chinese history, we see that the communal spirit of the 1970s gave way to an ethos of personal responsibility in the 1980s and 1990s, which today expresses itself as heightened self-interest in a capitalist market economy (which is, ironically, overseen by a Communist government).

Since the year 2000, vast sums of money have accrued from real estate development. As a consequence, a "surging consumer culture has emerged in the main urban centers, to which these increasing inequities add their particular features, such as gates and protected communities of high income housing (with names like Beverly Hills) for the rich, and spectacular privileged consumption zones, restaurants and nightclubs, shopping malls, and theme parks in many cities."[31] Rhetorically, the Chinese Communist Party seeks to prevent new capitalist class formations, but it has "also acceded to the massive proletarianization of China's workforce, the breaking of the 'iron rice bowl,' the evisceration of social protections, the imposition of user fees, the creation of a flexible labor market regime, and the privatization of assets once held in common."[32] These divergences from socialist ideology are mirrored in many Chinese universities, which are starting to exhibit forms of academic capitalism "resulting in a more hierarchical faculty structure" associated with leading Western research universities.[33]

In earlier chapters, we highlighted the shift in the costs of higher education from the state to the individual in China, as the government sought to double college and university enrollments and encourage its citizens to spend their savings in the domestic economy. In this respect, global convergence has only strengthened the neoliberal tendencies that emerged in the Deng era (but which are powered by China's historical legacy of entrepreneurialism and acceptance of highly tiered class structures). In such an environment, one wonders if its humanistic tradition can ever be recovered authentically. In the West, liberal education assumes autonomy and freedom, and students traditionally take responsibility for their decisions (and mistakes). In China, emphasis is still placed on cultivating students through highly articulated programs of study, which tend to be much less independent.[34] It is true that the study of Chinese history, philosophy, and literature are leading to a renewed interest in the humanist calling at Fudan University and elsewhere, but American institutions of higher education operating in the country face serious challenges adhering to the principles of freedom of speech and inquiry once enshrined in the educational traditions of the United States.

The Nanjing Center operated by Johns Hopkins University, for instance, has faced "restrictions on political discussion: the halting of an on-campus public screening of a documentary about the Tiananmen Square uprising of 1989 and a ban on off-campus distribution of a journal started by an American student with articles by classmates." The Chinese government claims to recognize the need to teach the creativity and innovation associated with liberal learning, but it remains unwilling to allow itself to become the object of that scrutinizing gaze. Above all, a "liberal education imbues future citizen-leaders with the values and skills that are necessary to question, not merely serve, concentrations of power and profit,"[35] and therefore a legitimate return of humanistic learning in China may still be far off.

As part of its global ambitions, China would like to see the renminbi (RMB) become a world currency rivaling the U.S. dollar and the euro. While that prospect may seem remote, it does speak to Chinese intentions. A 2014 article in the government-sanctioned *China Daily* declares that the RMB "will become the world's third largest currency after the U.S. dollar and euro within five years as the country accelerates the promotion of its currency unit."[36] Because the Chinese currency ranks fifth in the world, China may have a better chance of reaching that goal than getting the world to adopt the Chinese language by way of its Confucius Institutes.

Even as the political and economic heft of the English-speaking world wanes, it is unlikely that Chinese will replace English as the world's lingua franca because of the difficulty involved in learning the thousands of ideographs required for basic written communication and the tones needed for speaking Chinese. Instead, China is adopting a whole host of Western academic norms and values as it seeks to build better research universities, which begs the question of "how to follow a model based on Western norms and ideals and yet at the same time retain one's own cultural distinctiveness."[37]

As countries around the world move toward the adoption of a universal university model, the problem of retaining some cultural and institutional uniqueness is serious. In the United States as well, the obsession with "best practices" means that colleges and universities increasingly look alike in terms of their organization and governance. When an oddball institution does manage to survive, all too often a new president or provost will initiate a process of "restructuring" or "reorganization" by way of strategic planning, so that it eventually looks like every other one. Thus, the standardization represented in these examples poses a significant threat to institutional diversity, both at home and abroad.

By way of conclusion, this chapter enumerates the harms associated with a neoliberal paradigm shift in American higher education and demonstrates that despite well-known shortcomings, countries around the world continue to adopt neoliberal ideology and its practices. As the Chinese government reshapes its education delivery system to more closely resemble those found in the West (particularly the United States), it is sanctioning a process of acculturation that includes, in this case, the transference of the values of intellectual freedom, peer review, and shared governance. Ironically, while elite colleges and universities in the United States are still recognized as the best the world offers, they are adopting corporate cultures that are antithetical to traditional academic principles of public service. The influx of business practices has bloated American colleges and universities with overpaid administrators who have denigrated the faculty, made questionable partnerships with corporate interests, and engineered generational tuition increases to bankroll it all. In the afterword that follows, several suggestions are put forth that may help to restore the palace of American higher learning in a new era of global convergence.

. . . .

Restoring the Palace

ALTHOUGH THIS STUDY has traced the development of Chinese higher education over thousands of years and found focus around the profound transformations in that country over the last century (as foreign models of higher learning were adopted and discarded), this is a book about the downward trajectory of American higher education.

While we have used China as a foil for American higher education, which makes for an interesting case study, the consequences of the global convergence that the Middle Kingdom has experienced are felt by many briskly developing economies. India, South Korea, Vietnam, Indonesia, Singapore, and a host of other Asian nations are beginning to attain the production levels of advanced industrial economies. Many of these countries are also intent on bolstering their higher education systems so that they may contend on an equal footing with peer institutions in the United States, United Kingdom, Australia, France, and other parts of the world.

As scholars and former administrators have been warning for decades, the American university is falling into disrepair — even though it retains a residual reputation for excellence that was built in the decades preceding the 1980s. When you read their arguments and observe the American higher education system from the point of view of a faculty member, it is hard to find fault with their assessments of decay. In addition to excellent books by Toby Miller, Henry Giroux, Gaye Tuchman, Bill Readings, Derek Bok, and many others, the popular media and blogosphere are overflowing with first-rate critiques that attempt to direct public attention toward the problems of chronic defunding, adjunctification, administrative expansion, corporatization, and unceasing tuition increases. And yet, such clarion cries of crisis largely go unheeded, and that is tragic because tenured faculty members are now so inconsequential in number that they are unable, and often unwilling, to mount any meaningful resistance on their own.

Therefore, the position that higher education in the United States occupies is very tenuous (as our historical survey shows) — not because of unassailable challenges resulting from the processes of globalization, but because of shortsighted policies that have intellectually bankrupted the American university. The primary mission of the university, to protect democracy, has been seriously imperiled, and traditional education values have been corrupted by neoliberalism (which commodifies higher education, encourages self-centered individualism, and emboldens a culture of profit that corrupts). To counter these ruinous trends, we need only to rediscover the values of the commonweal that the United States was founded upon. A government, operating with the consent of the people and working toward the best interests of the people, will ensure funding for, and access to, high-quality public primary, secondary, and higher education for everyone.

As we saw earlier, state funding for public higher education has been eviscerated. It is shameful that comprehensive colleges in the State University of New York system, for example, receive a meager 13 percent of their funding from the state of New York. If the United States is going to compete internationally, its states must pony up for public higher education as their treasuries refill following the hard times of the Great Recession. Fully refunding public institutions of higher learning would allow them to jettison huge fundraising bureaucracies, sports teams, and the hiring of fancy consultants to create brands for the marketplace — all of which compromise the central mission of the college and university: to educate.

On the federal level, increased funding for grant programs such as Pell would help to stave off the rising costs of higher education, and the current billion-dollar-per-year profit on federally subsidized student loans could be diverted to help finance investment in grants to provide better access to post-secondary education. In exchange for reinstated funding from federal and state governments, American colleges and universities must commit to dramatically lowering tuitions and fees—and at the same time to restoring the tenure-track lines that have been lost since the 1960s, when more than 70 percent of professors were tenure eligible.

Public outrage at the exploitation of adjunct faculty members is starting to resonate in Washington, D.C., and for good reasons: as we have seen, most American adjunct professors are not paid a living wage, lack office space, sign semester-by-semester contracts, teach at multiple campuses, lack basic faculty rights and freedoms, have no voice in curricular matters or in governance, and are non–tenure eligible. The situation has become so dire that adjunct faculty members are organizing to petition the Labor Department's Wage and Hour Division about "wage theft" for the hours of preparation and grading that they spend outside of the classroom (which are unpaid).[1] Our students also suffer under a neoliberal model of education delivery that relies so heavily on part-time professors, who through no fault of their own lack the continuity of support and mentoring opportunities available to tenure-track faculty (due to the investments that these institutions make in their full-time professors).

By hiring a new wave of qualified tenurable faculty members out of the contingent ranks, college and university administrations can be streamlined as faculty members return to help run day-to-day operations. With more tenured professors on campus, the faculty might also regain its share in institutional governance, which has been so diminished in recent years. Moreover, through the restoration of tenure, the current practice of bringing in administrators who have no investment in the institution, do not know their colleagues, and who serve at the whim of a president or provost could be largely eliminated. In brief, trimming unnecessary executive, administrative, and management positions (along with their support apparatuses)—and simultaneously increasing the number of tenured faculty members—will contribute to a rebuilding of American higher education.

If one believes that the fitness of the professoriate is an important measure of the quality of a college or university, then an accurate breakdown of the constitution of the faculty is a telling testament to any institution's dedication to its students. The number of full-time faculty members should be compared with the number of executive, administrative, and management positions on campus. Choosing to attend an institution of higher learning with a high percentage of tenured faculty, and the fewest number of administrators, suggests that students and their parents will see more of their tuition dollars going directly to instruction and student services (tutoring, counseling, etc.).

These student services help to define the American college and university in the twenty-first century, and they are expensive. However, they should be maintained or even bolstered, for any good institution of higher learning will ultimately be built around its students. Consequently, students and parents should persistently query campus administrators as to how many of their faculty members hold adjunct positions, instructorships, or lectureships versus tenurable appointments — and demand transparency and accountability for rising tuition costs.

We must take stock of the important values once entrenched and ask ourselves how they can best be made workable for the realities of the twenty-first century. Those principles included a commitment to decentralized campus governance, a clear majority of tenurable professorships, streamlined bureaucracies, faculty oversight of the curriculum, and perhaps most critically, instilling a sense of personal and public responsibility. We should work to realize the ideal of ensuring that higher learning is accessible to all citizens — and recognize that cuts to government funding for technical and community colleges, four-year liberal arts colleges, master's granting institutions, and research universities of all types are incompatible with quality educational delivery.

At the moment, we see that chronic federal and state defunding translated into flat wages for professors and therefore their flight from public to private universities. Although journalists covering higher education were slow to blame slick-talking executives for rising college tuitions, which increased 1,200 percent over the last thirty years, we can no longer afford to ignore the fact that the number of university administrators grew a whopping 369 percent since the mid-1970s.[2] The overly generous salaries and benefits they receive are incommensurate with the nonprofit tax status that most American institutions of higher learning benefit from. It would be naïve, however, to believe that administrators would trim their own ranks, so pressure from students, parents, and faculty members must be applied firmly and transparency insisted upon. The future of elite higher education in the United States depends on many factors, but the ability to attract "a large and continuing flow of talented graduate students from abroad to help fill a university's graduate rosters and staff its labs"[3] is essential. When the United States can no longer do that, its position as global leader will have collapsed.

Global convergence in higher education need not mean backsliding into obscurity; it could become instead the impetus that invigorates debate and prompts reform. Returning to China one final time, we see that the country's best hope for the future of higher education lies in its ability to emulate more closely some of the defining ideals found in the American academy between 1945 and 1980. Most notably, China must ensure campus democracy, protect free speech, increase transparency, and institute a fair promotion and tenure system. In order to do all these things, China must also rid its higher education system of the neoliberalism that has infected it since Deng Xiaoping's reforms of the 1980s, which gave rise to increased tuitions and fees that are starting to limit educational access and promote a classism at odds with the government's socialist propaganda.

In my view, American higher education must respond in a similar manner, though admittedly for different reasons: rid the academy of neoliberal ideology and practice and embrace the values and traditions that once made the American university a celebrated space that served the public and protected its government "of the people, by the people, for the people." On a certain level, therefore, restoration simply requires that we recognize the paradigm shift that began in the 1980s—and insist on a new exemplar that does not mindlessly imitate the features of the American university during its pinnacle but instead seeks ways to accommodate them to the new world of convergence in which we live.

History demonstrates that such profound national shifts in social consciousness are possible. For example, following the Great Depression in the late 1920s and 1930s, the civically minded policies of the New Deal replaced those that led to the Gilded Age of the late nineteenth century. Americans may yet again shift their perceptions in the wake of the Great Recession by pushing back on the rhetoric of accountability, one of neoliberalism's many guises. Boaventura de

Sousa Santos argues that progressives might meet the "new with the new" instead of returning to a vision of the university from the past, for to do so would be to ignore its failures before the 1960s. Meeting the "new with the new" means for Santos the jettisoning of neoliberal globalization, because it is based on the systematic destruction of national projects like the public university. In its place, Santos calls for a "counterhegemonic globalization of the university-as-public-good" as a counterbalance against the mercantilization of the academy.[4]

While not "all ties with industry are suspect,"[5] close affiliations with corporate entities pose a threat to shared governance, to the nonbiased selection of faculty members for endowed chairs, and to academic programs that are funded by large corporate or private donations. The practice of creating and selling patents may also compromise the traditional nonprofit, student-centered focus of American colleges and universities. Therefore, the Bayh-Dole Act of 1980 should be revisited, for the corporatization of research must be halted. Michael Crow's call for the adoption of his ideal of the "New American University" should be rejected wholesale for what it really is: a prime example of legitimizing the processes of commercialization and corporatization around market-based for-profit principles.

Yet, we can do more, and we should. Global convergence provides an opportunity for American higher education to return to the primary duty of supplying the country with members of a civically informed electorate who can defend their democracy from the forces that would challenge it. To that end, the liberal arts (our most important inheritance from the classical past) must figure prominently in any new paradigm of American higher education. That new paradigm might dialectically progress out of the current corporate model of the university—and those features that made American colleges and universities celebrated centers of teaching, learning, and scientific research during the mid-twentieth century. Through such dialectical synthesis, we may remove the ashes that have dimmed the halls of American institutions of higher learning and initiate enduring reforms that anticipate a globalization in which nation-states cooperate rather than compete in the development of the university.

In that progression, STEM fields should suffer no diminution, since the United States graduates fewer students in science and engineering than most other advanced industrialized countries. Prudent STEM investments must never become a substitute for funding the liberal arts, as has been the case for generations now. There are plenty of reasons why governments and corporations fear citizens trained to think critically and skeptically about power and its rhetoric, yet these abilities are hallmarks of liberal education indispensable to the survival of any true republic. In our New Gilded Age, where will that democratic impulse thrive, if not in our colleges and universities?

Neoliberalism can therefore have no enduring place in higher education, for it privileges mercantile prerogatives over the interests of faculty and students. It is crucial for faculty members of all ranks to speak out, and to write accessibly, so as to expose its many deficiencies. While neither the "shrinking US share of global enrollments nor the rising share of foreign students in American universities should be a cause for special concern," the individualistic, class-based, market-minded ethos that has infiltrated the academy certainly is worrisome. Indeed, there exists "a far, far nobler prospect of freedom to be won than that which neoliberalism preaches. There is a far, far worthier system of governance to be constructed than that which neoconservatism allows."[6]

Additionally, we should treat university and college ranking systems for what they are, inaccurate measures of public opinion, rather than objective scientific evaluations. Until now, competition (rather than cooperation) among institutions of higher learning for prominent slots on various rankings systems has encouraged the adoption of tendentious criteria. Yet, as it stands today, no reliable method exists "that allows students to determine where they will learn the most."[7] Students may be deceived by ranking systems regarding the actual quality of education that an institution provides just as easily as by glossy for-profit college promotion materials, because they tend to know so little about the colleges and universities they are attending or considering, even with the Integrated Postsecondary Education Data System now available online.

For-profit colleges have been highly successful in the United States because they provide educational opportunities during times that more traditional institutions eschew, such as weekends, early mornings, and late nights. However, as noted earlier, many of them employ shady practices to secure loans so expensive that often their students are unable to repay—even if they manage to graduate—and they also cost more on average than their public counterparts. The federal government would do well to better regulate student loan disbursements at for-profit institutions of higher learning, since their enrollees borrow the largest percentage of student loans each year. The vocational training offered by for-profit colleges could be provided by community colleges more cost effectively, but two-year public institutions lacked even the funding needed to meet increased demand for vocational retraining following the Great Recession.

Irrespective of what the rest of the world does, the United States must also rid itself of the unconvincing performance indicators "used to assess and measure individuals, departments, and universities against each other." The new managerialism this practice represents has replaced "elected deans and marginalized faculty senates and academic councils," and contributed to a general decline in collegiality in the academy.[8] Yet business practices have become so alarmingly normalized in global higher education that they can be found not only in the United States but also in Australia, Canada, New Zealand, and a host of other countries,[9] as we have seen. Consequently, it will not be easy to extricate these and other commonly accepted imperatives from the business world and replace them with those that are more "edu-centric" (such as tenure, which ensures a means to challenge management prerogatives that impinge on the ability of faculty members to educate their students).

In sum, democratic values rather than commercial ones should inform American higher education. Yes, colleges and universities need to equip students to productively enter the workforce, but they should also teach students to "contest workplace inequality, imagine democratically organized forms of work, and identify and challenge those injustices that contradict and undercut the most fundamental principles of freedom, equality, and respect for all people who constitute the global public sphere."[10] We should look forward to a "new university" based on a multicultural vision that incorporates humanist thought, as well as a diversity of representation in terms of students and faculty.

Regrettably, the current culture of teaching and learning in the American academy (constructed out of shared norms, values, standards, expectations, and priorities) "is not powerful enough to support true higher learning."[11] College and university teaching is a delicate art that sometimes requires putting students under pressure and making clear explanations of complex ideas.[12] Unluckily, teaching often gets eclipsed at research universities and is seemingly undervalued even at undergraduate institutions—perhaps due in part to the glut of adjunct professors and newly minted PhDs, whose difficulties on the academic job market are the result of a shrinking percentage of tenurable positions.

My hope is that the broad comparative and historical perspective adopted in this study provides convincing support for the following argument: if the status quo is maintained, American colleges and universities will gradually squander their global preeminence as faculty publication rates slow, public fiscal support for higher education dwindles, and the ranks of the tenured professorship decline precipitously. In the near-to-mid term, the growing number of doctorate degrees awarded outside of the United States will undoubtedly diminish the gap between U.S. universities and those in other countries.[13]

Yet, if we just change our minds, and reject the misguided policies that have realigned American higher education around corporate values, then global convergence can benefit higher learning in the United States as it does rapidly industrializing nations, albeit in different ways. Keeping in place some of the advances in practical research that have come with closer ties to industry and returning the humanities to a central place in our colleges and universities will go a long way in restoring the palace. Were we to combine these steps with the restitution of public funding in the name of the commonweal, the United States might once again earn the inspiring epithet bestowed by Absalom Peters back in 1851—"a land of colleges."

NOTES

Introduction. Palace of Ashes

1. William Blake, "London," in *The Complete Poetry and Prose of William Blake*, ed. David Erdman (Princeton: Princeton UP, 1991), 26.
2. Amy Roberts and Gregory Ching, "Concepts, Contributions, and Challenges of the Contemporary University Community in Taiwan," in *The Internationalization of East Asian Higher Education*, ed. John Palmer et al. (New York: Palgrave Macmillan, 2011), 44.
3. Pierre Dardot and Christian Laval, *The New Way of the World: On Neo-liberal Society* (New York: Verso, 2013), 4–5.
4. Dardot and Laval, 14.
5. Henry A. Giroux, *Neoliberalism's War on Higher Education* (Chicago: Haymarket Books, 2014), 29–30.
6. Giroux, 6.
7. See my blog at askmyprofessor.org.
8. Robert Rhoads, Xiaoyang Wang, Xiaoguang Shi, and Yongcai Chang, *China's Rising Research Universities: A New Era of Global Ambition.* (Baltimore: Johns Hopkins UP, 2014), xiii.
9. Robert A. Rhoads, "The New Militarism, Global Terrorism, and the University: Making Sense of the Assault on Democracy 'Here, There, Somewhere.'" *InterActions* 3.1 (2007): 18.
10. David K. Chan, "Internationalization of Higher Education as a Major Strategy for Developing Regional Educational Hubs: A Comparison of Hong Kong and Singapore," in *The Internationalization of East Asian Higher Education*, ed. John Palmer et al. (New York: Palgrave Macmillan, 2011), 12.
11. Roberts and Ching, 42.
12. John Palmer and Young Ha Cho, "Does Internationalization Really Mean Americanization? A Closer Look at Major Korean Universities' International Policies," in *The Internationalization of East Asian Higher Education*, ed. John Palmer et al. (New York: Palgrave Macmillan, 2011), 133–135.
13. Karin Fischer, "For Some Foreign Students, U.S. Education Is Losing Its Attraction," *New York Times*, May 25, 2014.
14. Palmer and Cho, 141.
15. Jae-Jon Jon and Eun-Young Kim, "What It Takes to Internationalize Higher Education in Korea and Japan: Mediated Courses and International

Students," in *The Internationalization of East Asian Higher Education*, ed. John Palmer et al. (New York: Palgrave Macmillan, 2011), 168–169.

16. Kelly Field, "Obama Plan to Tie Student Aid to College Ratings Draws Mixed Reviews," *Chronicle of Higher Education*, August 22, 2013.

17. Jonathan Cole, *The Great American University: Its Rise to Preeminence, Its Indispensable National Role, and Why It Must Be Protected* (New York: Public Affairs, 2009), 60–69.

18. Robert Paul Wolff, *The Ideal of a University* (New York: Beacon, 1969), 3, 10, 28, 43.

19. Robert Paul Wolff, "The Philosopher's Stone: The Ideal University," http://robertpaulwolff.blogspot.com.

20. Donald Kennedy, *Academic Duty* (Cambridge: Harvard UP, 1997), viii.

21. Kennedy, 1.

22. Colleen Flaherty, "Outsourced in Michigan," *Inside Higher Ed*, July 21, 2014.

23. Stanley Aronowitz, *The Knowledge Factory: Dismantling the Corporate University and Creating True Higher Learning* (Boston: Beacon, 2001), 66–67.

24. Haizheng Li, "Higher Education in China: Complement or Competition to US Universities?," in *American Universities in a Global Market*, ed. Charles Clotfelter (Chicago: U of Chicago P, 2010), 289.

25. James Adams, "Is the United States Losing Its Preeminence in Higher Education?," in *American Universities in a Global Market*, ed. Charles Clotfelter (Chicago: U of Chicago P, 2010), 64–65.

26. Charles Clotfelter, *American Universities in a Global Market* (Chicago: U of Chicago P, 2010), 22.

27. Li, 277–278.

Chapter 1. From Mandarins to Mao Zedong

1. Weifang Min, "Chinese Higher Education: The Legacy of the Past and the Context of the Future," in *Asian Universities: Historical Perspectives and Contemporary Challenges*, ed. Phillip G. Altbach and Toru Umakoshi (Baltimore: Johns Hopkins UP, 2004), 53–54.

2. Wing-Tsit Chan, *A Sourcebook in Chinese Philosophy* (Princeton: Princeton UP, 1964), 21.

3. Chan, 15–16.

4. *Great Learning* (大學), *Doctrine of the Mean* (中庸), *Analects* (論語), and *Mencius* (孟子).

5. *Book of Documents* (尚書), *Book of Changes* (易經), *Spring and Autumn Annals* (春秋), *Book of Rites* (禮記), and *Classic of Poetry* (詩經).

6. Chan, 18.

7. Chan, 32.

8. Chan, 44.

9. Chan, 20.

10. Chan, 39.

11. Chan, 17.

12. Anthony Welch and Hongxing Cai, "Enter the Dragon: The Internationalization of China's Higher Education System," in *China's Higher Education Reform and Internationalization*, ed. Janette Ryan (New York: Routledge, 2011), 9–10.

13. Benjamin Elman, *A Cultural History of Civil Examinations in Late Imperial China* (Berkeley: U of California P, 2000), xvii.

14. Elman, *A Cultural History*, 5.

15. Min, 55.

16. Elman, *A Cultural History*, xxiv.

17. J. Michael Farmer, *The Talent of Shu: Qiao Zhou and the Intellectual World of Early Medieval Sichuan* (Albany: SUNY P, 2008), 75.

18. Elman, *A Cultural History*, 9.

19. Elman, *A Cultural History*, 8.

20. Chan, 27–28.

21. Elman, *A Cultural History*, 15.

22. Elman, *A Cultural History*, 56.

23. Elman, *A Cultural History*, 36–38.

24. Elman, *A Cultural History*, 267–268.

25. Kent R. Guy, "Fang Po and the Ch'in-ting Ssu-shu-wen," in *Education and Society in Late Imperial China, 1600–1900*, ed. Benjamin Elman and Alexander Woodside (Berkeley: U of California P, 1994), 165.

26. Guy, 167.

27. Guy, 170.

28. Ruchang Zhou, *Between Noble and Humble: Cao Xueqin and the Dream of the Red Chamber*, ed. Ronald Gray and Mark Ferrara (New York: Peter Lang, 2009), 90.

29. Pamela Kyle Crossley, "Manchu Education," in *Education and Society in Late Imperial China, 1600–1900*, ed. Benjamin Elman and Alexander Woodside (Berkeley: U of California P, 1994), 352–353.

30. Crossley, 356–357.

31. Benjamin A. Elman, "Changes in Confucian Civil Service Examinations from the Ming and the Ch'ing Dynasty," in *Education and Society in Late Imperial China, 1600–1900*, ed. Benjamin Elman and Alexander Woodside (Berkeley: U of California P, 1994), 116–117.

32. Susan Mann, "The Education of Daughters in the Mid-Ch'ing Period," in *Education and Society in Late Imperial China, 1600–1900*, ed. Benjamin Elman and Alexander Woodside (Berkeley: U of California P, 1994), 20–21.

33. Mann, 23–24.
34. Elman, "Changes," 116–117.
35. Elman, "Changes," 117.
36. Elman, "Changes," 117.
37. Zhou, 138.
38. Elman, A Cultural History, 297.
39. Zhou, 84.
40. Elman, A Cultural History, 293.
41. Catherine Jami, "Learning Mathematical Sciences during the Early and Mid-Qing," in Education and Society in Late Imperial China, 1600–1900, ed. Benjamin Elman and Alexander Woodside (Berkeley: U of California P, 1994), 239–240.
42. Franklin Parker, People's Republic of China: Brief History and School Policy (Flagstaff: Northern Arizona University Center for Excellence in Education, 1986), 6.
43. Rui Yang, "Transformation of China's Higher Education System," in China's Higher Education Reform and Internationalization, ed. Janette Ryan (New York: Routledge, 2011), 9–10.
44. Min, 56–57.
45. Ruth Hayhoe, China's Universities, 1895–1995: A Century of Cultural Conflict (New York: Routledge, 1996), 15.
46. Elman, A Cultural History, 621–624.
47. Yang, "Transformation," 38–39.
48. Anthony Welch and Hongxing Cai, "The Internationalization of China's Higher Education System," in China's Higher Education Reform and Internationalization, ed. Janette Ryan (New York: Routledge, 2011), 12–13.
49. Leslie Stone, "Preparing for the Twenty-first Century: Liberal Education and Undergraduate Educational Reform at Sun Yat-sen University," in China's Higher Education Reform and Internationalization, ed. Janette Ryan (New York: Routledge, 2011), 72.
50. Yang, "Transformation," 39–40.
51. Michael Agelasto and Bob Anderson, Higher Education in Post-Mao China (Hong Kong: Hong Kong UP, 1998), 2.
52. Min, 59–60.
53. Chang Tu Hu, "Higher Education in Mainland China," Comparative Education Review 4, no. 1 (1961): 159–160.
54. Wei Li and Dennis Tao Yang, "The Great Leap Forward: Anatomy of a Central Planning Disaster." Journal of Political Economy 113, no. 4 (2005): 842.
55. Li and Yang, 841.
56. Min, 61–62.
57. Shih Ming Hu, "Education in the People's Republic of China (Mainland) from 1949 to 1969," American Historical Association History Education

Project Occasional Paper Series, ed. Eli Seifman (Stony Brook: History Education Project, 1972), 35.

58. Barry Burton, "The Cultural Revolution's Ultraleft Conspiracy: The 'May 16 Group,'" *Asian Survey* 11, no. 11 (1971): 1035.

59. Jung Chang, *Wild Swans: Three Daughters of China* (New York: Doubleday, 1991), 419.

60. Agelasto and Anderson, 2.

61. Min, 62–63.

62. Jin Xiao, "Higher Adult Education: Redefining Its Roles," in *Higher Education in Post-Mao China*, ed. Michael Agelasto and Bob Anderson (Hong Kong: Hong Kong UP, 1998), 194–195.

63. Rui Yang, "Indigenizing the Western Concept of University: The Chinese Experience." *Asia Pacific Education Review* 14 (2013): 91.

Chapter 2. A Shared Humanistic Heritage

1. Ralph Pounds, *The Development of Education in Western Culture* (New York: Appleton-Century-Crofts, 1968), 23.

2. Samuel Noah Kramer, "Schooldays: A Sumerian Composition Relating to the Education of a Scribe." *Journal of the American Oriental Society* 69 no. 4 (1949): 199.

3. Kramer, 200–201.

4. Edward J. Power, *A Legacy of Learning: A History of Western Education* (Albany: SUNY P, 1991), 4–5.

5. Pounds, 36–37.

6. Frederick M. Binder, *Education in the History of Western Civilization* (Toronto: Collier-Macmillan, 1970), 2–3.

7. Power, 12–14.

8. Binder, 34.

9. Henri Irénée Marrou, *A History of Education in Antiquity* (Madison: U of Wisconsin P, 1982), 109.

10. Power, 20–21.

11. Power, 22–23.

12. Pounds, 48.

13. Power, 29.

14. Power, 30.

15. Plato, *The Republic of Plato*, trans. Francis MacDonald Cornford (Oxford: Oxford UP, 1945), 227–232.

16. W. H. Cowley and Don Williams, *International and Historical Roots of American Higher Education* (New York: Garland, 1991), 8.

17. Cowley and Williams, 9.

18. Cowley and Williams, 15.

19. Power, 54.

20. Nick Huggett, "Zeno's Paradoxes," *Stanford Encyclopedia of Philosophy*, 2010.

21. Harry G. Good and James D. Teller, *A History of Western Education* (London: Collier-Macmillan, 1969), 41.

22. Good and Teller, 47–48.

23. Mehdi Nakosteen, *The History and Philosophy of Education* (New York: Wiley, 1965), 125–128.

24. Pounds, 69.

25. Pounds, 70–71.

26. Cowley and Williams, 22–23.

27. Cowley and Williams, 25–26.

28. Cowley and Williams, 29–30.

29. Good and Teller, 65.

30. Will Durant, *The Age of Faith: A History of Medieval Civilization — Christian, Islamic, and Judaic — from Constantine to Dante* (New York: Simon and Schuster, 1950), 451.

31. Durant, 467.

32. Durant, 468.

33. Pounds, 94–95.

34. Pounds, 90–91.

35. Pounds, 93–94.

36. Binder, 68.

37. Power, 111–112.

38. Cowley and Williams, 31.

39. Cowley and Williams, 33.

40. Cowley and Williams, 33.

41. Nakosteen, *History and Philosophy*, 191–192.

42. Mehdi Nakosteen, *History of Islamic Origins of Western Education: A.D. 800–1350* (Boulder: U of Colorado P, 1964), 156.

43. Nakosteen, *History of Islamic Origins*, 187.

44. Durant, 236–237.

45. Nakosteen, *History of Islamic Origins*, 189–190.

46. Pounds, 88–89.

47. Pounds, 96.

48. Nakosteen, *History of Islamic Origins*, 194.

49. Christopher J. Lucas, *American Higher Education: A History* (New York: St. Martin's, 1994), 72.

50. Lucas, 74.

51. Cowley and Williams, 50.

52. Pounds, 117.

53. Binder, 132–133.
54. Cowley and Williams, 52.
55. Lucas, 79.
56. Lucas, 81.
57. Lucas, 84.
58. Cowley and Williams, 62–63.
59. Lucas, 88.
60. Good and Teller, 156–157.
61. Lucas, 99–100.
62. Rutgers and William and Mary were the exceptions.
63. www.wm.edu/about/history/.
64. Cowley and Williams, 67–68.
65. Frederick Rudolph, *The American College and University: A History* (Athens: U of Georgia P, 1990), 4–5.
66. Rudolph, 4–5.
67. Rudolph, 10–11.
68. Rudolph, 26.
69. Rudolph, 21–22.
70. Rudolph, 36–38.
71. Binder, 251.
72. John Brubacher and Willis Rudy, *Higher Education in Transition: A History of American Colleges and Universities, 1636–1976* (New York: Harper and Row, 1976), 59.
73. Harold T. Shapiro, *The Larger Sense of Purpose: Higher Education and Society* (Princeton: Princeton UP, 2005), 41.
74. Shapiro, 40–42.
75. Shapiro, 63.
76. Brubacher and Rudy, 59.
77. Brubacher and Rudy, 61.
78. Brubacher and Rudy, 70.
79. Donald Tewksbury, *The Founding of American Colleges and Universities before the Civil War with Particular Reference to the Religious Influences Bearing upon the College Movement* (New York: Archon, 1965), 204.
80. Nakosteen, *History and Philosophy*, 494–495.
81. Cowley and Williams, 121.
82. Cowley and Williams, 137.
83. Brubacher and Rudy, 174.
84. Jonathan R. Cole, *The Great American University: Its Rise to Preeminence, Its Indispensible National Role, Why It Must Be Protected* (New York: Public Affairs, 2009), 23–24.
85. Cole, 23.

86. John J. Corson, *Governance of Colleges and Universities* (New York: McGraw-Hill, 1960), 97–98.

87. Lucas, 204.

88. www.aaup.org/report/1940–statement-principles-academic-freedom -and-tenure.

89. Cowley and Williams, 182.

90. Lucas, 227–228.

91. Cowley and Williams, 193–194.

92. Lucas, 229.

93. Shapiro, 72.

Chapter 3. The Chinese Moment

1. Ruth Hayhoe, *China's Universities and the Open Door* (New York: Sharpe, 1989), 30.

2. Kjeld Erik Brodsgaard, "The Democracy Movement in China, 1978–1979: Opposition Movements, Wall Poster Campaigns, and Underground Journals." *Asian Survey* 21, no. 7 (1981): 759.

3. Brodsgaard, 763.

4. Hayhoe, *China's Universities*, 39–40.

5. Hayhoe, *China's Universities*, 43.

6. The 1st Five-Year Plan covered the years 1953 to 1957.

7. Shi Ming Hu and Eli Seifman, *Education and Socialist Modernization in the People's Republic of China, 1977–1986* (New York: AMS, 1987), 37.

8. Hu and Seifman, 35–36.

9. Hu and Seifman, 43–44.

10. Jin Xiao, "Higher Adult Education: Redefining Its Roles," in *Higher Education in Post–Mao China*, ed. Michael Agelasto and Bob Anderson (Hong Kong: Hong Kong UP, 1998), 199–201.

11. Xiao, 202.

12. Elizabeth Economy and Michael Levi, *By All Means Necessary: How China's Resource Quest Is Changing the World* (Oxford: Oxford UP, 2014), 21–22.

13. Ruth Hayhoe, "The Tapestry of Chinese Higher Education," in *Chinese Education: Problems, Policies, and Prospects*, ed. Irving Epstein (New York: Garland, 1991), 115–116.

14. Teresa Wright, "CCP Restraints on Student Behavior in the Spring of 1989," in *Higher Education in Post–Mao China*, ed. Michael Agelasto and Bob Anderson. (Hong Kong: Hong Kong UP, 1998), 380.

15. Teresa Wright, *The Perils of Protest: State Repression and Student Activism in China and Taiwan* (Honolulu: U of Hawaii P, 2001), 1–2.

16. Wright, "CCP Restraints," 394.

17. Kai-ming Cheng, "Reforms in the Administration and Financing of Higher Education," in *Higher Education in Post–Mao China*, ed. Michael Agelasto and Bob Anderson (Hong Kong: Hong Kong UP, 1998), 23–24.

18. Cheng, 12.

19. Cheng, 19.

20. Ka-ho Mok, "Globalization and Educational Restructuring: University Merging and Changing Governance in China." *Higher Education* 50 (2005): 67.

21. Jason Lane and Taya Owens, "Fostering Economic Competitiveness in China and the US: Untangling the Web of Competing Regulations and Interests," in *Survival of the Fittest: The Shifting Contours of Higher Education in China and the United States*, ed. Qi Li and Cynthia Gerstl-Pepin (New York: Springer, 2014), 21–22.

22. Yinmei Wan, "Expansion of Chinese Higher Education Since 1998: Its Causes and Outcomes." *Asia Pacific Education Review* 7, no. 1, 22.

23. Juann Hung and Rong Qian, "Why Is China's Savings Rate So High? A Comparative Study of Cross-Country Panel Data." *Working Paper Number 2010-07*, Congressional Budget Office, Washington, D.C., 2010.

24. Wan, 23.

25. Wan, 23.

26. Wan, 22.

27. Susan Caskie, "The Rise of Youth Suicide in China: Stress Over School-work Has Driven Up the Youth Suicide Rate," *The Week*, November 1, 2013.

28. Ka-ho Mok and Kok Chung Ong, "Transforming from 'Economic Power' to 'Soft Power': Transnationalization and Internationalization of Higher Education in China," in *Survival of the Fittest: The Shifting Contours of Higher Education in China and the United States*, ed. Qi Li and Cynthia Gerstl-Pepin (New York: Springer, 2014), 135.

29. Mok and Ong, 135.

30. Mok and Ong, 138.

31. Haizheng Li, "Higher Education in China: Complement or Competition to US Universities?," in *American Universities in a Global Market*, ed. Charles Clotfelter (Chicago: U of Chicago P, 2010), 269.

32. Davide Cantoni, Yuyu Chen, David Y. Yang, Noam Yuchtman, and Y. Jane Zhang, "Curriculum and Ideology." National Bureau of Economic Policy Research, nber.org, May 29, 2014.

33. Cantoni et al.

34. Anthony Welch and Hongxing Cai, "Enter the Dragon: The Internationalization of China's Higher Education System," in *China's Higher Education Reform and Internationalization*, ed. Janette Ryan (New York: Routledge, 2011), 14.

35. Welch and Cai, 17.

36. Li, 270.

37. Hongyi Lai, "China's Cultural Diplomacy: Going for Soft Power," in *China's Soft Power and International Relations*, ed. Hongyi Lai and Yiyi Lu (New York: Routledge, 2013), 92.

38. Lai, 93.

39. Elizabeth Redden, "Confucius Controversies," *Inside Higher Education*, July 14, 2014.

40. Weifang Min, "Chinese Higher Education: The Legacy of the Past and the Context of the Future," in *Asian Universities: Historical Perspectives and Contemporary Challenges*, ed. Phillip Altbach and Toru Umakoshi (Baltimore, Johns Hopkins UP, 2004), 71.

41. Li Wang, *The Road to Privatization of Higher Education in China: A New Cultural Revolution?* (New York: Springer, 2014), 35.

42. Wang, 46–47.

43. Wang, 48–49.

44. Wang, 53.

45. Wang, 1–2.

46. Outline of China's National Plan for Medium and Long-term Education Reform and Development (2010–2020). www.aei.gov.au/news.

47. Outline of China's National Plan.

48. Outline of China's National Plan.

49. Outline of China's National Plan.

50. Simon Marginson, "The Confucian Model of Higher Education in East Asia and Singapore," in *Higher Education in the Asia–Pacific: Strategic Reponses to Globalization*, ed. Simon Marginson, Sarjit Kaur, and Erlenawati Sawir (New York: Springer, 2011), 54.

51. Li, 301.

52. Qiang Zha and Jing Lin, "China's Move to Mass Higher Education: Analyzing the Policy Execution with a 'NATO-Scheme,'" in *Survival of the Fittest: The Shifting Contours of Higher Education in China and the United States*, ed. Qi Li and Cynthia Gerstl-Pepin (New York: Springer, 2014), 38.

53. Zha and Lin, 38.

54. Welch and Cai, 18–25.

55. Rui Yang, "Advanced Global Strategy in China: The Case of Tsinghua," in *Higher Education in the Asia–Pacific: Strategic Reponses to Globalization*, ed. Simon Marginson, Sarjit Kaur, and Erlenawati Sawir (New York: Springer, 2011), 156.

Chapter 4. Crisis in the American Academy

1. David Francis Mihalyfy, "Higher Ed's For-Profit Future," *Jacobin: A Magazine of Culture and Polemic*, www.jacobinmag.com/2014/06/higher-eds-for-profit-future/, June 7, 2014.

2. Bruce Wilshire, *The Moral Collapse of the University: Professionalism, Purity, and Alienation* (Albany: SUNY P, 1990), 80–81.

3. E. Han Kim and Min Zhu, "Universities as Firms: The Case of US Overseas Programs," in *American Universities in a Global Market*, ed. Charles Clotfelter (Chicago: U of Chicago P, 2010), 165–167.

4. Jennifer Washburn, *University, Inc.: The Corporate Corruption of Higher Education* (New York: Basic Books, 2006), xiii.

5. *Oxford English Dictionary* (Oxford: Oxford UP, 2010), 377.

6. "The Adjunct Project," *Chronicle of Higher Education*, adjunct.chronicle.com, 2013.

7. Debra Leigh Scott, "How Higher Education in the US Was Destroyed in 5 Basic Steps," *AlterNet*, http://www.alternet.org/how-higher-education-us-was-destroyed-5-basic-steps, October 16, 2012.

8. Robert E. Martin and R. Carter Hill, "Baumol and Bowen Cost Effects in Public Research Universities," www.pdx.edu/sites/www.pdx.edu.econ/files/Measuring_Baumol_and_Bowen_Effects_in_Public_Research_Universities__NewDataFinal.pdf, March 2014.

9. Jon Marcus, "New Analysis Shows Problematic Boom in Higher Ed Administrators," *Huffington Post*, www.huffingtonpost.com/2014/02/06/higher-ed-administrators-growth_n_4738584.html, February 6, 2014.

10. Michelle Jamrisko and Ilan Kole, "Cost of College Degree in U.S. Soars 12 Fold: Chart of the Day." *Bloomberg*, www.bloomberg.com/news/articles/2012-08-15/cost-of-college-degree-in-u-s-soars-12-fold-chart-of-the-day, August 15, 2012.

11. Jordan Weissmann, "A Truly Devastating Graph on State Higher Education Spending," *Atlantic*, www.theatlantic.com/business/archive/2013/03/a-truly-devastating-graph-on-state-higher-education-spending/274199/, March 20, 2013.

12. "25 Years of Declining State Support for Public Colleges," *Chronicle of Higher Education*, http://chronicle.com/article/25-Years-of-Declining-State/144973/, March 3, 2014.

13. "25 Years of Declining."

14. Scott, "How Higher Education."

15. Andrew Delbanco, *College: What Was, Is, and Should Be* (Princeton: Princeton UP, 2014), 99.

16. Benjamin Franklin, Proposals Relating to the Education of Youth in Pensilvania, www.archives.upenn.edu/primdocs/1749proposals.html, Philadelphia, 1749.

17. Charles Clotfelter, *American Universities in a Global Market* (Chicago: U of Chicago P, 2010), 1.

18. Kevin Carey, "Americans Think We Have the World's Best Colleges. We Don't." *New York Times*, www.nytimes.com/2014/06/29/upshot/americans-think-we-have-the-worlds-best-colleges-we-dont.html?_r=0&abt=0002&abg=0, June 28, 2014.

19. Jonathan R. Cole, *The Great American University: Its Rise to Preeminence, Its Indispensible National Role, Why It Must Be Protected* (New York: Public Affairs, 2009), 145.

20. Cole, 154.

21. Cole, 154.

22. Peter Lunenfeld, "Ronald Reagan Stuck it to Millennials: A College Debt History Lesson No One Tells." *Salon*, www.salon.com/2014/07/05/ronald_reagan_stuck_it_to_millennials_a_college_debt_history_lesson_no_one_tells/, July 5, 2014.

23. Roger Geiger, "Research Universities in a New Era," in *Higher Learning in America: 1980–2000*, ed. Arthur Levine (Baltimore: Johns Hopkins UP, 1993), 70–71.

24. Derek Bok, *Universities in the Marketplace: The Commercialization of Higher Education* (Princeton: Princeton UP, 2003), 12.

25. Cole, 155.

26. David Breneman, "Liberal Arts Colleges: What Price Survival?," in *Higher Learning in America: 1980–2000*, ed. Arthur Levine (Baltimore: Johns Hopkins UP, 1993), 95–96.

27. Breneman, 92.

28. Patrick M. Callan, "Government and Higher Education," in *Higher Learning in America: 1980–2000*, ed. Arthur Levine (Baltimore: Johns Hopkins UP, 1993), 14–15.

29. Margaret Gordon, "The Economy and Higher Education," in *Higher Learning in America: 1980–2000*, ed. Arthur Levine (Baltimore: Johns Hopkins UP, 1993), 31.

30. Bok, 191.

31. Bok, 4.

32. Christopher Newfield, *Unmaking the Public University: The Forty Year Assault on the Middle Class* (Cambridge: Harvard UP, 2008), 5–6.

33. Washburn, 139.

34. Benjamin Ginsberg, *The Fall of the Faculty: The Rise of the All-Administrative University and Why It Matters* (Oxford: Oxford UP, 2011), 215.

35. Ginsberg, 31.
36. Frank Donoghue, *The Last Professors: The Corporate University and the Fate of the Humanities* (New York: Fordham UP, 2008), 78.
37. Ginsberg, 24–25.
38. Toby Miller, *Blow Up the Humanities* (Philadelphia: Temple UP, 2012), 27.
39. Ginsberg, 136.
40. Jordan Weissmann, "The Ph.D. Bust: America's Awful Market for Young Scientists — in 7 Charts," *Atlantic*, www.theatlantic.com/business/archive /2013/02/the-phd-bust-americas-awful-market-for-young-scientists-in-7 -charts/273339/, February 20, 2013.
41. Christopher Newfield, "The View from 2020: How Universities Came Back." *Journal of Academic Freedom* 2 (2011): 6.
42. Ginsberg, 116.
43. Ginsberg, 116–117.
44. The bolded text in this quotation is part of the original document.
45. "A Test of Leadership: Charting the Future of U.S. Higher Education." *A Report of the Commission Appointed by Secretary of Education Margaret Spellings*, www2.ed.gov/about/bdscomm/list/hiedfuture/reports/pre-pub-report.pdf, 2006, vii.
46. "A Test of Leadership," viii.
47. "A Test of Leadership," ix.
48. "A Test of Leadership," 3.
49. Susan Mettler, "College, the Great Unleveler," *New York Times*, http:// opinionator.blogs.nytimes.com/2014/03/01/college-the-great-unleveler/, March 1, 2014.
50. Steven Salzberg, "For-Profit Universities: The Yugos of Higher Education." *Forbes*, www.forbes.com/sites/sciencebiz/2010/09/27/for-profit-universities -the-yugos-of-higher-education/, September 27, 2010.
51. Salzberg.
52. "A Test of Leadership," 23.
53. Mark S. Ferrara, *Barack Obama and the Rhetoric of Hope* (Jefferson, NC: McFarland, 2013).
54. Trish Kahle, "Welcome to Neoliberal U," *Socialist Worker*, socialistworker .org/2013/08/29/welcome-to-neoliberal-u, August 29, 2013.
55. Rudy Fichtenbaum and Hank Reichman, "Obama's Rankings Won't Solve Crisis in US Academy." *Times Higher Education*, www.timeshighereducation .co.uk/comment/opinion/obamas-rankings-wont-solve-crisis-in-us -academy/2007156.article, September 12, 2013.
56. *Department of Education Budget for the Fiscal Year 2015*, www.whitehouse.gov /sites/default/files/omb/budget/fy2015/assets/education.pdf.
57. Cole, 452.

58. Michael Lind, "The American Century Is Over: How Our Country Went Down in a Blaze of Shame," *Salon*, www.salon.com/2014/07/12/the _american_century_is_over_how_our_country_went_down_in_a_blaze _of_shame/, July 12, 2014.

Chapter 5. Global Convergence and Competition

1. Martin Wolf, "In the Grip of a Great Convergence." *Financial Times*, www.ft.com/cms/s/0/072c87e6–1841–11e0–88c9–00144feab49a.html, January 4, 2011.

2. Michael Spence, *The Next Convergence: The Future of Economic Growth in a Multi-speed World* (New York: Farrar, Straus and Giroux, 2011), 4.

3. Kishore Mahbubani, *The Great Convergence: Asia, the West, and the Logic of One World* (New York: Public Affairs, 2013), 12.

4. Spence, 4.

5. Mahbubani, 47.

6. Mahbubani, 87.

7. Mahbubani, 7.

8. Kemal Gürüz, *Higher Education and International Student Mobility in the Global Knowledge Economy* (Albany: SUNY P, 2011), 317.

9. Gürüz, 318–319.

10. Christopher Newfield, "The View from 2020: How Universities Came Back." *Journal of Academic Freedom* 2 (2011): 7.

11. Gürüz, 198–199.

12. Robert Rhoads, Xiaoyang Wang, Xiaoguang Shi, and Yongcai Chang. *China's Rising Research Universities: A New Era of Global Ambition* (Baltimore: Johns Hopkins UP, 2014), 2.

13. Rhoads et al., 5.

14. Rhoads et al., 19.

15. Rui Yang, "Indigenizing the Western Concept of University: The Chinese Experience." *Asia Pacific Education Review* 14 (2013): 91.

16. Rhoads et al., 24.

17. Robert A. Rhoads, "The U.S. Research University as a Global Model: Some Fundamental Problems to Consider." *Interactions* 7, no. 2 (2011): 1.

18. David K. Chan, "Internationalization of Higher Education as a Major Strategy for Developing Regional Educational Hubs: A Comparison of Hong Kong and Singapore," in *The Internationalization of East Asian Higher Education*, ed. John Palmer et al. (New York: Palgrave MacMillan, 2011), 13.

19. www.iu.qs.com/university-rankings/academic-survey-responses-2013/.

20. www.timeshighereducation.co.uk/world-university-rankings/2013-14 /world-ranking/range/276–300.

21. Amy Roberts and Gregory Ching, "Concepts, Contributions, and Challenges of the Contemporary University Community in Taiwan," in *The Internationalization of East Asian Higher Education*, ed. John Palmer et al. (New York: Palgrave MacMillan, 2011), 42–44.
22. Güruz, 90.
23. Güruz, 90.
24. Ka-ho Mok, "Globalization and Educational Restructuring: University Merging and Changing Governance in China." *Higher Education* 50 (2005): 59–60.
25. Güruz, 184
26. Güruz, 184.
27. Anne Corbett, *Universities and the Europe of Knowledge: Ideas, Institutions and Policy Entrepreneurship in European Union Higher Education 1955–2003*. (New York: Palgrave Macmillan, 2005), 195.
28. Anthony R. Welch and Rui Yang, "A Pearl in the Silk Road? Internationalizing a Regional Chinese University," in *The Internationalization of East Asian Higher Education*, ed. John Palmer et al. (New York: Palgrave MacMillan, 2011), 63.
29. Roberts and Ching, 42.
30. John D. Palmer and Young Ha Cho, "Does Internationalization Really Mean Americanization? A Look at South Korean Universities' Internationalization Policies," in *The Internationalization of East Asian Higher Education*, ed. John Palmer et al. (New York: Palgrave MacMillan, 2011), 123.
31. Mary Shepard Wong and Shuang Frances Wu, "Internationalization of Higher Education in East Asia: Issues, Implications, and Inquires," in *The Internationalization of East Asian Higher Education*, ed. John Palmer et al. (New York: Palgrave MacMillan, 2011), 199–200.
32. Alfred N. Whitehead, *The Aims of Education and Other Essays* (New York: Free Press, 1967), 93.
33. Stanley Aronowitz, *The Knowledge Factory: Dismantling the Corporate University and Creating True Higher Learning* (Boston: Beacon, 2001), 1.
34. Aronowitz, 123.
35. Carol G. Schneider, "Liberal Education: Slip-sliding Away," in *Declining by Degrees: Higher Education at Risk*, ed. Richard H. Hersh and John Merrow (New York: Palgrave Macmillan, 2005), 66.
36. Toby Miller, *Blow Up the Humanities* (Philadelphia: Temple UP, 2012), 123.
37. Schneider, 64–65.
38. Henry A. Giroux and Susan Searls Giroux, *Education: Race, Youth, and the Crisis of Democracy in the Post–Civil Rights Era* (New York: Palgrave Macmillan, 2004), 249–250.

39. Giroux and Giroux, 263.
40. Pilar Mendoza, "A Mission of Amenities, Not Education." *Academe*, www
.aaup.org/article/mission-amenities-not-education#.VP03BUKprzI,
Nov.–Dec. 2010.
41. Gaye Tuchman, *Wannabe U: Inside the Corporate University* (Chicago: U of
Chicago P, 2009), 208.
42. Tuchman, 204.
43. Stefan Theil, "Reinventing the Global University." *Newsweek*, www
.newsweek.com/reinventing-global-university-87861, August 8, 2008.
44. http://barretthonors.asu.edu/honors-faculty/.
45. http://barretthonors.asu.edu/welcome/resources-for-facultystaff
/who-are-honors-faculty.
46. Michael Crow, "The Research University as Comprehensive Knowledge
Enterprise: The Reconceptualization of Arizona State as a Prototype
for a New American University." *Seventh Glion Colloquium Montreux*,
June 2009, 2.
47. Crow, 3.
48. Crow, 7.
49. Crow, 4.

Chapter 6. Pricing the Paradigm Shift

1. Robert A. Rhoads, "The U.S. Research University as a Global Model: Some
Fundamental Problems to Consider." *Interactions* 7, no. 2 (2011): 8.
2. Rhoads, 9.
3. Rhoads, 20–21.
4. Lesbian, gay, bisexual, and transgender.
5. Henry A. Giroux and Susan Searls Giroux, *Take Back Higher Education: Race,
Youth, and the Crisis of Democracy in the Post–Civil Rights Era* (New York:
Palgrave Macmillan, 2004), 257.
6. Debra Leigh Scott, "How the American University Was Killed," *Homeless
Adjunct*, https://junctrebellion.wordpress.com/2012/08/12/how-the
-american-university-was-killed-in-five-easy-steps/, August 12, 2012.
7. Lawrence Wittner, "Why Are Campus Administrators Making So Much
Money?," *History News Network*, http://historynewsnetwork.org/article
/156375, July 18, 2014.
8. Benjamin Ginsberg, *The Fall of the Faculty: The Rise of the All-Administrative
University and Why It Matters* (Oxford: Oxford UP, 2011), 164.
9. Wittner.
10. Derek Bok, *Universities in the Marketplace: The Commercialization of Higher
Education* (Princeton: Princeton UP, 2003), 108.

11. James D. Adams, "Is the United States Losing Its Preeminence in Higher Education?," in *American Universities in a Global Market*, ed. Charles Clotfelter (Chicago: U of Chicago P, 2010), 64–65.

12. Charles Clotfelter, *American Universities in a Global Market* (Chicago: U of Chicago P, 2010), 10–11.

13. Karin Fischer, "U.S. Seen as Weak on Global Research Collaboration," *Chronicle of Higher Education*, www.nytimes.com/2014/07/21/us/us-seen-as-weak-on-global-research-collaboration.html, July 20, 2014.

14. William Deresiewicz, "Don't Send Your Kid to the Ivy League," *New Republic Magazine*, www.newrepublic.com/article/118747/ivy-league-schools-are-overrated-send-your-kids-elsewhere, July 21, 2014.

15. Deresiewicz.

16. J. Krishnamurti, *Education and the Significance of Life* (San Francisco: Harper, 1981), 14–15.

17. Ginsberg, 175.

18. Lion Feuchtwanger and Adrian Feuchtwanger, *Against the Eternal Yesterday: Essays Commemorating the Legacy of Lion Feuchtwanger* (Los Angeles, Figueroa Press, 2009), 65.

19. "SUNY Applied Learning Workshop." SUNY Oswego Metro Center, September 18–19, 2014.

20. Heather Eggins, "Globalization and Reform: Necessary Conjunctions in Higher Education," in *Globalization and Reform in Higher Education*, ed. Heather Eggins (Berkshire: Open UP, 2003), 2–3.

21. Michael Spence, *The Next Convergence: The Future of Economic Growth in a Multispeed World* (New York: Ferrar, Straus and Giroux, 2011), 29.

22. Spence, 49.

23. Spence, 156.

24. Rui Yang, "Indigenizing the Western Concept of University: The Chinese Experience." *Asia Pacific Education Review* 14 (2013): 91.

25. Robert Rhoads, Xiaoyang Wang, Xiaoguang Shi, and Yongcai Chang, *China's Rising Research Universities: A New Era of Global Ambition* (Baltimore: Johns Hopkins UP, 2014), 163.

26. Rhoads et al., 164.

27. Rhoads et al., 165–166.

28. Rhoads et al., 167–168.

29. Keith Bradsher, "Next Made-in-China Boom: College Graduates," *New York Times*, www.nytimes.com/2013/01/17/business/chinas-ambitious-goal-for-boom-in-college-graduates.html, January 16, 2013.

30. David McNeill, "Academic Scandal Shakes Japan," *New York Times*, www.nytimes.com/2014/07/07/world/asia/academic-scandal-shakes-japan.html, July 6, 2014.

31. David Harvey, *A Brief History of Neoliberalism* (Oxford: Oxford UP, 2010), 147.
32. Harvey, 150.
33. Rhoads et al., 175.
34. Leslie Stone, "Preparing for the Twenty-first Century: Liberal Education and Undergraduate Educational Reform at Sun Yat-sen University," in *China's Higher Education Reform and Internationalization*, ed. Janette Ryan (New York: Routledge, 2011), 83.
35. Jim Sleeper, "Liberal Education in Authoritarian Places," *New York Times*, www.nytimes.com/2013/09/01/opinion/sunday/liberal-education-in-authoritarian-places.html, August 31, 2013.
36. "China's RMB to be Next World Currency—Four Challenges to Be Faced," *China Daily*, http://en.people.cn/n/2014/0724/c98649-8760270.html, July 24, 2014.
37. Rhoads et al., 177.

Afterword. Restoring the Palace

1. Joseph Fruscione, "When a College Contracts 'Adjunctivitis,' It's the Students Who Lose," *PBS Newshour*, July 25, 2014.
2. Thomas Frank, "Behind the Three-Decade Scheme to Raise Tuition, Bankrupt Generations, and Hypnotize the Media," *Salon*, www.salon.com/2014/06/08/colleges_are_full_of_it_behind_the_three_decade_scheme_to_raise_tuition_bankrupt_generations_and_hypnotize_the_media/, January 8, 2014.
3. Charles Clotfelter, *American Universities in a Global Market* (Chicago: U of Chicago P, 2010), 17–18.
4. Boaventura de Sousa Santos, "The University in the 21st Century: Toward a Democratic and Emancipatory University Reform," in *The University, State, and Market: The Political Economy of Globalization in the Americas*, ed. Robert A. Rhoads and Carlos Alberto Torres (Stanford: Stanford UP, 2006), 80–82.
5. Derek Bok, *Universities in the Marketplace: The Commercialization of Higher Education* (Princeton: Princeton UP, 2003), 204.
6. David Harvey, *A Brief History of Neoliberalism* (Oxford: Oxford UP, 2010), 206.
7. Bok, 162–163.
8. Jan Currie, *Universities and Globalization: Critical Perspectives* (London: Sage, 1998), 4.
9. Jan Currie and Lesley Vidovich, "Micro-Economic Reform through Managerialism in American and Australian Universities," in *Universities and Globalization: Critical Perspectives*, ed. Jan Currie (London: Sage, 1998), 154.

10. Henry A. Giroux and Susan Searls Giroux, *Take Back Higher Education: Race, Youth, and the Crisis of Democracy in the Post–Civil Rights Era* (New York: Palgrave Macmillan, 2004), 10.

11. Richard P. Keeling and Richard H. Hersh, *We're Losing Our Minds: Rethinking American Higher Education* (New York: Palgrave Macmillan, 2011), 152–153.

12. Andrew Delbanco, *College: What It Was, Is, and Should Be* (Princeton: Princeton UP, 2012), 170.

13. Richard B. Freeman, "What Does Global Expansion of Higher Education Mean for the United States?," in *American Universities in a Global Market*, ed. Charles Clotfelter (Chicago: U of Chicago P, 2010), 402.

INDEX

Civil War, American, 72–75

classical learning, 119, 146, 148; in ancient world, 46, 51–53, 55–58; in China, 23, 32; in Early Modern Period, 61–64; in Islamic world, 58–60, 156; in US higher education, 18, 43, 70, 72, 115, 147, 177

C9 League, 89

colleges: Christian, 35, 66–67; colonial, 16, 43, 68–70, 106, 115; community (two-year), 6, 15, 77, 79–80, 120, 130, 175, 179; liberal arts, 16, 74–76, 80, 150; technical, 73–74, 146, 175. See also private colleges and universities; public colleges and universities; specific colleges

colonialism, 2, 31, 35, 145. See also colleges: colonial

commodification of higher education, 3–4, 17, 107, 126, 142, 154, 165, 173; history of, 47, 65, 116–17

Common Core, 93, 159

commonweal, 106, 144, 152, 173, 180; in China, 24; as common good, 11, 78, 113, 115, 118, 165; higher education as public good, 1, 5, 13, 17, 109, 143–44, 149, 154, 160, 177

community colleges (two-year), 15, 77, 79–80, 120, 130, 175, 179; in China, 6

Confucianism, 4, 34, 36, 41, 50, 102; central principles of, 19–23; in civil service examinations, 26, 43

Confucius (孔子), 24–25, 46; Analects, 21–23; in Chinese education, 50, 91, 114, 116

Confucius Institutes, 97–98, 170

Constantine, 54–55

consumers, 4–5, 113, 145, 157

contingent faculty, 10, 12, 80, 107, 109–13, 126, 174; at Arizona State University, 150, 155. See also adjunctification

corporatization, 8, 63, 113, 118–19, 121–22, 130, 147; and adjunct crisis, 107, 159; audit practices of, 125, 149–50, 171–72, 177; corrupting influence of, 110, 143, 148, 157–59, 163, 180; in institutional governance, 1, 5, 12, 17, 108–9, 125, 142

Crow, Michael, 150–55, 177

Crusades, 16, 58

cultural displacement, 145, 147–48, 158

cultural imperialism, 9, 32, 37, 145

Cultural Revolution, Great Proletarian (文化大革命), 40–42, 82–85, 100, 103, 156

cuneiform, 44

Dartmouth College, 68, 73

defense industry, 78, 118

democracy, 16, 71, 149, 173; on campus, 112, 121, 146, 159, 173; in China, 14, 82–83, 87, 95, 103, 176; depletion of, 8, 177; origins of, 45–46

Deng Xiaoping (邓小平), 82–83, 85, 96, 100, 155–56, 169, 176

denominationalism, 16, 74, 106, 156–57

deprofessionalization, 13, 110, 123, 133, 159

Development Plan, 100–101, 104

Dewey, John, 34, 122, 146

doctoral degrees, 15, 78, 103, 111, 126–27, 161; in China, 84, 96, 103

Dream of the Red Chamber (红楼梦), 28

Duke University, 122

Duncan, Arne, 131–32

education in the marketplace, 3, 5, 10, 118–19, 121, 129, 163, 173; international, 97, 139, 143, 146; as neoliberalism, 152, 162. See also commodification of higher education